Introduction to Ethnic Studies

Second Edition

Richard Lowy
University of California–Riverside

KENDALL/HUNT PUBLISHING COMPANY
4050 Westmark Drive   Dubuque, Iowa 52002

Acuña, Rodolfo, pp. 178, 184, 186, 187: From *Occupied America: A History of Chicanos, 3rd ed.*, by Rodolfo Acuna. Copyright © 1988, pp. 13,147–150. Reprinted by permission of Pearson Education, Inc.

Adams, Howard, pp. 95, 96: From *Tortured People: The Politics of Colonization, Revised Edition*, by Howard Adams 1999, published by Theytus Books Ltd. Penticton, BC, Canada. Reprinted by permission.

Almaguer, Tomás, pp. 174, 175, 176, 177, 179, 180, 185: From "Historical Notes on Chicano Oppression: The Dialectics of Racial and Class Domination in North America," by Tomás Almaguer. Reprinted by permission of Tomás Almaguer.

Banks, James A., pp. 59, 216, 217, 223, 226: From *Teaching Strategies for Ethnic Studies, 4th E*, by James A. Banks, Allyn & Bacon, 1987, pp. 469, 470, 473, 430. Reprinted by permission of James A. Banks.

Blauner, Bob, pp. 84, 85: From "Colonized and Immigrant Minorities" and "Internal Colonialism and Ghetto Revolt" from *Still The Big News: Racial Oppression in America* by Bob Blauner. Used by permission of Temple University Press. © 2001 by Bob Blauner. All Rights Reserved.

Chan, Sucheng, pp. 203, 204: From *Asian Americans: An Interpretive History, 1/e* by Sucheng Chan. © 1991 Gale, a part of Cengage Learning, Inc. Reproduced by permission. www.cengage.com/permissions.

Fenton, Steve, pp. 16, 20, 24, 25: From *Ethnicity* by Steve Fenton. Reprinted by permission of Polity Press, Ltd.

Fredrickson, George M., p. 54: From *Racism* by George M. Fredrickson. © 2002 Princeton University Press, 2003 paperback edition. Reprinted by permission of Princeton University Press.

Gonzales, Rodolfo "Corky," pp. 164–165: From "I am Joaquín" by Rodolfo Corky Gonzales. Reprinted by permission of Escuela Tlatelolco.

Hraba, Joseph, pp. 75, 76, 77, 78, 79, 80, 214, 215, 216, 219, 220, 221, 222, 223: From *American Ethnicity, 2E* by Hraba. © 1994 Wadsworth, a part of Cengage Learning, Inc. Reproduced by permission. www.cengage.com/permissions.

Marger, Martin N., pp. 108, 109, 210, 211, 212, 213, 214, 218, 219, 221, 222, 225, 226, 227: From *Race and Ethnic Relations, 5/e* by Marger. © 2000 Wadsworth, a part of Cengage Learning, Inc. Reproduced by permission. www.cengage.com/permissions.

Muñoz, Carlos Jr., pp. 165, 166: From *Youth, Identity, Power: The Chicano Movement*, by Carlos Muñoz Jr, 1990. Reprinted by permission of Verso.

Newman, Richard and Marcia Sawyer, pp. 136, 138, 139, 140, 142, 143: From *Everybody Say Freedom* by Richard Newman and Marcia Sawyer, copyright © 1996 by Richard Newman & Marcia Sawyer. Used by permission of Plume, an imprint of Penguin Group (USA) Inc.

Nicholson, Philip Yale, pp. 27, 52: *Who Do We Think We Are? Race and Nation in the Modern World*, by Philip Yale Nicholson. Armonk: M. E. Sharpe, 1999, pp. 7, 13, 95, 96.

Omi, Michael and Howard Winant, pp. 26, 27, 63, 71, 72: Copyright © 1986. From *Racial Formation in the United States: From the 1960's to the 1980's* by Michael Omi and Howard Winant. Reproduced by permission of Routledge/Taylor & Francis Group, LLC.

Samora, Julian and Patricia Vandel Simon, pp. 183, 184: *History of the Mexican-American People (Hard)* by Samora, Julian. Copyright 1993 by Univ. of Notre Dame Press. Reproduced with permission of Univ. of Notre Dame Press in the format Textbook via Copyright Clearance Center.

Smedley, Audrey, pp. 25, 26, 52: From *Race in North America*, by Audrey Smedley, Copyright © 1998 by Westview Press, Member of Perseus Books Group. Reprinted by permission of Westview Press, a member of Perseus Books.

Stannard, David E., pp. 96, 104, 105, 109: From *American Holocaust: Columbus and the Conquest of the New World* by David E. Stannard, copyright © 1992 by David Stannard. Used by permission of Oxford University Press, Inc.

Takaki, Ronald, p. 179: *Iron Cages: Race and Culture in 19th Century America* by Ronald Takaki. New York: Alfred A. Knopf, Inc., 2000, pp. vii–viii.

Zia, Helen, pp. 204, 205: Excerpts from "Surrogate Slaves to American Dreamers" from *Asian-American Dreams* by Helen Zia. Copyright © 2000 by Helen Zia. Reprinted by permission of Farrar, Straus and Giroux, LLC.

Contents

Dedication

I dedicate *Introduction to Ethnic Studies* with love, respect, and appreciation:

To the memory of my parents

    Peter H. Lowy

    Ruth S. Lowy

To my brother

    Robert Lowy

To my sister

    Judy Jacobson

To my mentors, who never wavered in their intellectual support for me and whose kindness, respect, commitment, and genuine humanity have sustained me and taught me the importance of mentoring and caring for the students I am privileged to teach:

    The late Dr. Maurice Jackson

    Dr. Alfredo Mirandé, Ethnic Studies Chair

Acknowledgments for the Second Edition

Before the publication of *Introduction to Ethnic Studies* in 2006, Dale Emery accepted a position with another publishing company and Amanda Smith became my primary contact person with Kendall/Hunt.

I have also had the good fortune to discuss the preparations for the second edition of *Introduction to Ethnic Studies* with Shelly Walia, who became the new Acquisitions Editor for Kendall/Hunt. Her support and encouragement have only added to my appreciation and respect for the entire staff of Kendall/Hunt in making the publication of my book possible.

I continue to owe a debt of gratitude and deepest appreciation to Liliana Aguayo, whose fantastic, dedicated, and skillful work made it possible for the initial typing of my handwritten manuscript into the first edition of *Introduction to Ethnic Studies*. For the second edition of my book, I have carefully made every effort to proofread, edit, and correct every mistake, typographical error, and inconsistency in the text based upon the suggestions of my staff at Kendall/Hunt and my desire to improve the text. I have interpolated additional references into the bibliography, although only a few were added to the sources in several chapters. I have also added additional DVDs to the list of Ethnic Studies Films. Once again, I thank Liliana Aguayo for incorporating the corrections for the second edition into the manuscript and thus facilitating the preparation of the text for publication.

I have benefited spiritually, intellectually, and as a human being from my association with many colleagues, professors, teaching assistants, students, and friends. I wish I could praise and acknowledge the following people individually, but since my space is necessarily limited, I will list them individually in alphabetical order. Thank you to all of you, and to those not explicitly listed, you are in my heart as well.

Parvin Abyaneh, Estella Acuña, Sabrina Alimahamed, Jerome Anderson, Andrea Armstrong-Henson, Manuel Barajas, Ravin Brazfield, Victor Brazfield, Lorie Broomhall, Diana Bustamante, Roberto Calderon, Adriana Church-Camacho, Arlene Cano, Michelle Cardenas, CoriAndre Crane, Al Chavez, Mike Chavez, "Chippie," Raoul Contreras, Katie Dailey, Daniel Diaz, Reina Diaz, Sandy Díaz, "Diego," Rachell Enriquez, Martha Escobar, Debbie Evans, Alfredo Figueroa, Rosanna Gaines, Maria Garcia, Ed Gomez, Choki Gomez-Díaz, Veronica Guevara, Yordanos Haile, Mokerrom Hossain, Carla Jackson, Jolena Jordan, Ziaul Karim, Yuko Kukihara, Grace Larias, Angel Lopez, Enrique Lopez, José Lopez, Nasrin Mokerrom, Christina Navoa, Pam Norman, Guy Osburn, Terie Osburn, Lehong Phan, Elvia Ramírez, "Riley," Maria Rincón, Marijke Rutherford, Ron Schneck, Leonard Simon, Yolanda Stanley, Jon Taleb, April Tellez, Beto Tijerina, Karen Tolbert, Camile Tomlin, Marisela Trujillo, Edith Morris-Vásquez, Elsa Valdez, Shelly Walia, Michelle Willens, Beth Wilson, Jake Wilson, Jane Yoon, Eloy Zarate, and Cherry Zaydahr.

About the Author

I began teaching for what was then the Ethic Studies Program in winter 1989 at the request of Dr. Alfredo Mirandé. While my primary responsibility has been to teach the large Ethnic Studies 1: Introduction to the Study of Race and Ethnicity classes, I have also taught the courses Chicano Sociology, Martin Luther King, Jr., Black & Chicano Bibliography, Comparative Race Relations, Political Economy of Race & Class, Research Methodology, Native American Policy in the 20th Century, and Native American Law. I have worked with students on numerous directed studies projects, internships, one senior thesis, and one honor thesis.

My personal biography, my intellectual training, my theoretical mind, and my primary mentors from California State University at Long Beach, San Diego State University, and the University of California have all oriented me to a career in university teaching.

My career in teaching has been developing slowly through part-time positions in sociology and ethnic studies from 1986 to the present. I have been able to develop and hone my intellectual understandings of the course subject matter and, more important, the dynamics of lecturing, classroom, and student interaction through the repeated opportunities I have had to teach. I have proven to be a very humanistic, caring, and student-oriented professor who is able to teach at an intellectually challenging level while remaining in touch with and sensitive to the needs of students. I have also worked closely with students on individual directed studies and internship projects and have always encouraged students intellectually and emotionally through my willingness to write letters of recommendation on behalf of students seeking further opportunities beyond the undergraduate level.

From 2000–2001 to the present, I have been the faculty advisor for the Chicano newspaper *Nuestra Cosa,* which is published quarterly through Chicano Student Programs by students, who also do the layout and distribution to the community.

In November 1993, at a CUC-sponsored breakfast, the University honored me as the 1993–1994 Non-Senate Distinguished Teaching Award recipient.

I continue to seek excellence in teaching and in working effectively with students from every conceivable racial, ethnic, and class background.

Introduction

Although ethnic studies and its various subdisciplines are of relatively recent origin, having evolved over the past forty years or so from various combinations of individual courses in traditional disciplines as well as in the programs, departments, institutes, and research centers that were created in response to the demands of student and community activists, there is nevertheless a huge and ever-growing literature and countless numbers of textbooks devoted to the topics of race relations; race and ethnicity; race, class, and gender; and every possible variation on these and other topics related to the field of multiculturalism.

Introduction to Ethnic Studies is not meant to replace or supercede any of the excellent ethnic studies–related textbooks, anthologies, readers, or specialized substantive books in the field of race and ethnic relations or the vast array of excellent books that have been published across the many traditional disciplines in the social sciences, humanities, or sciences. In fact, I have attempted to recognize that regardless of the political and ideological positions associated with ethnic studies in its activist and/or intellectual developmental stages, the field is of necessity derived from a wide array of activism, collective struggle, oral traditions, research, and pre-1960s writings related to the historical and contemporary struggles of oppressed peoples and groups worldwide and in the U.S. sociocultural and political context.

Introduction to Ethnic Studies is written from a humanistic, leftist, and radical perspective that derives from an activist pedagogy positing that knowledge is neither neutral nor disinterested, but is partisan and from the perspective and interests of the oppressed, who in their struggles for voices, recognition, liberation, social justice, and full citizenship seek not just to understand the world, but to change it.

The discourse of *Introduction to Ethnic Studies* is structured around an ethnic studies philosophical, conceptual, and theoretical framework and the recognition that the historical reality of prejudice, stereotyping, racism, and institutionalized inequality still has its contemporary manifestations despite the generalized belief that in the United States, racism is either greatly diminished or a thing of the past.

The text of *Introduction to Ethnic Studies* emphasizes the centrality of racism to the disciplines of ethnic studies, the role of assimilation and internal colonialism as fundamental processes that have affected White ethnic immigrants and populations of color, and provides historical and contemporary racial overviews of Native Americans, African Americans, Chicanos, and Asian Americans.

In Chapters 1 and 2, I develop an introductory overview of the historical context and political framework out of which ethnic studies developed and evolved as well as the fact that the concepts, definitions, and theories in ethnic studies are value-laden because the discipline itself is shaped by the dialectical relationship between political and social activism; the dynamics of departmental and university units relative to academic freedom and rules governing promotion, tenure, and merit; and the fact that the ideas and knowledge in textbooks are processed in the interaction between diverse faculty and their students, representing a complex web of racial, ethnic, class, gendered, and community experiences.

Chapters 3 through 6 contain the heart of the conceptual and theoretical analysis that is fundamental for understanding basic paradigms in ethnic studies. The presentations on ethnicity and race and theorizing ethnicity and race: assimilation and internal colonialism are based upon the approach I have developed in my teaching for Ethnic Studies 1: Introduction to the Study of Race and Ethnicity. Each chapter is supplemented by references or citations that provide access to the conceptual and theoretical literature that I have drawn upon through the years and that are suitable in whole or part for students to pursue on their own or for class assignments.

Chapters 7 through 10 present historical and contemporary overviews of the major racial groups that are covered in the curriculum of the Ethnic Studies Department for which I teach. Each racial group chapter has an introduction in which I place the group in its historical or sociological context and lay the foundation for discussing the political–economic dynamic of contact, oppression, and the racialized response and consequences for the group in question.

The Bibliography contains citations for every work that is directly quoted, paraphrased, or mentioned in the text as a valuable or representative reference.

Finally, I will conclude this introductory overview of my book by quoting from Chapter 3, "Racism," to describe what ethnic studies is as a set of disciplines and whom the discipline is for:

> Ethnic studies, to reiterate, has hybrid origins in the historical struggles of racially oppressed populations—both before and during the era of Jim Crow segregation; anticolonial, nationalist independence movements, internal colonial struggles, the civil rights movement, and the anti-imperialist–anticapitalist battles throughout the nineteenth and twentieth centuries—and in the universities where teachers, students, researchers, and activists have demanded, fought for, written about, researched, and struggled for the classes, programs, research centers, and disciplines that now constitute the diverse subfields and curricula that individually and collectively constitute ethnic studies.

> Ethnic studies in the United States is of recent origin but its intellectual roots and political praxis encompass the universal brutality of the Middle Passage; the conquests of the Taino, the Mexica, the Incas, and Indians of North America; the slave revolts and resistance of Toussant, Denmark Vessey, Nat Turner, Fredrick Douglass, Gabriel Prosser, Harriet Tubman, W. E. B. DuBois, and Malcolm X; the struggles for justice of Joaquin Murieta, Tiburcio Vázquez, Mexicano braceros and farmworkers, Dolores Huerta, Reies Lopez Tijerina, Corky Gonzales, César Chavez, and the disenfranchised Chicano/as throughout Mexico and occupied America; and the legacies of Pontiac, Tecumseh, Osceola, Geronimo, Crazy Horse, Sitting Bull, John Trudell, the people of Sand Creek, Wounded Knee, and every Indian boarding school. Those who lived as second-class citizens, those who died without a trace, those exploited as cheap labor, those denied the right to vote, those excluded—from the Chinese and Japanese to the Filipino, those who were lynched, those who were brutalized in racist courts and prisons, those women raped and sterilized, those denied burial in cemeteries after dying for their country, those who fought for civil rights, those who still fight today—these are the people, groups, and causes that are the substance of every course and subfield in ethnic studies.

Overview of Ethnic Studies

Chapter One

Key Terms

anticommunist right

anti–Vietnam war movement

Christian right

civil rights struggles

cold war America

de facto segregation

de jure segregation

ethnic studies

free speech movement

Jim Crow racism

neoconservatives

racist right

right-wing backlash

youth counterculture

Key Lesson

Following World War II, the political era of **cold war America** pitted the United States against the Soviet Union, Red China, and the emerging nations of the third world or the nonaligned movement. Joseph McCarthy engaged in an anticommunist witch hunt and the beginnings of civil rights activism focused the world's attention on racial injustice in the segregated South, which called attention to the hypocrisy of America's advocacy of democracy for the emerging nations of Africa, Asia, the Caribbean, and Latin America. The progressive and radical movements of the 1960s were in part a reflection of the baby-boom generation coming of age, White and working-class minorities attending colleges and universities, and the generational confrontation of youth counterculture, civil rights, radical nationalism, anti-war activism, feminism, and ecology against American materialism, cold war ideology, mainstream values, and the military–industrial complex. Out of the 1960s the demands for new and relevant educational curricula led to the movements for Black, Chicano, Asian, Indian, and women's studies and ultimately to the creation of **ethnic studies** disciplines around the nation. Political backlash, rearticulation of conservative ideologies, and the failure of radical agendas to be structurally realized have led to the more or less permanent recognition that **de jure segregation** and overt, biologically based racism and prejudice are wrong, but have created controversy over the meaning of affirmative action, feminism, group rights, and multiculturalism in the university and American culture.

My initial purpose is to introduce you to the discipline of ethnic studies and to reassure you that what may at first come across as a field rooted in controversy, divisiveness, and contentiousness due to the critical examination of issues of race, ethnicity, class, and gender in European and American historical and contemporary experience is in fact an opportunity to gain access to a vast and growing body of material that is both scholarly and challenging due to the multidisciplinary and interdisciplinary nature of the substantive material and the variety of theoretical and methodological approaches that have informed the curriculum of ethnic studies.

The field of ethnic studies is relatively new compared to the more traditional university fields that make up the physical and biological sciences, the social sciences, and the humanities. While there have always been individuals, groups, and organizations that responded to social oppression, exploitation, and domination, the formal creation of ethnic studies as an integral part of the university had its origins in the protest and social justice movements of the 1960s and 1970s.

For those of you who would like to understand the context that shaped the social, political, and cultural movements out of which the various disciplines of ethnic studies emerged, I would recommend that you read Terry H. Anderson's *The Movement and the Sixties;* and Douglas T. Miller's *On Our Own: Americans in the Sixties.*

If you are specifically interested in the nature of the various fields that make up ethnic studies or in the substantive, theoretical, and political debates that have developed in various university settings as a result of the institutionalization of the new disciplines in the humanities and social sciences, I would refer you to: Johnnella E. Butler and John C. Walter, Editors, *Transforming the Curriculum: Ethnic Studies and Women's Studies;* and *Color-Line to Borderlands: The Matrix of American Ethnic Studies,* edited by Johnnella E. Butler.

Because my overview of the field of ethnic studies is preliminary and somewhat cursory, I want to list some of the factors that I argue are important for the development and political nature of ethnic studies. Because ethnic studies is historically rooted in political and social protest that emerged in the post–World War II Joe McCarthy communist witch hunts and the African American civil rights struggle to bring down southern **Jim Crow racism** and **de facto discrimination** in the rest of the country, it should not come as a surprise that it was largely the traditional left and the emergence of the baby-boom generation to college-age and political awareness that ushered in a quantum leap in activism as **civil rights struggles,** the **free speech movement,** the **youth counterculture,** and a host of new social movements and attempted transformations reverberated throughout 1960s and 1970s America. Much of the struggle to deal with racism in America has not been freely welcomed by the social or political elites whose self-proclaimed role is to act as gatekeepers for the establishment and protectors of the institutional status quo.

Ethnic studies, Black studies, Chicano studies, Asian studies, Indian studies, and women's studies have been created in struggle and controversy around the nation. The specifics of how protest has been reacted to in various contexts, regions, and circumstances depend upon a variety of factors that must be examined historically and empirically.

In listing key issues that have shaped the evolution of ethnic studies over the past thirty-five years or so, it is my contention that there has been an ongoing attack against the progressive agenda of the 1960s due to the emergence of right-wing social and political strategies that have tried to contain and control the liberal and leftist efforts of activists in the post–Vietnam War and post-Watergate era of the Nixon administration. The United States lost its ability to dominate the course and development of world events beginning in the 1970s, and despite the claims of cold war warriors and establishment pundits, minorities and women have not fared well in the university or in the political and economic realm that has been referred to as the new world order, globalization, and the post–September 11, 2001, War on Terrorism.

The following list of factors is meant to provide a basis for understanding why ethnic studies emerged when it did and the subsequent influences that have affected the political climate in which human rights, civil rights, women's rights, worker's rights, and gay/lesbian/bisexual/transgender rights have developed into ethnic studies and related subfields:

- Originated in the protest movements of the 1960s and 1970s, such as the **anti–Vietnam War movement.**

- Sought greater diversity in the university and educational relevance for students of color.

- Demanded and created new curricula, programs, and departments in colleges and universities.

- Almost from the beginning of minority inclusion and curricular reform, there were conservative challenges and a **right-wing backlash** to the protests of the late 1960s as a result of America's loss of hegemony politically and economically due to the Vietnam War, Watergate, the oil crisis, and other events toward the end of the Carter presidency.

- The emergence of the **neoconservative** movement, the **Christian right,** the **racist right,** and the **anticommunist right** of the cold war were reinforced by the Iran Hostage Crisis, the success of the Sandinistas in Nicaragua, and the Soviet Union's invasion of Afghanistan.

- During the 1970s with the *Bakke* decision and the polemical nature of school busing and support for neighborhood schools, the unfinished 1960s agenda began to erode.

- During the Reagan and Bush presidencies, rollbacks in civil rights gains became more frequent and outrageous during the decade of the 1980s.

Although President Bush was defeated by Bill Clinton, who served two terms, the political climate was repressive despite Clinton's much more progressive agenda on race and his much more tolerant attitudes toward African Americans. Some people have argued that Clinton had to become more centrist or even right-leaning in order to deal with the well-organized and well-financed neoconservative and right-wing Christian movements. President Clinton referred to himself as a New Democrat, and many found his social positions to begin to mirror the right wing in Washington following the loss of the House of Representatives to the conservative right in 1994.

Events throughout the 1990s reflected a more hardline right-wing agenda based on family values, anti-immigrant movements, and calls for welfare reform and major reforms in affirmative action policy. A summary of these issues is reflected by the following concerns:

- Newt Gingrich and the neoconservative "Contract for America" after the 1994 midterm elections.

- Proposition 187 and the focus on illegal aliens and their alleged role in undermining jobs, education, health care, and welfare that citizens were supposedly not receiving.

- Political correctness became a heated issue across college campuses and in the national talk-show radio culture as the backlash against liberal and radical politics became nastier.

- Anti–affirmative action debates and Proposition 209 fueled the concerns of White males and groups claiming that they constituted "reverse racism."

- The backlash that began in the 1980s with the "English only" movement continued into the 1990s with attacks against bilingual education, Proposition 227, and many advocating that recent immigrants (Mexicans) should be subject to total immersion into English.

- Welfare reform became a code word for attacking people of color, the poor, and specifically Black women.

- The debate about the "underclass" in America that had begun in the late 1980s was a reminder to many of the controversies of the Moynihan debate about the Black family pathology and "victim blaming" from the 1960s.

- The debate about race and IQ brought about by the much published book *The Bell Curve* struck many as an explicit endorsement of racism and a new eugenics that argued that improving the sociocultural environment for Blacks was a waste of time and money.

Other issues during the 1990s and into the twenty-first century have further suggested how the hopes of 1960s activists continued to be dashed against the realities of a rigid, authoritarian, punitive right that pushed for hardline stances regarding the prison industrial complex, the targeting and profiling of minority youth and gangs, and the profiling of religious minorities in response to Islamic fundamentalism and later the George W. Bush post-9/11 War on Terrorism. These issues can be summarized as follows:

- A massive increase in the number of prisons built and staffed throughout the state of California during the decades of the 1980s and 1990s took place, while access to college and university education became both difficult and more expensive because of a failure to fund the needed growth in new campuses.

- Civil libertarians across the nation have continued to call attention to the racist nature of the U.S. criminal justice system and the disproportionate numbers of people of color subject to imprisonment and the death penalty.

- The application of "three strikes" legislation has been used to target racial minorities for harsh prison sentences for minor crimes.

- During the 1980s, youth gangs began to proliferate in California due to the increased availability of cocaine, crack, and other dangerous drugs along with guns, which resulted in the targeting of Black and Latino youths as "gang members" subject to harsher or enhanced sentencing in the criminal justice system and a trend toward more young people being put on trial as adults rather than as juveniles.

- The notion of "racial profiling" throughout American society has become a well-documented reality in which men and women of color experience daily suspicion, questioning, or surveillance from law enforcement personnel, store and shop clerks, and others who find their presence or behavior troubling.

- The term *DWB,* or *Driving While Black* (or Brown), has been used throughout the 1990s to the present to indicate how minorities experience this form of "everyday racism."

- The notion of profiling has increasingly become a part of media coverage of violent acts associated with internal or international terrorism, such as the first attack on the World Trade Center, the Oklahoma City bombing, and the 9/11 attack on the "Twin Towers."

- The erosion of civil liberties has troubled many people in the post-9/11 War on Terrorism during the first term of President George W. Bush and the passage of two Patriot Acts, the harsh rhetoric of Attorney General John Ashcroft, the reorganization of over one hundred government agencies into the office of Homeland Security, and the detention of enemy combatants at the U.S. military base on Guantánamo Bay, Cuba.

- Liberals, radicals, activists, and progressives have found the political climate in the United States during the presidency of George W. Bush to be repressive, reactionary, or authoritarian due to:

  • The contested 2000 election highlighted by the Florida scandal and ultimate declaration that Bush won by only about 500 votes, giving him the needed electoral votes even though Al Gore won the popular vote.

  • Events that followed the September 11, 2001, attacks on the World Trade Center and led to the Bush policy of preemptive military intervention and the new War on Terrorism.

  • The wars in Afghanistan and Iraq, particularly the claim by the Bush administration that Saddam Hussein had weapons of mass destruction as a basis for attacking Iraq and "taking out" Saddam Hussein.

■ During the post–civil rights years, most Americans believe that racism has been virtually eliminated in U.S. society, and despite the proclamation of greater tolerance and multicultural inclusion, scholars and activists continue to document what has been called a more subtle but very real form of "new racism," "modern racism," or "color-blind racism."

This list of issues is derived from academic and political discourses that reflect a very critical and perhaps radical value orientation with regard to how ethnic studies developed; the importance of promoting an agenda of social activism, social justice, and multiracial inclusion; radical examination of U.S. history and policies; and a sustained critique of the dominant social structure and core institutions.

By explicitly acknowledging that the field of ethnic studies is inherently political, I would seemingly place myself in the unenviable position of denying students an objective and value-neutral vantage point for dealing with and evaluating the role of race and ethnicity in the American experience. But I would argue that the role of ethnic studies in the university is different than the traditional view of elitist or consensus views of history. Traditional modernist notions about knowledge, epistemology, and methodology were predicated on the application of the scientific method and universally accepted disciplinary paradigms to all realms of enquiry. However, the social sciences and humanities have increasingly moved from positions of objectivity to perspectives of intersubjectivity, interpretative understanding, positionality and standpoint epistemology, and phenomenology and the social construction of reality.

In short, ethnic studies does not promote universally valid propositions that are independent of specific, particular, local, or unique conditions that must be understood and interpreted from the point of view of groups of individuals whose experiences and interpretations of reality must be incorporated into our own emerging worldviews and social and political projects.

As students who represent the complex diversity that is so central to real U.S. history and the multicultural mosaic of the present, it is your responsibility to acknowledge the diverse viewpoints and experiences that you inherently bring to this classroom and to the university. Ethnic studies begins with the recognition that there is no absolutely privileged version of American history. Rather, every historical claim is subject to critique, reevaluation, fresh interrogation, and analysis from the perspective of the present as well as our multiple future projects and concerns.

In addition, U.S. society is not monolithic but is stratified in terms of multiple interest groups, social classes, diverse interlocking institutions, and complex culturally and spatially distributed groupings, communities, and individuals whose racial, ethnic, and gendered identities intersect and diverge in infinitely complex ways.

The controversial nature of ethnic studies flows from a paradox of our socially generated humanity. On the one hand we are all absolutely unique from our DNA to our socialization and individual self-consciousness and identity. And yet, our social reality structures us into society in terms of placing us into a particular period of time and particular experiences of development and exposure to cultural, class, religious, linguistic, gendered, and political circumstances.

Ethnic studies is therefore a reflexive discipline that allows us to question who we are, where we or our families come from, what communities and causes we identify with, how we relate to our social and political surroundings, and how we can develop and grow within the complex net of relationships that we encounter.

As you begin your exposure to and relationship with ethnic studies, therefore, recognize that the discipline incorporates multiple political and ideological viewpoints into its debates, subject matter, theories, paradigms, methodologies, and subdisciplines.

Two other sources of subjectivity and interpretation derive from the individual professor who teaches each and every course: his or her academic training and experiences, and his or her ethnic, racial, class, and gendered identity. Also, as I alluded to previously, ethnic studies is usually taught from the *perspective* and *collective experience* of racial, ethnic, class, and gendered *oppression* and *exclusion* or *marginalization* of groups rather than from the *dominant White* or *Anglo male* and *privileged traditional* and *elitist* discourses of the *powerful.*

There is also variation within ethnic studies regarding how much emphasis individual faculty place on the celebration of race and ethnic accomplishments and achievements that validate a group's humanity, capability, and upward mobility or inclusion in the face of historical or contemporary prejudice, stereotyping, scapegoating, racism, and discrimination versus what has come to be called "victim" or "oppression" studies. There are disadvantages to approaches that celebrate multiculturalism by overemphasizing assimilation, loss of racial or ethnic identity, or privileging the standards and values of the dominant or hegemonic social order. But to stress only the history and experiences of racism, classism, sexism, and marginalization of racial groups under diverse circumstances can lead to a perception by students of what unfortunately has come to be called "white bashing," which causes some students to close their minds to any exposure of racism and injustice in society.

Ethnic studies must critique dominant and biased approaches to history and it must represent the voices and experiences of the oppressed and marginalized. But this can be done by a fair and balanced discourse that acknowledges opposing value orientations, political viewpoints, and conflicting or contradictory paradigms and theoretical approaches.

Finally, it is important to accept the fact that one ethnic studies course, one professor, and one set of assigned readings can not even begin to represent the depth and wealth of material that is available on race and ethnicity. Not only do we have scholars who have specialized in important subfields such as African American, Asian American, Native American, and Chicano/Latino studies, but some individuals can literally spend a whole career dealing with the complexities of narrow topics such as slavery, immigration, labor, culture, law, race, the Holocaust, women and gender, policing, and countless other topics that affect race and ethnicity.

I want to conclude this chapter with my recommendations to all students, including:

- Keep an *open mind* and an *open heart.*

- *Examine* and be *aware* of your *emotional* and *intellectual* reactions to *concepts, theories,* and *historical* material.

- Don't interpret this class as a *personal attack against you,* but as an *invitation* to a *critical field* of *study, scholarship,* and *political engagement* with *history* and *contemporary social and institutional arrangements.*

- There are many ways to teach about *racial* and *ethnic reality,* since the topic is *vast* and can require years of *study* and *thought* to *fully master* all its *complexity* and *ramifications.*

- All of you can *contribute* to *applying* the *knowledge* and *ideas* from ethnic studies to your ongoing *interactions, organizational and institutional affiliations, social and political involvements,* and in your chosen *jobs, fields of endeavor,* or *professional development.*

Questions, Exercises, and Topics for Discussion and Debate

1) Discuss the meaning of Jim Crow racism and distinguish between de jure segregation and de facto segregation.

2) What is meant by the term *cold war,* and why would American racism and race relations at home affect America's image and reputation abroad?

3) Discuss the 1960s in America. What events, movements, and circumstances do you feel affected the nation in significant and long-lasting ways? What was the meaning of the 1960s for White college students, working-class people of color, women, and the poor?

4) What are the disciplines of ethnic studies? What factors led to the demand for minority studies courses, programs, and departments?

5) Discuss the political and social context of the late 1960s and the 1970s. Why did Whites react politically against minority studies, affirmative action, and the movements of the 1960s?

Concepts, Definitions, and Theories

Chapter Two

Key Terms

concepts

data

definitions

factually valid information

the packaging and selling of
commodified knowledge in textbooks

liberal or reformist multiculturalist
ideology

the lived politics of race, ethnicity, class,
and gender

revisionist racial and ethnic histories

theories

Key Lesson

The publication of a textbook represents a compromise between an author's personal, professional, and disciplinary intent and the organizational, business, and marketability requirements of a publishing company. Race and ethnic relations books combine factual information, data, revisionist racial and ethnic histories, and objective definitions, concepts, and theories with a liberal or reformist multicultural ideology. Often the voice of the author is muted, objectified, marginalized, or silenced. But in the discipline of ethnic studies, multiple, subjective, perspectival, complex, value-laden political points of view are preferred to neutral or objective representations of data, facts, knowledge, concepts, or theory. The use of textbooks in ethnic studies disciplines by faculty, students, and departments occurs in an inherently political context. The discourse, debate, discussion, and incorporation of race and ethnic knowledge is potentially political, contested, and ideological because ethnic studies emerged in a context of conflict and struggle, and the educational and pedagogical climate of ethnic studies cannot remain neutral or disinterested. The politics of publishing, curricular development, pedagogy, and the transfer of knowledge between faculty, classroom, and community is an inherently political act.

There is a fundamental difference between those scholars who write textbooks on the topic of "race and ethnicity" or "race relations" and teachers, professors, and scholar/activists who utilize such intellectual tools in the context of teaching their students, developing their own knowledge base, or promoting and advocating social change, political struggles, and collective movements for justice, full equality, or popular democracy.

Most textbooks dealing with race relations are more or less interchangeable in terms of their organization of material, their structure, the concepts and theories presented, and the substantive history, facts, **data,** and problems dealt with for a variety of racial and ethnic populations in the United States (and occasionally regionally or around the world). Textbooks are usually produced in conjunction with publishing enterprises whose *business* is to provide **the packaging and selling of commodified knowledge** consisting of relevant material for undergraduate or graduate students in various academic disciplines in the social sciences and humanities. Most race relations textbooks are created in the prevailing tolerant, **liberal or reformist multicultural ideology,** that will provide students with the latest and most objective basic **concepts, definitions,** representative **theories** and paradigms, up-to-date **revisionist racial and ethnic histories, factually valid information,** current assessment of debates and controversies, and evaluation of future trends based on the best available scholarly research.

There is nothing wrong with this state of affairs, and it would be ideal for the ongoing education of college and university students, but those intellectuals, scholars, and activists in the various ethnic studies fields are involved in disciplines that increasingly must build upon concepts, theories, data, and academically reliable information, but *also* politicized frameworks, ideologically discrepant perspectives, and a need to challenge students with application of knowledge in the real world of experience, research at the community level, internships, and the competing experiences of students representing diverse racial, ethnic, gendered, and class backgrounds.

What I am saying, therefore, is that the field of ethnic studies is in need of a new style of textbook that must combine relevant definitions, concepts, and theories with historical and contemporary information about race and ethnicity, but in a manner that is more explicitly political.

Many factors must be considered when discussing the field of ethnic studies and the structure of integrated or separate subdisciplines that evolved on different college or university campuses in different states, regions, or sections of the United States and even around the world. Many of the protests and militant struggles that initially challenged the legitimacy of high school or college curricula and practices regarding the treatment of students of color or the lack of diversity in higher education caught administrators totally off guard or by surprise. Whether at the high school or university level, attempts to placate the militant demands for Black, Chicano, Indian, or Asian studies meant that faculty without the needed training would have to attempt to put together new courses or set up programs that were unprecedented within the business-as-usual status quo. In other cases, radical student or community demands for relevant minority course content were reinforced by activist and/or sympathetic faculty who were well aware of why such changes were urgently needed.

At the college level, controversy over the militant demands for Black, Chicano, and Indian studies was generated by the insistence of activists that nonuniversity faculty teach courses even if they did not have Ph.D.s or even master's degrees. In some cases faculty were condemned by politicians, the media, and the public because they were considered extreme in their politics and their activist teaching, which violated the conservative, traditional, and elitist canons of disinterested and objective scholarship. This was certainly the case with Angela Davis at UCLA, who was a long-term activist, extremely well trained intellectually, and a communist.

Many faculty who accepted the role of teaching Black, Mexican, Indian, or Asian studies courses, or of administering such programs, often had been trained in traditional academic disciplines and had little or no formal training in the rapidly developing ethnic or racial fields. Often faculty were recruited with the provision that they would hold joint appointments in their chosen discipline and the ethnic studies program in order to protect them in case the new programs were abolished, cut, or integrated into existing departments. The climate of the 1960s and 1970s was extremely volatile since the demands for change were coming from minority high schoolers, community activists, and working-class first-generation-to-attend-college students. Faculty and students taught each other. Demands for minority support services and student unions led to accusations that the new racial programs were separatist and that students and faculty on campuses were not academically qualified.

In addition to all the possible combinations of the above scenarios being played out around the country in the context of various racial demographics and political circumstances, the disciplines of ethnic studies had to legitimize their courses, their intellectual rationales, their campus missions, and their career tracks and objectives of faculty with regard to teaching, research, publications, committee work, and campus/community service, which affect decisions concerning tenure, retention, and merit.

The institutionalization of race and ethnic studies was a new phenomenon that challenged the mechanisms of funding, course creation and development, and governance of the university by chancellors, presidents, deans, academic senates, and other bodies. It would take many years to sort out and stabilize the new departments, programs, research institutes, and even new directions in graduate study that would evolve as a response to the demands of activist students and faculty in traditional departments affected by the rise of, and interest in, ethnic studies.

Minority studies and women's or gender studies, it can safely be asserted, changed the face of the social sciences and humanities forever. But the political activism and youthful exuberance out of which these curricula developed could not grow in the university without themselves being affected by changes in the political culture of the larger society or by subsequent generations of students and faculty.

The struggles for ethnic and women's studies over the past thirty-five years or so is now about stabilizing the disciplines, recruiting faculty who are themselves not a product of historical activism and struggle, but rather the product of the programs that were created as well as the people who must carry on the insurgent struggles that have yet to be completed in the university and throughout society.

There are few if any textbooks that place ethnic studies knowledge in a proper historical, political, or social context. My purpose is not to carry out that endeavor but to point out, descriptively, the inherently political climate that has affected the production of ethnic studies knowledge, facts, concepts, theories, and agendas both inside the university and throughout society.

The evolution of ethnic studies is as much about *how* information is used in every department—which consists of relationships among and between faculty members, their students, and the university and community-at-large—as it is about the *validity* and *reliability* of our textbooks that are foundational, but not determinative, of what we do to fulfill our academic and political mandate.

In the following chapters I will present my version of key concepts, definitions, theoretical paradigms, and historical and contemporary overviews on African Americans, Native Americans, Chicanos, and Asian Americans. This work is based upon a large body of scholarly research, writing, and intellectual production. But I have not attempted to compile or synthesize what is available in countless sources. Rather, I will develop a limited overview of ethnic studies while constantly urging my readers to study, raise their consciousness, grow politically, and seek to promote social and economic justice, cultural diversity and awareness, critical analysis of contemporary society, and social transformation of U.S. hegemonic global capitalism that is the by-product of historical Eurocentrism, conquest, colonialism, imperialism, and agendas that continue to rob all of us of our common humanity derived from the realization of justice and shared community.

Questions, Exercises, and Topics for Discussion and Debate

1) The field of ethnic studies should be informed and built upon a foundation of objective, empirically based information, that any disinterested scholar or person can agree upon. Explain why you agree with or do not accept this proposition.

2) Should textbooks reflect the values, biases, and political point of view of the author, or present an objective representation of multiple, clearly articulated points of view for the student to internalize? Explain your answer.

3) What do you think is meant by the phrase: **"the lived politics of race, ethnicity, class, and gender"?**

4) What does the author mean when he speaks about "the packaging and selling of commodified knowledge in textbooks"?

Ethnicity and Race

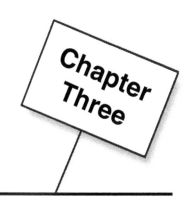

Chapter Three

Key Terms

the American dilemma

assimilation

colonization

criteria for membership

domination

enslaved Indians and Africans

ethnic differences as learned

ethnic group

ethnic identity

ethnic loyalty

ethnicity

European expansion

European immigrants

indentured servants

monogenesis

myth of the melting pot

nation

nationality

nation-state

polygenesis

pre-capitalist mercantile system

race

racial group

racism

settler colonies

slaveholders

subordination

voluntary labor

Key Lesson

The concepts of **ethnicity, race,** and **nation** or **nation-state** are fundamental to the discipline of ethnic studies. Ethnicity and **ethnic identity** are predicated upon learned social behavior, multiple **criteria for membership** in the **ethnic group** or community among which physical appearance or race are only one characteristic, and a strong linkage to the theory of assimilation, voluntary migration, and the melting pot. Race is defined narrowly as a sociohistorical concept that derives from folk knowledge. Over time, religious or biological knowledge is transformed into popular or pseudo-scientific theories of classification that, though arbitrary, separate dominant from subordinated others who may be subject to conquest, colonization, enslavement, dispossession of land, forced removal, denial of rights and citizenship, and even genocide or extermination. Ethnicity is a culturally variable concept and can be voluntarily embraced or lost over time as responses of group members to social conditions in the host society. Race is ascribed to individuals as a result of appearance and sociohistorical context in a society in which group members have been forcefully subordinated on their own land, as in the case of classical colonization or settler colonialism, or through involuntary migration to a host society through enslavement, annexation, or involuntary labor in a context of internal colonialism. Thus the differential treatment of voluntary ethnic immigrants and involuntary racial migrants within a pluralistic multiethnic or multiracial society establishes the context for theorizing ethnic assimilation or racialized exclusion. The dynamics of ethnic prejudice and stereotyping versus racial prejudice, stereotyping, and **racism** as ideological and structural conditions of oppression under varied political economic conditions is fundamental to the discipline of ethnic studies.

> Race: a group of persons (animals or plants) connected by *common descent* or origin; a tribe, nation, or people regarded as of common stock.
>
> Nation: an extensive aggregate of persons, so closely associated with each other by *common descent,* language or history as to form a distinct race of people, usually organized as a separate political state and occupying a definite territory.
>
> Ethnic: (an adjective) pertaining to nations not Christian; pertaining to a race or nation; having common racial, cultural, religious or linguistic characteristics especially designating a racial or other group within a larger system.
>
> (Fenton, 2003, p. 14)

The discipline of ethnic studies in the United States is rooted in a number of historical, political, and ideological contradictions. The material base of colonial expansion was the competition between emerging European nation-states in a **pre-capitalist mercantile system** that pitted well-to-do adventurers, explorers, and trader/investors and the powers of monarchs, kings, queens, and state institutions against one another and that relied upon the involuntary and **voluntary labor** of citizens, **indentured servants, enslaved Indians and Africans,** and the occupation of lands and indigenous peoples in the Caribbean, North America, Mexico, Central America, South America, Asia, and Africa from the mid-1400s through the eighteenth century.

Ironically, the ideological justification, rationalization, or retrospective historical description of the process of expansion, conquest, and colonization has been predicated on the emerging Eurocentric notions of liberty, religious freedom, economic opportunity, and ideas of white supremacy, civilizational superiority, the spreading of the Christian message of salvation to those living in darkness and superstition, and the rights of conquest and just wars along with discovery as a framework for the expansion of capitalism.

In the context of **European expansion** and **colonization,** relationships of **domination** and **subordination** emerged around the world, based on the development of **settler colonies** and the imposition of military, economic, political, legal, religious, and cultural hegemony through violence, coercion, and even cooperative relationships with indigenous people living at various levels of development with the land, other peoples, and the cosmos.

Throughout the western hemisphere, but particularly during the time of colonization in North America by the Spanish, English, French, and Dutch—followed by the independent United States, which successfully won the revolution against England—native Indian civilizations, societies, and tribes were subjected to a continuous onslaught of deadly diseases, cultural genocide, military and civilian occupation, violence, the rape of their women, and the loss of their original sovereignty through treaties, forced removal, loss of land based upon false promises, bad-faith negotiations, the destructive introduction of alcohol, and the private depredations of U.S. citizens and the ever-increasing population of **European immigrants** during the nineteenth century. The United States used its newly won freedom and developing institutions to expand territorially in the name of "Manifest Destiny," and to fulfill the interests of **slaveholders,** land-hungry immigrants, industrialists, speculators, corporate capitalists, railroad magnates, and the exploiters and developers of resources such as timber, coal, oil, hydroelectric power, copper, and agricultural lands. This abbreviated and perhaps overly blunt assessment of European colonialism and U.S. racial history is a necessary context for understanding the concepts of race and ethnicity in relationship to modernity and the nation-state.

At the time that the civil rights movement was actively confronting the reality of Jim Crow racism and de jure and de facto segregation, and the insurgent struggles of American Indians, Chicanos, and Asians were calling attention to the injustices of genocide, reservations, boarding schools, relocation, termination, annexation, subordination, violation of the Treaty of Guadalupe Hidalgo, exploitation of farmworkers' labor, and exclusion and subordination of Asians in the nineteenth and twentieth centuries, most Americans knew very little of the long history of racial or even ethnic injustice. The **myth of the melting pot,** notions of ethnic amalgamation and **assimilation,** and the view that America welcomed immigrants to her shores, provided economic opportunity, and granted legal equality became the basis of the belief that racially oppressed populations would soon become successfully incorporated if they could only emulate and follow the example of other groups such as the Germans, Catholics, Mormons, Italians, Jews, Greeks, Irish, and countless other immigrants who did not fit the Anglo-Saxon Protestant mold, but who, through hard work, self-sacrifice, and education, were able to see their own children and grandchildren become successful citizens in the land of the free and the home of the brave.

The ideology and normatively accepted value of incorporation through assimilation was itself a twentieth-century viewpoint that was developed within the emerging social sciences such as anthropology, sociology, and social work to counter the overt, biologically based racism that was so much a part of the beliefs and ethos of nineteenth- and early twentieth-century thought. By the twentieth century, racial segregation of Blacks was virtually ubiquitous in all parts of the country, Indians were wards of the federal government, Asians were excluded from immigrating to the United States, and Mexicans were for the most part subordinated throughout the states of the Southwest. At the same time, millions of recent Eastern and Southern European immigrants who had come to America between the 1890s and 1920s to work in the emerging industrialized factories of the East, Midwest, and North were living in ethnic slums, tenement apartments, and in conditions that were unsafe, unsanitary, and highly oppressive for men, women, and especially children. This is the context in which social activists, social scientists, social workers, and politicians began to view immigrants as members of cultural groups rather than in exclusively racial terms. Progressives developed a framework of helping to reform urban slums and neighborhoods by teaching immigrants the values and behaviors that would allow them to adapt to the American way of life and to adjust to the economic, political, and other institutions in society. This recognition of **ethnic differences as learned** attitudes and behaviors that had been brought from the country and culture of origin to America was distinctly different from the racist ideology of innate biological make-up as destiny and predictor of intelligence, criminality, violence, sexuality, and other self-fulfilling prophecies based on stereotypes and dominant-group prejudices that were so highly institutionalized, that racial minorities—even when individuals were exemplary in conduct, education, intellect, and breeding—could not collectively find acceptance, mobility, or structural integration into mainstream society.

The relationship between American racist ideology and institutional practice and the view that the United States represents a unique but highly successful social experiment in which diverse peoples from every conceivable ethnic background can throw off or reject foreign heritage and loyalty in order to voluntarily accept citizenship in the great melting pot that was popularized by Israel Zangwill in his 1908 play "The Melting Pot" is the basic contradiction that led the great Swedish sociologist/economist Gunnar Myrdal to speak of the **"American dilemma"** as the contradiction between the abstract values of the American creed, which emphasized decency, and American racist practices based upon violence, discrimination, and denial of full citizenship and justice to racial minorities.

In Zangwill's play "The Melting Pot," the following familiar sentiment was voiced:

America is God's crucible, where all the races of Europe are melting and reforming!

Germans, Frenchmen, Irishmen, and Englishmen, Jews and Russians—into the crucible with you all! God is making the American.

(Gerstle, 2001, p. 31)

In contrast to Zangwill, consider the following quote from Stephen Steinberg's book *The Ethnic Myth: Race, Ethnicity, and Class in America* (1989):

Ethnic pluralism in America has its origins in conquest, slavery, and exploitation of foreign labor, conquest, first in the case of the native Americans who were systematically uprooted, decimated and finally banished to reservation wastelands; and second, in the case of Mexicans in the Southwest who were conquered and annexed by an expansionist nation. Slavery, in the case of the millions of Africans who were abducted from their homelands and forced into perpetual servitude on another continent. Exploitation of foreign labor in the case of the tens of millions of immigrants who were initially imported to populate the nation's land mass, and later to provide cheap labor for industrial development.

(Steinberg, 1989, p. 5)

To conclude this overview for my discussion of race and ethnicity, I will again quote Stephen Steinberg:

To say that ethnic pluralism in America had its origins in conquest, slavery, and exploitation is not to deny that in the course of American history ethnic diversity has come to assume positive value. Nor is it to deny that minorities have often reaped the benefits of an affluent society, notwithstanding the circumstances of their origins. Nevertheless, it is imperative to come to terms with the essentially negative basis on which pluralism developed. Only in this way is it possible to begin to understand why virtually all of the nation's racial and ethnic minorities have confronted intense and virulent bigotry, why all had to struggle to preserve their ethnic identities and institutions, and why the history of race and ethnicity has been fraught with tension, rivalry, and conflict.

(Steinberg, 1989, p. 6)

Sources on Race and Ethnicity

The concepts of race and ethnicity are fundamental to the field of ethnic studies. Each can be defined in simple enough terms to allow necessary comparisons or contrasts in meaning to be reasonably specified. But race and ethnicity are by no means simple terms either with respect to conceptual definitions, historical usage, theorization, or political and ideological application by societal members or by scholars and researchers in various social science and humanities disciplines.

I will begin by providing a list of sources that I have found to be of value, even though my own development of these concepts will not reflect the range of information that is available in these as well as countless other sources and textbooks.

I have found the textbook *Race and Ethnic Relations: American and Global Perspectives* (Fifth Edition) by Martin N. Marger to be a good source for conceptual definitions, theory, and comparative overviews of key American and global ethnic and racial groups. Another textbook that is useful for understanding race and ethnicity in the context of the impact of Europeans in the New World and the history of the United States from the colonial era to about 1990 is James S. Olson, *The Ethnic Dimension in American History* (Second Edition). A very useful text with a strong conceptual and theoretical approach to race and ethnicity and comparative case studies is Stephen Cornell and Douglas Hartmann, *Ethnicity and Race: Making Identities in a Changing World.* The book *Hate Prejudice and Racism* by Milton Kleg is not only an excellent source for information on ethnic groups and race but also for discussions about race and racism; prejudice and attitudes; stereotyping; discrimination, aggression, and scapegoating; hate groups and haters; and hate prejudice and education. Although the book *Uprooting Racism: How White People Can Work for Racial Justice* by Paul Kivel could be cited in the chapter on "racism," I include it here as a useful conceptual, theoretical, and practical guide for understanding race and ethnicity and for applying basic ethnic studies concepts to the understanding of history and contemporary affairs for the purpose of creating racial awareness, multicultural sensitivity, and transformation of self, community, and society.

The following books provide excellent coverage on concepts related to ethnicity, race, and nationalism as well as theoretical and historical coverage of the concept of race in the United States:

Steve Fenton, *Ethnicity*

Thomas F. Gossett, *Race: The History of an Idea in America*

Audrey Smedley, *Race in North America: Origin and Evolution of a Worldview* (Second Edition)

Anthony D. Smith, *Nationalism*

Stephen Steinberg, *The Ethnic Myth: Race, Ethnicity, and Class in America*

Sources on the Concept of Race

Other than the concept of "racism," there is probably no term in the field of ethnic studies that is as controversial, emotionally loaded, or theoretically and historically provocative as "race." While the race concept is directly relevant for understanding the history and evolution of racism in all its modern, Eurocentric, ideological, institutional, and structural manifestations, I will limit myself here to sources that pertain to the meaning of race, while suggesting that many controversies within and between laypeople, scholars, scientists, activists, and members of racialized communities and populations demand that we all become more informed intellectually, socially, and politically in order to more fully be able to evaluate, interpret, and understand the multiple perspectives that issues related to race continue to provoke.

The following books deal with race in terms of its history, definitions, anthropological and cultural usage, relevance in the ancient world, and sociological and political topics:

Alexander Alland, Jr., *Race in Mind: Race, IQ, and Other Racisms*

Robert Bernasconi and Tommy L. Lott, Editors, *The Idea of Race*

Luigi Luca Cavalli-Sforza, *Genes, People, and Languages*

David M. Goldenberg, *The Curse of Ham: Race and Slavery in Early Judaism, Christianity, and Islam*

Stephen Gregory and Roger Sanjek, Editors, *Race*

Kenan Malik, *The Meaning of Race: Race, History and Culture in Western Society*

Ashley Montagu, *Man's Most Dangerous Myth: The Fallacy of Race* (Sixth Edition)

Brian Niro, *Race*

Steve Olson, *Mapping Human History: Genes, Race, and Our Common Origins*

Stephen Oppenheimer, *The Real Eve: Modern Man's Journey Out of Africa*

Frank M. Snowden, Jr., *Before Color Prejudice: The Ancient View of Blacks*

Frank M. Snowden, Jr., *Blacks in Antiquity*

Milford Wolpoff and Rachel Caspari, *Race and Human Evolution: A Fatal Attraction*

Ethnicity

As the quotes at the beginning of the chapter suggest, the concept of ethnicity shares some of the same semantic space as those of race and nation.

Steve Fenton argues that "the idea of an ancestry group of a people linked by common descent however loosely that is thought of, is the core idea of all three terms" (Fenton, 2003, pp. 23–24).

He summarizes the uniqueness of race, nation, and ethnicity by first stating their core commonalty in terms of "descent and communities" (p. 23).

- Race includes two more points:

    1) The idea that "logical" groups are instances of abstractly conceived divisions of humankind.

    2) The idea that race makes explicit reference to physical or "invisible" differences as the primary marker of difference and inequality.

- Nation includes one more point:

    1) The assumption that nations are or should be associated with a state or state-like political form.

- Ethnicity requires three qualifications:

    1) That the group is a kind of sub-set within a nation state.

    2) That the point of reference of difference is typically culture rather than physical appearance.

    3) Often that the group referred to is "other" (foreign, exotic, minority) to some majority who are presumed not be "ethnic." (Fenton, p. 23)

Stephen Cornell and Douglass Hartmann provide a good diagram in their book *Ethnicity and Race: Making Identities in a Changing World,* which demonstrates that race and ethnicity share some commonality while differing in other key essentials.

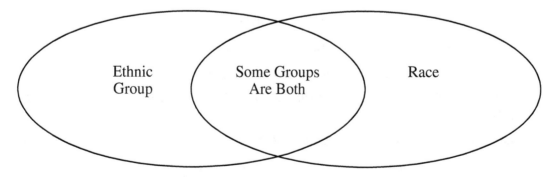

Figure 3.1

Cornell and Hartmann list the differences between ethnic group identity and racial identity as follows:

Ethnic Group

- Identity is based on putative common descent, claims of shared history, and symbols of peoplehood

- Identity may originate in either assignment by others or assertion by selves

- Identity may or may not reflect power relations

- Identity may or may not imply inherent differences in worth

- Identity is usually constructed by both selves and others

Race

- Identity is based on perceived differences

- Identity typically originates in assignment by others

- Identity typically reflects power relations

- Identity implies inherent differences in worth

- Identity is constructed by others (at point of self-construction, group becomes ethnic group as well as race)

(Cornell and Hartmann, 1998, p. 35)

Another race relations textbook that I found useful (see Jaret) provided three possible relationships between the concepts of race and ethnicity:

1) Ethnic groups are subcategories within a race.

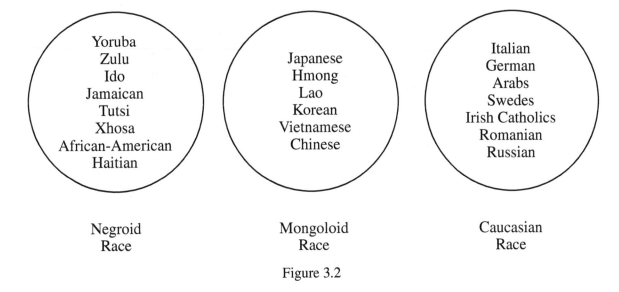

Yoruba
Zulu
Ido
Jamaican
Tutsi
Xhosa
African-American
Haitian

Negroid
Race

Japanese
Hmong
Lao
Korean
Vietnamese
Chinese

Mongoloid
Race

Italian
German
Arabs
Swedes
Irish Catholics
Romanian
Russian

Caucasian
Race

Figure 3.2

The groups listed in each "racial" category presumably have phenotypic similarities despite ethnic/cultural differences in terms of history, customs, language, religion, and any number of socially learned behaviors and criteria for identification and group loyalty.

   2) **Racial groups** are a type or subcategory of ethnic groups.

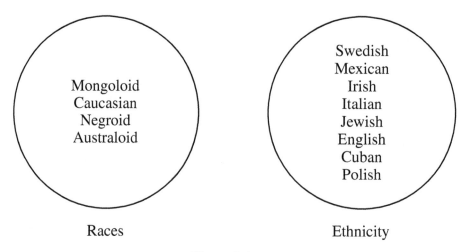

Jews   Polish Americans   Anglo Americans
Chinese Americans   Chicanos
Swedish Americans   American Indians   Black Americans
Asian Americans   Italian Americans

Figure 3.3

The ethnic groups listed may all be characterized by unique national origins, religions, languages or dialects, food preferences, and numerous other community-based criteria as a basis for identity and **ethnic loyalty.** Race is not the basis by which these groups can be singled out as unique even though appearance may be one among many factors determining identity. Therefore, ethnicity is the primary focus for identity, and racial differences may be a subcategory within or between any of the ethnic groups under consideration.

   3) Race and ethnic groups are really two kinds of groups, so we really shouldn't consider either one to be a subtype of the other.

Mongoloid
Caucasian
Negroid
Australoid

Swedish
Mexican
Irish
Italian
Jewish
English
Cuban
Polish

Races   Ethnicity

Figure 3.4

In terms of this scheme, alleged racial groups are represented as large classifications or unique families with no further breakdown in terms of specified similarities or differences. Likewise, any number of ethnic populations or groups can be listed but with no analysis of racial heritage, descent, or necessary physical appearance.

   It is clear that one can create any number of schemes by which to categorize and distinguish various relationships between ethnicity and race.

   I want to devote the remainder of this section specifically to the criteria that in whole or part are helpful for understanding the meaning of ethnicity. In the book *Hate Prejudice and Racism,*

Milton Kleg lists fourteen criteria that were developed by Thermstrom and colleagues in the *Harvard Encyclopedia of American Ethnic Groups* (1980) as a basis for selecting the groups for the encyclopedia. While not exhaustive and certainly open to critique, the criteria for ethnicity include:

1) Common geographic origin

2) Migratory status

3) Race

4) Language

5) Religious faith or faiths

6) Ties that transcend kinship, neighborhood, and community boundaries

7) Shared traditions, values, symbols

8) Literature, folklore, music

9) Food preferences

10) Settlement and employment patterns

11) Special interests in regard to politics in the homeland and the United States

12) Institutions that specifically serve and maintain the group

13) An internal sense of distinctiveness

14) An external perception of distinctiveness

These criteria in all their possible permutations and combinations provide a good concrete starting point for conceptualizing ethnic group differences within different nation-states or social systems.

A generic definition of ethnicity that Kleg provides is the following:

Any group sharing a *common culture* and *feeling of kind* or oneness.

(Kleg, 1993, p. 33)

Kleg cites a definition from the 1950s by Brenton Berry to expand upon the above meaning. Berry's definition of ethnic group states the following:

A human group bound together by ties of cultural homogeneity. Complete uniformity, of course, is not essential; but [t]here (sic) does prevail in an ethnic group a high degree of loyalty and adherence to certain basic institutions, such as family patterns, religion, and language. The ethnic group often possesses distinctive folkways and mores, customs of dress, art, and ornamentation, moral codes and value systems, and patterns of recognition. . . . Above all, there is a consciousness of kind, a we-feeling.

(Kleg, 1993, p. 34)

Some or all of Berry's criteria of ethnicity must inform any definition. A weakness of this antiquated definition is a static and a historical listing of ethnic criteria and an implicit functionalist theoretical bias.

Kleg does point out a useful criteria that may apply to ethnic groups but is perhaps more relevant for defining racially oppressed groups. He cites the bond among African Americans in terms of "a common history of victimization, including chattel slavery, followed by segregation, discrimination, and acts of violence" (Kleg, p. 34).

I indicated earlier that the concepts of ethnicity, nationality, and race overlap. Kleg quotes a composite definition of nationality by Henry Pratt Fairchild that is virtually the same as Berry's definition for ethnic group. Fairchild's definition of nationality states:

> A human group bound together by specific ties of cultural homogeneity. A true nationality is animated by a consciousness of kind (q.v) and has a fundamental similarity in its mores (q.v). There need not be, and seldom is, complete uniformity in all cultural traits; but there must be conformity, or at least sympathy and cooperation, with reference to a number of the basic institutions such as language, religion, dress, and ornamentation, recreation, moral code, political system, family pattern and ethical ideas (q.v). The members of a nationality feel a bond of sympathy to each other different from that they experience toward the members of another nationality . . .
>
> (Kleg, 1993, p. 35)

Fairchild's definition shares the same weaknesses that I specified for Berry's definition of ethnic group. What I want to point out is that Fairchild is really indicating for culturally homogenous nation-states criteria of identification, uniqueness, and loyalty that are identical to Berry's criteria for unique groups that differ from the mainstream or normatively assimilated dominant culture. Fairchild is referencing the modal national culture and values that may differ between nation-states such as the United States, Nigeria, Israel, Vietnam, or other countries (regardless of the actual ethnic divisions within each country).

The concept of ethnicity, ethnic group, ethnic identity, or ethnic loyalty is complicated by the real-world dynamics of individual or group migration; the experiences of individuals and groups within specified historical epochs and geographical regions; the processes of intergenerational communication, socialization, and collective memory; the nature and intensity of forms of victimization, oppression, and persecution; the treatment individuals and groups receive as they gain access to social institutions or greater class mobility; and the alteration of ethnic or racial reality due to interethnic relationships, mixed marriages, diluted sense of ethnic identification, multiple ethnic or group loyalties, or voluntary identification with the national identity of the dominant society.

The variations on these themes can become analytically and conceptually complicated with respect to the history, sociological processes, and phenomenological experiences of ethnic communities and individual persons. In attempting to move beyond complications and controversies surrounding the meaning of ethnicity and ethnic affiliation, Milton Kleg proposed a paradigm that began with a definition of ethnic group that approximated Berry's definition. His paradigm or ethnicity model recognized five interrelated categories (Kleg, p. 37):

1) ethnic group

2) subethnic group

3) composite ethnic group

4) individuals or groups of heritage

5) groups of faith

I do not intend to develop Kleg's paradigm but to place definitions and theories of ethnicity in a larger contemporary framework that draws upon the work of Steve Fenton.

Steve Fenton concludes his study of ethnicity by claiming that there cannot be a theory of ethnicity nor can "ethnicity" be regarded as a theory. He makes two claims:

1) . . . there is not a single unitary phenomenon "ethnicity" but rather an array of private and public identities which coalesce around ideas of descent and culture. But the contexts in which these identities are found are multifold and multiform. This does not mean sim-

ply that there are "ethnicities" rather than "ethnicity" that is the "same" phenomenon in different situations. Rather it means that the contexts are sufficiently different so as to give an entirely different sense, force and function to ethnic identities according to the social, economic and political site of their emergence or their rise to "importance."

(Fenton, pp. 179–180)

2) . . . in the "contexts of ethnicity," it is the context that matters more than the ethnicity . . . the significance or salience of ethnic identities is, in many if not most instances, influenced by external coordinates of the ethnic action rather than by internal characteristics of the ethnic identity itself. . . . It suggests that our attention should be primarily turned to these "coordinates" which form part of an explanation of why "ethnicity" has become a focus of action . . . our interest then is not just in "ethnicity" but in ethnicity as a component of the sociology of modernity.

(Fenton, p. 180)

In the discipline of ethnic studies it is important to provide basic definitions of key terms that form the basis of theoretical frameworks that have been proposed by historians, sociologists, and scholars concerned with empirically investigating or solving persistent social problems in the political, cultural, or economic framework of a society or nation-state.

As Fenton argues, we cannot ultimately define ethnicity, ethnic group, or ethnic identity independently of the social and historical context that shapes and structures the existence and meaning of the groups that we want to understand. Since context is fundamental and dialectically related to how ethnic identities and communities will be structured, we must study the history and external coordinates that shape each specific ethnic context.

It is axiomatic in ethnic studies that theory is both value-laden and political. As a reflexive discipline, ethnic studies scholars and activists view race, ethnicity, class, and gender to be by-products of processes associated with modernity, the rise of modern nation-states, the development of an emerging global market, the transition from mercantile capitalism to free-market, monopoly, and transnational capitalism, and the contact and oppression of indigenous societies through conquest, enslavement, colonization, exploitation of labor, genocide, imperialism, neo-colonialism, and globalization.

This is the larger context that conditions the development of ethnicity and race under constantly changing circumstances in which those representing the power structures and institutions of various societies, nations, and regions in the evolving world system confront and impact the lives of the racial and ethnic other.

The ethnic studies scholar must be aware of history, sociological, and political processes, and the prevailing dynamics of domination and hegemony in relation to subordination and oppression. But beyond their role as academics, researchers, and honest scholars, the prevailing concern of those in the field of ethnic studies is not just to understand injustice, domination, oppression, or exploitation, but to change it.

Race

Indeed, the very existence of physical differences among populations is accepted as a concrete evidence of race. And we have been conditioned to respond automatically to the presence of certain varying physical features as indicators of race and the differences it connotes.

(Smedley, 1999, p. 1)

Race, then, originated, not as a product of scientific investigations but as a folk concept; it initially had no basis, no point of origin, in science or the naturalistic studies of the times. The folk idea was subsequently embraced, beginning in the mid- to late-eighteenth century, by naturalists and other learned people and given credence and legitimacy as a supposed product of scientific investigations. The scientists themselves undertook efforts to document the existence of the differences that the European cultural worldview demanded and had already created.

(Smedley, 1999, pp. 26–27)

The social sciences have come to reject biologistic notions of race in favor of an approach which regards race as a social concept.

(Omi and Winant, 1986, p. 60)

Race consciousness, and its anticipation in theories of race, is largely a modern phenomenon. When European explorers in the New World "discovered" people who looked different than themselves, these "natives" challenged existing conceptions of the origins of the human species, and raised disturbing questions as to whether *all* could be considered in the same "family of man." Religious debates flared over the attempt to reconcile the Bible with the existence of "racially distinct" people. Arguments took place over creation itself as theories of **polygenesis** questioned whether God had made only one species of humanity (**"monogenesis"**). Europeans wondered if the natives of the New World were indeed human beings with redeemable souls. At stake were not only the prospects for conversion, but the types of treatment to be accorded them. The expropriation of property, the denial of political rights, the introduction of slavery and other forms of coercive labor as well as outright extermination, all presupposed a worldview which distinguished European—children of God, human beings, etc.—from "others." Such a worldview was needed to explain why some should be "free" and others enslaved, why some had rights to land and property while others did not.

(Omi and Winant, 1986, p. 58; boldface added)

The concept of race is central to the discipline of ethnic studies because its initial folk meaning evolved and reinforced expansionist European nation-states in their historical encounters and subsequent conquests of indigenous peoples around the world.

In time, the concept of race came to replace religious notions of inclusion in Christendom based upon theological orthodoxy, which in Spain was further defined by the notion of clean bloodlines *(limpieza de sangre)* by which Catholics could distance themselves from newer converts, and especially from Jews who feigned conversion to maintain social status while secretly practicing Judaism. With the development of systematics and classification in naturalism and biology, the concept of lineage or group origins of humanity became linked to lower species of organisms. Thus, the attempt to understand order in nature became a basis to create a rigid hierarchical ordering of different classes of humanity. The folk knowledge of differences when combined with scientific efforts to make sense of nature used Europeans as the epitome of human civilization, spirituality, and aesthetic beauty in relation to classifying indigenous, pagan and "less evolved" peoples as inferior, uncivilized, and barbarous heathens.

The historical evolution of the notion of race is paralleled by the rise and development of the nation-state. Likewise, racism as institutional practice, the social and cultural manifestations of racial inequality, and the changing ideological rationalizations and justifications of such practices cannot be understood apart from the structural changes that have accompanied modernity.

The social reality of race as a taken-for-granted natural relationship based on difference and inequality between Europeans and populations of color has long been reflected in the ideology of racism, which makes it possible for people *not to see oppression* as a humanly produced outcome but rather to rationalize their own willing participation in all such practices as literally conforming to a law of nature that can no more be altered than the law of gravity. Thus when racism was brutal throughout the eighteenth and nineteenth centuries in particular, even the most preeminent and educated representatives of the dominant status quo did not argue against prejudice, bigotry, or intolerance. This was true even in the twentieth century, according to Philip Yale Nicholson:

Prejudice, bigotry, and intolerance had nothing to do with the racial and national expression of group identification in this era. Those words were infrequently used. They were almost unknown concepts. The perceived truth about race and nation were confirmed by science and enforced by laws, albeit with the passing of time, and with alterations in law and science. Today the word bigot is used to describe the expression of racial and national identity commonly used by yesterday's presidents, Supreme Court justices, prime ministers, and most scientists, writers, and intellectuals. Until the rapid break down of formal colonial and racial structures of the post-World War II era, such words as *bigot* or *prejudice* that depicted racist thinking or behavior negatively were used almost exclusively by their victims or by those who tried to protect them from abuse.

(Nicholson, 2001, pp. 95–96)

The idea of race and the ideology of racism coexist in an interesting configuration in time. As Omi and Winant acknowledge:

From the very inception of the Republic to the present moment, race has been a profound determinant of one's political rights, one's location in the labor market, and indeed one's sense of "identity." The hallmark of this history has been *racism,* not the abstract ethos of equality, and while racial minority groups have been treated differently, all can bear witness to the tragic consequences of racial oppression.

(Omi and Winant, 1986, p. 1)

Racism, whether acknowledged or not, contributed to the oppression of Indians, Blacks, Asians, and Mexicans. In the post–civil rights present, people are finally willing to be able to acknowledge the racism of the past, but do so, according to Omi and Winant, in order to

. . . offer a vision of the contemporary US as an egalitarian society, one which is trying to live up to its original principles by slowly extending and applying them to the gnawing issue of race. In such a vision recent history is seen as a period of enlightened progress—an unfolding drama of the social, political and economic incorporation of minorities which will not be thwarted or reversed. The "colorblind" society, it is argued, will be the end result of this process.

(Omi and Winant, 1986, pp. 1–2)

With the previous definitions, history, and theory as background, I want to specify what is important about the concept of race for ethnic studies.

- There is a paradoxical relationship between lay or folk ideas about race and so-called scientific knowledge claims.

- What *race* a person "*is*" appears to be obvious from looking at him or her (phenotype or typological thinking).

- Racial differences have a *naturalness* that seems to *affirm* the very *existence* of races (folk wisdom or racial commonsense worldview).

- People claim that there always have been and that there will always be races (misrepresentation about human origins and a rationalization for the unpleasantness of racial problems or conflict).

- The concept of race as folk beliefs about human variability is different from society to society, thus demonstrating the *social construction of race* rather than a *biologically natural* or *inevitable classification system* with *built-in* or *preordained* grounds for *affirmation* or *denying humanity* to any group within the human family.

- When applied to variant or phenotypically distinct populations as if they were separate biological species, the concept of race fails to recognize the genetic compatibility of human males and females to mate (either voluntarily or through coercion) and to produce fertile offspring, barring reproductive or physical anomalies.

- All attempts to create meaningful *classification systems* based upon race—whether by naturalists, biologists, anthropologists, or sociologists—have been *arbitrary* because racial variations are *not discrete* and the *criteria* for race do not vary concomitantly between individuals or populations.

- Despite the fact that the *human species* and all of its *variant subpopulations* cannot be validly isolated *scientifically* unless one provides a *normative* rather than *natural* reason to do so, *race as a socially constructed category* continues to be salient within the context of human beliefs about ethnicity, culture, race, and nationality.

- Modern science has rejected typological thinking in favor of studying and comparing *gene frequencies* among subpopulations.

- Classification for the purpose of *excluding people* from the *human species* is no longer recognized as having *any* scientific validity.

- The concept of "pure races" is *not valid* and there have probably *never been* pure races in the historical or distant past.

- Popular racial divisions that distinguish broad categories such as caucasoid, negroid, australoid, or mongoloid are largely imprecise and arbitrary.

The Sociological Meaning of Race

I have made a number of references to the thesis that race is a *social construction* and a *socio-historical concept*. While most social scientists, sociologists, and race relations experts are interested in both lay and expert scientific opinions about race, the sociological analysis of race does not have to concern itself with the *scientific accuracy* of racial conceptions. The sociological analysis of race is fundamentally interested in the *social* and *political consequences* of people's *ideas* and *beliefs* about *racial distinctions*.

Whatever the biological *validity* or *invalidity* of the concept of *race*, what is most *important* and *significant* for *intergroup relations* is the *social meaning* of *race*.

- People attach *significance* to the concept of *race* and consider it to reflect *real* and *important* clues about how to *interpret* social *divisions* and *distinctions* among *human groups*.

- As long as people *believe* that *differences* in *selected traits* are *meaningful,* they will *act* on the basis of those *beliefs*.

- The sociologist W. I. Thomas is remembered, among other things, for his "definition of the situation": "If men [people] define situations as real, they are real in their consequences."

- A belief in the "*inferiority*" of a racial group may lead to a *self-fulfilling prophecy* if that belief is culturally embedded, institutionally legitimate, and collectively acted upon by the people of a society.

- Race is a human invention that is not *socially reproduced identically within or across different sets of social arrangements* regardless of the state of scientific knowledge.

- The racial categories of one society need not *agree* or *correspond* to those of another society.

- The *social meaning* of *race* is constantly *subject to change* through *contestation* and *political struggle.*

- When the people in a society *buy into* a *social vision* about *racial differences,* they *believe* that *perceived physical differences* between groups *correspond* to *social* or *behavioral differences.*

Conclusion

Whatever laypeople, professionals, bureaucrats, scientists, politicians, educators, or any one else mean when they use the terms *ethnicity* and *race,* these concepts are historically, theoretically, empirically, politically, and ideologically important for defining the scope and application of ethnic studies in terms of teaching, research, and praxis in social and political contexts.

The concepts of ethnicity and race cannot be defined independently of the historical and sociological processes out of which they emerge and through which they are transformed.

The overlap in meaning of race and ethnicity make it difficult to discuss these terms in relation to different ideal-type models of society. But the commonality in meaning requires that ethnic and racial relationships not be trivialized.

Often, today's assimilated or even dominant ethnic groups were defined and treated as racial populations that were subjected to prejudice, stereotyping, scapegoating, violence, exploitation, and exclusion yesterday in relation to a previous social order.

Many groups that are defined and assumed to be racial in today's social meaning of the term in reality can be subdivided in ethnic and cultural qualities that are significant. Not all Black people in the United States share an African American historical trajectory. Cubans, Brazilians, Puerto Ricans, Dominicans, West Indians, and diverse African immigrants can be differentiated in countless ways based on language, dress, food preferences, sports interests, musical tastes, religion, and political loyalties and commitments.

The same may be true of Native Americans, Asians from diverse social and ethnic origins, and Latinos who may have a shared language but represent different national origins and a full range of physical differences.

With such complicated racial and ethnic diversity in the United States and throughout every region and nation in the world, it is no wonder that so many groups and individuals have had to overcome so many forms of prejudice, stereotyping, and racism throughout the long history of modernity.

The next chapter will be devoted to an analysis of prejudice and stereotyping and will provide a context for discussing the meanings of racism in the chapter to follow.

Questions, Exercises, and Topics for Discussion and Debate

1) Discuss the meaning of the terms *ethnicity, race, nation,* and *nation-state.*

2) What is the relationship between ethnicity, ethnic identity, ethnic differences as learned, and assimilation or ethnic amalgamation?

3) Discuss the meaning of the concept of race for ethnic studies: Include:
   a) The folk meaning of race
   b) Classification systems based upon race
   c) The meaning of "pure races"
   d) The social construction and social reality of race

4) What is the relationship between ethnicity, voluntary migration, indentured servants, and European immigrants in relation to the melting pot and assimilation theory?

5) How do race, colonization, involuntary migration, and innate biological make-up as destiny relate to the ideology of racism and the enslavement of Indians and Africans?

6) Discuss the meaning and implications of monogenesis and polygenesis with reference to racism.

Prejudice and Stereotyping

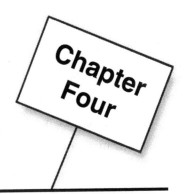

Chapter Four

Key Terms

attitudes

beliefs

"color-blind" racism

degradation, scapegoating, or dehumanization

ethnic and racial discourse

false or incorrect information

feelings

groups of people

liberal consensus

mass communications

media hegemony

multiculturalism

overgeneralizations

partial, distorted, erroneous, or caricatured information

prejudice

prejudice reduction paradigm

propaganda

rearticulation of racist ideology

social categories

stereotyping

Key Lesson

The historical reality of ethnicity and race is not a natural or constant biologistic destiny that persists in historical time despite social and cultural transformations of the evolving nation-states system. The failure of ethnic and racial distinctions to disappear from the medieval era and the Renaissance through the modernistic Enlightenment and the Industrial Revolution went against the predictions of classical sociologists such as Marx, Durkheim, and Weber. **Prejudice** was originally associated with notions such as provincialism, superstition, and irrationality that Enlightenment rationalists used to define the persistence of religious thought in the era of progress, science, and secular social engineering of society. But modernity also saw the rise of Eurocentric thought, expansion, colonization, and racism. By the twentieth century, the progressive theorists from sociology and anthropology began to criticize biologistic racial thinking and they recognized that ethnic group behavior was learned and subject to rapid change as groups were successfully assimilated into the host society. The study of prejudice and **stereotyping** also paralleled developments in mass media and the recognition that individuals and groups could be either educated or propagandized by media content. After World War II a liberal consensus emerged in which hatred, scapegoating, discrimination, and racism were viewed as malleable and subject to change through education, media campaigns, and transformation of attitudes, emotions, cognitions, and group or individual prejudices and stereotypes. While the reduction of ethnic and racial prejudice is critically important for creating a healthy society based upon humanistic and democratic values of inclusion and tolerance, it has become clear that racial prejudice and stereotyping are not the cause of structural inequality and that as biological racism and ideology are reduced or defined as outside of the polite social consensus, that cultural racism and the rearticulation of reactionary political agendas become more subtle and nuanced as "color-blind" racism and "victim blaming" are now couched in terms of values rather than genetics or nature.

Introduction

In the post–civil rights era—following the *Brown* decision of 1954 through the sit-ins; freedom rides; Birmingham; the march on Washington; the murders of Medgar Evers, four Black girls in a Birmingham church Sunday school class, Malcolm X, John F. Kennedy, and Martin Luther King, Jr.; the years of "long hot summers"; the passage of the 1964 Civil Rights Act, and the 1965 Voting Rights Act—most Americans came to finally understand (however indirectly) just how unjust, cruel, degrading, and racist the system of southern White supremacy or Jim Crow segregation was. This fragmentary and partial recapitulation of the dialectic of Black–White struggle serves to highlight a number of important points that are essential for understanding how White dominance in American history could become institutionalized so completely and for so long.

- For most Americans from White, European, immigrant backgrounds—until relatively recently—the so-called race problem was defined in terms of Black and White.

- Until the insurgent movements of the 1950s through the mid-1970s by Blacks, Chicanos, Indians, Asians, and women, dominant-group Americans did not consciously or actively think of the United States as a multicultural nation that had any need to remember, respect, celebrate, acknowledge, or incorporate the contributions of people of color or women into "their" history or in "their" educational system.

- When the representatives of the power structure or institutional leaders do acknowledge racism, institutional inequality, or egregious injustices, they, for the most part, cannot apologize, provide reparations, ask for forgiveness, or do anything that might "set a dangerous precedent" for some future group that might use a prior law or court decision as a basis for its call for justice.

- The dramatic transformation of racial practices and prejudices in the post–World War II period of the present have resulted in the rise of a new form of racism based upon an ideology of "color-blindness" in which individuals can appeal to "race-neutral" criteria as a basis for setting standards for social inclusion while denying that institutional mechanisms of inequality were or still are operating in the lives of people of color.

- The recognition of prejudice and stereotyping as fundamental concepts for social science research and investigation has been a major basis for reform and social transformation of the **attitudes, feelings,** and **beliefs** of members of the dominant society—particularly with reference to the role of mass media as organs of communication, influence, propaganda, and indoctrination as well as within the reform and transformation of American educational curricula.

- But the huge research and applied literature from the disciplines of psychology, social psychology, and mass communications—which have fueled decades of work in the realm of attitude change, race awareness training, multicultural sensitivity work, and prejudice and stereotype reduction programs—has often been framed in an overdetermined effort to target individuals or prejudiced groups that are deemed to be operating outside the mainstream society and its preeminent goals of assimilation, adjustment within mainstream institutions, and the promotion of mainstream values that do not too actively bring up the past or fuel conflict or divisiveness in the present.

In this chapter, I want to define and characterize the concepts of prejudice and stereotype that have been developed throughout much of the twentieth century as an alternative to the paradigms of biological racism, racial White supremacy, racist hierarchy, and ideologies of innate racial inferiority based upon folk knowledge, pseudo-science, and social Darwinism.

Sources on Prejudice and Stereotyping

The literature on prejudice and stereotyping is vast and impossible to cover in an introductory textbook or course outlining the field of ethnic studies. The amount of work that has been conducted in the area of stereotyping of racial and ethnic minorities in film, television, newspapers, radio, school textbooks, and children's books alone, would be insurmountable.

In today's world of global communications, the Internet, the World Wide Web, chatrooms, cyberspace, talk radio, computer games, desktop publishing, special-interest satellite channels, ideologically based publications, and rap music—just to name the most obvious media—it is clear that the effort to understand the original meanings of prejudice and stereotyping in a far simpler time, beginning seventy or eighty years ago, now require a grasp of **media hegemony** that is almost unimaginable.

The following works are more than adequate for understanding prejudice, stereotyping, and their relationship to racism.

Gordon W. Allport, *The Nature of Prejudice*

Donald Bogle, *Prime Time Blues: African Americans on Network Television*

Donald Bogle, *Toms, Coons, Mulattoes, Mammies, and Bucks: An Interpretive History of Blacks in American Films*

Eduardo Bonilla-Silva, *Racism without Racists: Color-Blind Racism and the Persistence of Racial Inequality in the United States*

Ward Churchill, *Fantasies of the Master Race: Literature, Cinema, and the Colonization of American Indians*

Arnoldo De León, *They Called Them Greasers: Anglo Attitudes Toward Mexicans in Texas, 1821–1900*

Lynn Duvall, *Respecting Our Differences: A Guide to Getting along in a Changing World*

Paulo Freire, *Pedagogy of the Oppressed*

James M. Jones, *Prejudice and Racism* (Second Edition)

Paul Kivel, *Uprooting Racism: How White People Can Work for Racial Justice*

Milton Kleg, *Hate Prejudice and Racism*

Robert G. Lee, *Orientals: Asian Americans in Popular Culture*

Donald Macedo, *Literacies of Power: What Americans Are Not Allowed to Know*

Michael Pickering, *Stereotyping*

Sheridan Prasso, *The Asian Mystique: Dragon Ladies, Geisha Girls, and Our Fantasies of the Exotic Orient*

Ruth Sidel, *Battling Bias: The Struggle for Identity and Community on College Campuses*

Christine E. Sleeter, *Multicultural Education as Social Activism*

Teun A. Van Dijk, *Communicating Racism: Ethnic Prejudice in Thought and Talk*

Prejudice

My understanding of prejudice for the emerging social sciences in the twentieth century begins with the critical paradigm shift away from biological racism, social Darwinism, and pseudo-science in the direction of the concept of culture as learned, and away from the provincial abso-lutism and ethnocentrism of White Anglo-Saxon Protestant values and expectations for ethnic immigrants and eventually racial minorities.

- Prejudice as a topic in the social sciences highlighted a major positional shift away from theories of innate and inborn differences toward a recognition that social behavior was not determined by an association with one's genetic make-up or any outward phenotypic traits, but through processes of interaction, nurture, opportunity, acceptance, and learning within a supportive environment.

- The focus on attitudes and the empirical conditions under which dominant individuals or groups acted, discriminated against, or scapegoated racial or ethnic minorities marked a major shift in the politics of White supremacy.

- In the era of massive migration of European ethnic groups to the United States—and at the time that reactionary politicians and social Darwinist scholars were calling for the exclusion of Asians and Eastern and Southern European immigrants, while fully institutionalizing the practices of Jim Crow segregation—reformers who were attempting to work with immigrants and their children in the slums, tenements, and ethnic ghettos attempted to help them to assimilate, adjust to, and learn about the American society.

- The rise of **mass communications** in the 1920s and 1930s ushered in studies of the new media and their potential for entertaining, educating, and influencing people in the mass society.

- During World War II, the issues of **propaganda** and the use of media to influence thought and action became critical in the battle against fascism and Nazism.

- After World War II, the struggle against communism and the battle for "the hearts and minds" of the people of the third world and the nonaligned nations, forced the United States to examine its own image and treatment of minorities in the larger international geopolitical context of the cold war.

- By the post–World War II era, the emerging **liberal consensus** was that dominant-group prejudice and stereotypes were equally, if not more, important as the cause of racial oppression in America than the traits of racialized groups.

- Gunnar Myrdal's monumental study "The American Dilemma" focused on Whites, rather than Blacks, as the major source of discrimination against minorities due to their failure to uphold core values of the American creed.

- Sociologists studied the attitudes, feelings, beliefs, and actions of Americans and stressed the value of positive interaction, cooperation, and education as the best way to influence values and change behavior.

- In the aftermath of World War II there was a concern with what came to be known as "the authoritarian personality" as a result of trying to understand how ordinary Germans had been so willing to follow Hitler in persecuting and scapegoating the Jews.

- The liberal **prejudice reduction paradigm,** assimilation, integration, and reform of the racist system was confronted and challenged by the militancy of Black nationalists, revolutionaries, and the emergence of radical identity politics in the late 1960s.

- The recognition by scholars and activists (including Martin Luther King, Jr.) that racism, poverty, and militarism were national and international problems led to an all-out attack on institutional racism, internal colonialism, neocolonialism, imperialism, and apartheid.

The topic of prejudice and stereotyping remains important but has undergone a major "make-over" due to the development of ethnic studies and the societal-wide movement toward multiculturalism—whether in a conservative, liberal, or radical form.

It is important to point out that there has also been a sustained backlash against the movements of the 1960s by those who stood for and defended the status quo; by many former activists who either "grew up," "sold out," or joined the neoconservatives and other right-wing movements between the 1970s to the present; and by the complacency, historical ignorance, or unfavorable political climate that the current generation of young people find themselves in.

The Meaning of Prejudice

The recognition of prejudice and stereotyping is important in the field of race relations because racial oppression or the creation of the "other" within a colony, nation-state, or society cannot be sustained without the legitimization of the superordinate or dominant race, religion, or ethnic group and the justified **degradation, scapegoating, or dehumanization** of those who have been conquered, colonized, violated, exploited, or excluded.

Prejudice is not the *cause* of *racism* but a *consequence* and *symptom* of racism's *persistence* and *continuing reality.* Prejudice and stereotypes, like the folk beliefs about race, constitute either the *a priori* common sense of an ethnic or national culture, or are created and sustained institutionally within a society by elites, power brokers, or individuals who must deal with complex conditions of racial and class conflict, struggle, or accommodation everyday.

Before providing a number of definitions of the term *prejudice,* I will quote Eduardo Bonilla-Silva, who has developed a discourse analysis of **"color-blind" racism** in which he explores the attitudes and beliefs of people in the post–civil rights era to show how people are able to rationalize racial inequality, deny any allegiance with racism, and even represent themselves as the victims of racism.

This is what Bonilla-Silva says:

Ideologies are about "meaning in the service of power." They are expressions at the symbolic level of the fact of dominance. As such, the ideologies of the powerful are central in the production and reinforcement of the status quo. They comfort rulers and charm the ruled much like an Indian snake handler, whereas rulers receive solace by believing they are not involved in the terrible ordeal of creating and maintaining inequality, the ruled are charmed by the almost magical qualities of a hegemonic ideology.

(Bonilla-Silva, 2003, pp. 25–26)

If these ideologies or prejudices represent "meaning in the service of power," then one of the consequences of speaking or believing them in the course of social discourse is that people not only reinforce the status quo by simply expressing their feelings and beliefs, but they align themselves with prevailing conditions and the unspoken power that is ready to act against those who might clearly see a need to act outside of the social relations that prejudice may serve to uphold. In discourse, the emotional and cognitive schemes that people express will also reflect reference group identification and social values that they are prepared to act upon.

Defining Prejudice

There are many definitions of prejudice and many theories about the function and purpose that prejudice serves. The definitions that I am providing are taken from Milton Kleg's *Hate Prejudice and Racism* (1993):

- Prejudice derives from the Latin word *praejudicium,* meaning previous judgment or a judgment made before the facts are examined.

- Prejudice has evolved to include "an attitude with an emotional bias."

- Prejudice can mean "any unreasonable attitude that is unusually resistant to rational influence."

- Prejudice is an irrational suspicion that is immune to information.

- In popular speech, prejudice has come to mean an attitude that involves the rejection of certain people based solely on their membership in a particular group (e.g., women) or based on certain identifying characteristics (e.g., skin color).

- Prejudice can be defined as an arbitrary belief or feeling toward an ethnic group or its individual members.

- Prejudice involves a judgment "based on a fixed mental image of some group or class of people and applied to all individuals of that class without being tested against reality."

- "Ethnic or racial prejudice can be defined as a readiness to act stemming from a negative feeling, often predicated upon a fixed over-generalization or totally false belief and directed toward a group or individual members of that group" (Kleg).

- Prejudice is defined as "an antipathy based upon a faulty and inflexible generalization. It may be directed toward a group as a whole or toward an individual because he/she is a member of that group" (Allport, 1958).

Given these definitions that capture overlapping meanings and some nuances of the term *prejudice,* I will specify my sense of *how* one can recognize prejudice in social discourse or interaction.

Prejudice is a term that applies to every potential interaction or discourse that any one might find themselves in. But our use of the word prejudice is confined to **ethnic and racial discourse.**

- Discourse involves our interactions in everyday life within the social encounters, discussions, debates, and arguments that we may find ourselves in.

- Prejudice is a potential disruption or break in the smooth taken-for-granted conversations and relationships that people engage in.

- Prejudice can also reinforce group norms, values, standards, and social or ideological boundaries that morally bind people to those sharing their interests and identities.

- I believe that emotionally charged or heated debates, arguments, or exchanges may be the result of people's prejudices being expressed and simultaneously revealing ideological, intellectual, and emotional rifts in the social or group order.

- Prejudice is recognizable if one hears or chooses to point out **overgeneralizations** about **social categories** or **groups of people.**

- Prejudice may be recognized by the strong or vigorous assertion or defense of **false or incorrect information.** This is contextually different than innocent mistakes or false information that one is willing to acknowledge when it is pointed out.

- An unwillingness to listen or to change one's mind in the face of counterarguments, information, or "reasonable" appeals may indicate prejudicial feelings, attitudes, or beliefs.

- Prejudice, almost by definition, involves the expression of **stereotypes** and rigid adherence to fixed and inflexible positions.

- A classic form of prejudice is the claim that "exceptions" or counterarguments for which one cannot answer within their own form of argumentation "only proves the rule."

Stereotypes as a Component of Prejudice

The topic of stereotypes is intimately associated with the structure and expression of prejudice. There are many books and studies that explore the nature of stereotyping in great detail. Besides studies of racial stereotypes that may be reflected by content analysis of movies, newspaper accounts, news, magazine shows, and other efforts at communication or interpersonal influence, the work that I find most useful for understanding stereotypes are studies of racial discourse, dialogue, or political and ideological perspectives.

The works of Teun A. van Dijk, Philamena Essed, Eduardo Bonilla-Silva, and David Wellman are excellent examples that deal with the expression and analysis of White, working-class, and minority discourse in terms of substantive content and themes that reflect the structure and semantic moves as well as the rhetoric and stories that people tell that situate their racial beliefs and experiences within the larger social and cultural structure of society.

I cannot summarize the vast array of information on stereotyping that is available, but I want to make a few points:

- Walter Lippmann described stereotypes as "pictures in our heads" that we do not acquire through personal experience.

- Stereotypes are exaggerations or caricatures of group behaviors.

- Stereotypes are "shorthand depictions" of the group.

- Stereotypes are "a special language" that functions to "reinforce the beliefs and disbeliefs of its users, and to furnish the basis for the development and maintenance of solidarity for the prejudiced."

- Stereotypes are the "evidence" provided to rationalize or intellectually justify or support prejudiced arguments.

- Stereotypes are the common generalizations that people share to simplify and to communicate about complex group and social realities.

- Stereotypes are oversimplistic and overexaggerated beliefs about a group, generally acquired second hand and resistant to change.

- Stereotypes are sustained despite numerous individual cases that clearly refute their validity.

- Stereotypes, like prejudice, can be positive or negative. Even what people intend to express as complimentary may be a reflection of **partial, distorted, erroneous, or caricatured information.**

Conclusion

The topic of prejudice and stereotyping remains important in contemporary society because of ongoing efforts to deal with racial, ethnic, religious, and gender bias that is expressed by individuals and groups with different sets of values, beliefs, and lifestyles.

Since the 1980s we have witnessed the birth or development of **multiculturalism** as a new paradigm to replace the liberal consensus that developed in twentieth-century social science. We have also seen a continuation of individual and group-based manifestations of racist violence, racial scapegoating, attacks against Jews, Muslims, Asians, gays, lesbians, and other groups or individuals who enter or leave the political context of American local, national, and international reality.

The country has become very polarized since the 1970s—partly due to the politics of the cold war; partly due to the effectiveness of the political right to organize around issues of anticommunism, family values, opposition to "illegal" immigration and bilingual education, pro-life and anti-feminist agendas, crime, and welfare reform; and partly due to patriotism in the aftermath of September 11 and the Bush–Cheney War on Terrorism. The attack on the universities based on the charges of "political correctness" and efforts to undermine ethnic and women's studies while trying to define affirmative action as "reverse racism" in order to promote "color-blind" racism and "meritocratic standards" while American society continues to be economically and racially divided between the "haves" and the "have-nots" are serious points of contention.

The civic discourse in the United States is increasingly not just a battle-ground for dominant group hegemony over racially oppressed people of color, women, and working-class people, but the organized right is increasingly winning against the forces of the left and those who struggle on behalf of communities and a fuller inclusionary democracy.

The realignment of the United States in relation to the forces of globalization, transnational capital, and the new world economic order have not ended racial inequality at home or between advanced capitalism and the underdeveloped nations of the Third world.

I view the battle against racial prejudice and stereotyping to be ongoing and unfinished. The only thing that has changed are the new forms and manifestations of racism and the **rearticulation of racist ideology** in the context of American hegemony.

Notable Quotes

Everybody has prejudices—you, me, your parents, teachers, neighbors, friends, acquaintances, relatives. Even great Americans and other famous people have prejudices. Some keep theirs hidden, but others let them show.

(Duvall, 1994, p. 14)

Prejudice is a positive or negative attitude, judgment, or behavior generalized to a particular person that is based on attitudes or beliefs held about the group to which the person belongs.

(Jones, 1997, p. 142)

We have inherited in our society a complex set of beliefs about race. These beliefs strongly state or unmistakably imply that non-white racial groups generally, and blacks in particular, are inferior to whites, lack the values systems whites hold, and may be either threatening to society (in the strong form) or undeserving of full status and participation in U.S. society. Against this backdrop of cultural signification and beliefs, it is easy to formulate biased judgments against the group and to employ these group-based beliefs in the assessment of individual group members. Prejudice engenders or results from such a system of thinking.

(Jones, 1997, p. 136)

Stereotypes play a vital role in our everyday life because they have been shown to affect what information we pay attention to and remember, how we interpret that information, and how we use it to form judgments. Finally, stereotypes can operate at an unconscious level and thus influence our thoughts, feelings, and behaviors without our awareness that this is happening. Because stereotypes play such a critical role in prejudice and can have subtle but powerful influences on our every thought and action, they are one of the most crucial elements in understanding the continuing power of prejudice.

(Jones, 1997, p. 202)

Stereotyping imparts a sense of fixedness to the homogenized images it disseminates. It attempts to establish an attributed characteristic as natural and given in ways inseparable from the relations of power and domination through which it operates. If a social group or category is stereotyped as inherently lazy, stupid, childish, or dishonest, the ascription acts not only as a marker of deviancy, making it marginal to the moral order, but also as a revalidation of that which it is measured against and found wanting. This two-foul movement is integral to the ways in which stereotypes function as a form of social control. The assessment that is offered in a stereotype is based on the leading precepts and preoccupations of those who reproduce them, and it is this assessment that underlies the perception and positioning of the "difference" it regards.

(Pickering, 2001, p. 5)

Questions, Exercises, and Topics for Discussion and Debate

1) Discuss the meanings of the term *prejudice* and why White attitudes, feelings, and cognitions about race and ethnicity in the twentieth century were important for establishing the liberal consensus on race.

2) Explain the meaning and characteristics of racial and ethnic stereotypes. What is the relationship between prejudice and stereotyping? What are the sources of stereotypes in a society, and how do stereotypes operate at the level of culture, media, the educational system, for the dominant group and individuals, and in the lives of people of color?

3) People often assert that stereotypes are either true or are based upon empirical and historical evidence. Do you accept or reject this proposition? Why? What are the social consequences of holding or believing stereotypes about race, ethnicity, class, and gender?

4) Is it possible to free oneself of racial prejudice and to consciously reject stereotyping? If stereotypes are socially produced and reproduced at the institutional level, what relationship do they have to reinforcing the status quo and the power structure in a multiracial society?

5) What is the impact of the diverse media of mass communication in modern society for either promoting or eliminating prejudice and stereotyping in American society?

6) Think about the groups with which you identify or to which you belong, given your family heritage, your ethnic or racial community and identity, and your social class and gender. How has your life been affected by the prejudices or stereotypes you hold? How has your life been affected by the prejudices or stereotypes of out-group members?

7) Reflect upon the relationship of prejudice and stereotyping to racism as an ideology and to racial discrimination, hate crimes, scapegoating, and racial profiling.

8) Discuss the political implications of multiculturalism and "color-blind" racism in the post–civil rights era.

Racism

Chapter Five

Key Terms

annihilation

color-blind racism

cultural racism

ethnic cleansing

ethnocentrism

Eurocentrism

everyday racism

extermination

genocide

hate crimes

holocaust

institutionalized inequality

institutionalized racism

new racism

prejudice

profiling

racial hierarchy

racialized exclusion

racism

racism as historical imposition

racist ideology

scapegoating

stereotyping

systematic discrimination

White privilege

white supremacy

Key Lesson

Various social psychological and social science terms and concepts describe the attitudinal predisposition of individuals and groups to act toward other persons or members of out-groups on the basis of biological traits, physical differences, or cultural distinctions that represent otherness or foreignness. Thus ethnic or racial prejudice—which is derived from ethnocentrism—influences the emotional judgments, intellectual or logical cognitions, and ideological schemata of persons who may act out against out-group members through a variety of behaviors ranging from discrimination, scapegoating, profiling, to blaming the victim. It is commonly assumed that prejudice, stereotyping, and ethnocentrism in a racialized and pluralistic society are the cause of historical or **institutionalized racism,** racial hierarchy, and numerous individual or collective forms of racist behavior. But there are no definitions of **racism** that limit the concept's meaning to individual prejudice, ethnocentrism, or stereotyping, which are causally prior to historical or contemporary practices such as Eurocentrism, White supremacy, White privilege, **everyday racism,** profiling, hate crimes, racialized exclusion, institutionalized inequality, genocide, holocaust, ethnic cleansing, and extermination or annihilation of racial populations. The exercise of racism involves dominant group power, institutional practices, reinforcement from a culturally racist pattern of belief, and the transmission of racist stereotypes and prejudice to individuals even in the face of dominant-group disapproval or negative sanctions. In the post–civil rights movement era, old-style racism, Jim Crow, or dominative racism has been rearticulated into **cultural racism,** new or modern racism, symbolic racism, and "color-blind" racism. But the real-world manifestations of past racism or ongoing racial hierarchy and inequality continue, even as the well-meaning either blame the victims of racism for their present problems or deny that anything that looks like racism is racism.

Introduction

The discipline of ethnic studies differs from other academic fields in a number of ways, which have been discussed in previous chapters. While ethnic studies may be highly dependent upon definitions, concepts, and theories that derive from anthropology, biology, literary criticism, history, economics, political science, and sociology, the substance and orientation of ethnic studies is not reducible to the assumptions or historical origins of particular fields connected to the humanities or social sciences.

Ethnic studies, to reiterate, has hybrid origins in the historical struggles of racially oppressed populations—both before and during the era of Jim Crow segregation; anticolonial, nationalist independence movements; internal colonial struggles; the civil rights movement; and the anti-imperialist–anticapitalist battles throughout the nineteenth and twentieth centuries—and in the universities where teachers, students, researchers, and activists have demanded, fought for, written about, researched, and struggled for the classes, programs, research centers, and disciplines that now constitute the diverse subfields and curricula that individually and collectively constitute ethnic studies.

Ethnic studies in the United States is of recent origin but its intellectual roots and political praxis encompass the universal brutality of the Middle Passage; the conquests of the Taino, the Mexica, the Incas, and Indians of North America; the slave revolts and resistance of Toussant, Denmark Vessey, Nat Turner, Frederick Douglass, Gabriel Prosser, Harriet Tubman, W. E. B. DuBois, and Malcolm X; the struggles for justice of Joaquín Murrieta, Tiburcio Vasquéz, Mexicano braceros and farmworkers, Dolores Huerta, Reies Lopez Tijerina, Corky Gonzales, Cesar Chavez, and the disenfranchised Chicano/as throughout Mexico and occupied America; and the legacies of Pontiac, Tecumseh, Osceola, Geronimo, Crazy Horse, Sitting Bull, John Trudell, the people of Sand Creek, Wounded Knee, and every Indian boarding school. Those who lived as second-class citizens, those who died without a trace, those exploited as cheap labor, those denied the right to vote, those excluded—from the Chinese and Japanese to the Filipino, those who were lynched, those who were brutalized in racist courts and prisons, those women raped and sterilized, those denied burial in cemeteries after dying for their country, those who fought for civil rights, those who still fight today—these are the people, groups, and causes that are the substance of every course and subfield in ethnic studies.

Ethnic studies is compelled by the richness and depth of its subject matter to be interdisciplinary, multidisciplinary, comparative, historical, contemporary, engaged, activist, and academically rigorous and objectively accurate.

Finally, I am of the opinion that the central conceptual and substantive focus of ethnic studies is the issue of racism and the necessity to demonstrate, document, and deconstruct the historical and contemporary manifestations of Eurocentrism throughout the world system.

Basic Questions

The concept of racism is central to ethnic studies because it is connected to so many other fundamental aspects of racial oppression, domination, Eurocentrism, and White supremacy. I shall begin my discussion of racism by raising some questions that help to focus attention on a number of theoretical and intellectual concerns.

1) What is racism? What components are associated with various definitions of racism?

2) Are prejudice and racism the same?

3) What is the locus of racism? Does racism operate at the level of individuals, small groups, social institutions, bureaucratic or corporate organizations, the mass media of communication, or throughout a whole society or social structure?

4) What is institutional racism? Are individuals accountable for the consequences of institutional racism?

5) What is cultural racism?

6) Can African Americans and other people of color be racist, or only Anglos, Caucasians, or European-descended people? Can people of color be racist toward other populations of color or in nations ruled by non-Europeans?

7) Is the phenomenon of racism of only historical significance?

8) Does racism still exist in the contemporary United States, and if so, to what extent?

9) Is racism getting worse in the contemporary world, as some members of oppressed or minority groups claim?

10) Is racism related to social inequality and unequal distribution of social prestige, wealth, social privilege, power, and quality of life?

11) Who benefits from racism, and how?

12) Does racism manifest itself in identical ways in different historical periods within a given society?

13) How can racism be minimized, meaningfully reduced, or ended?

Sources on Racism

The historical, theoretical, and contemporary literature on the topic of racism is immense and growing. The writing on race as a fundamental concept also tends to overlap most discussions of racism.

Additional discussion of racism can be found in the historical and contemporary autobiographies and biographies of individuals who have described their personal experiences and encounters with racism, discrimination, prejudice, and the institutions of social movement struggles through which the meanings of race, class, and gender are contested in diverse historical epochs.

Other sources where racism and racist practices are elaborated are the studies of insurgent racialized movements for racial liberation; decolonization; abolition of slavery; opposing de jure segregation or apartheid; protesting and organizing; struggles for sovereignty, civil rights, Black power, Chicano power, Asian American, or Native American identity; and issue-based struggles around topics such as labor and workers' rights; class and inequality; gender and sexism; the border and immigration; the criminal injustice system and the prison industrial complex; poverty, welfare, and health care; and education, language, and the curriculum. In providing a list of books that deal with various aspects of racism, I have created groupings that are not necessarily mutually exclusive or independent of each other. The topic of racism includes the following areas:

I. Historical overviews of racism

II. Eugenics, social Darwinism, and scientific racism

III. Definitional, conceptual, and theoretical discussions of racism

IV. Edited readers about various aspects of race and racism

V. Books about racial experience, everyday racism, elite racism, and reverse racism

VI. Racism in the post–civil rights era

VII. European racism, anti-Semitism, and the Holocaust

VIII. White power and White supremacy

I. Historical Overviews of Racism

1) Richard Drinnon

   Facing West: The Metaphysics of Indian-Hating and Empire Building

2) George M. Fredrickson

   Racism

3) George M. Fredrickson

   White Supremacy: A Comparative Study in American and South African History

4) Paul R. Griffin

   Seeds of Racism in the Soul of America

5) Reginald Horsman

   Race and Manifest Destiny: The Origins of American Racial Anglo-Saxonism

6) Benjamin Isaac

   The Invention of Racism in Classical Antiquity

7) Philip Yale Nicholson

   Who Do We Think We Are? Race and Nation in the Modern World

8) Ronald Sanders

   Lost Tribes and Promised Lands: The Origins of American Racism

9) George W. Stocking, Jr.

   Victorian Anthropology

II. Eugenics, Social Darwinism, and Scientific Racism

10) Elazar Barkan

   The Retreat of Scientific Racism: Changing Concepts of Race in Britain and the United States Between the World Wars

11) Stephen Fraser, Editor

   The Bell Curve Wars: Race, Intelligence and the Future of America

12) Stephen Jay Gould

   The Mismeasure of Man

Racism: The Problem of Agency, Social Structure, and Power

In the previous discussion of prejudice and stereotyping, one can discern an interesting paradox. Most discussions of prejudice indicate that it consists of socially learned attitudes; emotional predispositions that may direct one's actions; and ethnocentric tendencies based upon erroneous, false, and distorted information that are not subject to change. It is clear that the prejudiced individual is viewed as irrational for willfully not yielding to intellectual information based upon logic, objectivity, and a disinterested desire to correct false beliefs that can potentially place the prejudiced person beyond the forces of rational discourse and social control.

In other words, prejudice may reflect an irrational set of attitudes that have been acquired through primary or secondary socialization based upon one's identification with particular reference groups that are at odds with a wider normative social consensus in the social system given the fact that stereotypes are "pictures in our heads" that we do not acquire through personal experience and yet they constitute the "evidence" provided by people to rationalize or intellectually justify or support prejudiced arguments—the attempt to correct or reduce racial prejudice is a social control mechanism that society attempts to employ when society has been forced to confront the structural and institutional racism that was largely accepted and taken for granted in previous eras of history.

Individuals may not be held accountable for acquiring prejudice and stereotypes, but their stubborn persistence in holding on to such beliefs or identifying with groups whose complex ideologies may contribute to social deviance or violence becomes the basis for holding the individual or group morally accountable.

But how are racist institutions and discriminatory practices first established? Do irrational segments within a society consciously convince or persuade others that acting on their beliefs and feelings will somehow be good or profitable to the entire society? If racial prejudice and stereotyping can be reflexively critiqued and questioned at one point in time, how is it that racist stereotypes, prejudices, and actions can seemingly operate or exist in other periods as either prevailing social or cultural norms, self-evident assertions of truth, or legitimate and acceptable rationalizations and justifications for the racism of dominant individuals or groups in society?

Clearly, the creation of racism and its endurance in and through the operation of social institutions is not the product of irrational or intellectually inferior minds.

Racism may retrospectively be analyzed and evaluated as based upon prejudice and stereotypes that reflect social and cultural bias, or that demonstrate the operation of unconscious and dysfunctional psychodynamics that may be described as "sick," "perverted," or "morally reprehensible," but racism can only be understood in each historical epoch in which it operates as a product of social violence, institutional social arrangements, and culturally accepted forms of legitimation that—unless subject to organized oppositions, resistance, and counterhegemonic power—reproduced the dominant power structure and social practices of the society.

Racism as a Product of Modernity

It is not without significance that many contemporary scholars have concluded that race is a relatively recent concept in human history. The cultural structuring of a racial worldview coincides with the colonial expansion of certain Western European nations during the past five centuries, their encountering of populations very different from themselves, and the creation of a unique form of slavery. Expansion, conquest, exploitations, and enslavement have characterized much of human history over the past 5,000 years or so, but none of these events before the modern era resulted in the development of ideologies or social systems based on race. . . . This view, while referring only to the West, unambiguously challenges the claim that race classifications and ideologies were or are universal or have deep historical roots.

(Smedley, 1999, pp. 16–17)

Most historians regard the emergence of the expansionist Western nation-state in about 1500 as the beginning of a new era, the modern era. Few have thought about racism as an interrelated, defining part of the same era.

(Nicholson, 2001, p. 7)

The institutions and practices associated with racism and nationalism are never exactly alike, but common threads are interwoven among them. The nation-state that emerged over the past 500 years displaced religious and dynastic institutional mythology and came to be the prevailing system of political authority in the world. Racism shared the twists and turns of this modern world system of human organization with the nation, as its other half, in one double helix. Race and nation are inseparably linked and interdependent. One claims the devotion and loyalty of most of the world's people. The other contributes to that devotion by denying the humanity of most of the (rest of the) world's people. Racism sleeps when expropriation is missing or dimly perceived; it awakes in war, in conquest, and as a reaffirmation of irrational loyalty to national authority. Leaders explain what is real; their power to decide the fate of others confirms their truths, and those who accept and depend on their authority internalize those truths as the prevailing mythologies.

(Nicholson, 2001, p. 13)

. . . the social meaning of race in modern society emerges from the contradiction between an ideological commitment to equality and the persistence of inequality as a practical reality. The modern world grew out of the dissolution of feudalism and the emergence of capitalism. Capitalist ideology, as embodied in the Enlightenment, expressed hostility to the parochial, irrational nature of feudalism and proclaimed a belief in human equality and a universal society. In practice, however, the particular form of capitalist society placed limits on the expression of equality. Capitalism destroyed the parochialism of feudal society, but it created divisions anew; divisions, moreover, which seemed as permanent as the old feudal ones. As social divisions persisted and acquired, the status of permanence, so these differences presented themselves as if they were natural. The conviction grew that inequality, whether within Western society or between the West and the non-Western world, was in the natural order of things.

(Malik, 1996, p. 6)

The claim that race, racism, the nation-state, and nationalism are products of the modern era is in no way meant to minimize the ability of humanity in the ancient or premodern era to inflict pain, violence, or suffering on those defined as deviant, different, inferior, or barbarian. Any study of ancient city-states, nations, empires, and civilizations will bear witness that people are capable of inflicting pain and cruelty in every era of history.

But from the perspective of ethnic studies, modernity brought together a unique combination of material, cultural, and ideological forces that culminated in new forms of political organization, the emergence of capitalism, the development of trade and transnational markets, and forms of oppression that subjected indigenous peoples and racialized others to conquest, colonization, Eurocentric domination, cultural genocide and enslavement, and economic exploitation that were both quantitatively and qualitatively more oppressive than any comparable practices in the ancient world.

The historical study of racism is a primary tool in the intellectual arsenal of the ethnic studies scholar. Through historical and comparative analysis, it is possible to trace the unique conditions associated with the origin and transformation of social institutions, organized institutional practices that may differ from one nation-state to another in the world system, and the social, cultural, and normative emergence of dominant social values and rationales by which conduct is legitimized, explained, and rationalized.

As Malik discusses in the previous quotation, race and racism can be evaluated in structural and ideological terms as constituting a disjunction between the Enlightenment value of universal equality (which undermined feudal rigidity and absolutism) and the reality of institutional inequality between social classes within nation-states and the hierarchical racialization of the non-European others who were conquered, colonized, and annexed by nation-states without being allowed full citizenship or class access within the nation-state.

The significance of racism as a development within modernity is two-fold:

1) The transformation of European feudalism led to important social and economic changes that undermined the power of the Catholic Church; weakened the absolute authority of kings and monarchs; led to the development of towns, the displacement of serfs from commons lands so that the nobility and landholding gentry could privately develop their own estates; and through the advances in finance, banking, book-keeping, and new technology, the foundations were laid for the modern nation-state, exploration, conquest, colonization, mercantilism, slavery, and by the eighteenth and nineteenth centuries, the rise of the Industrial Revolution and the full manifestations of modern capitalism.

2) The material transformation of Europe, which could not have been completed without the domination of the people, land, and resources of the New World, nor the enslavement of Africans and the exploitation of the peasants and working class of Europe, was affected by developments in the realm of natural science and biology.

The work of classifiers and taxonomists led to new beliefs about the nature of human beings in Europe who were defined as spiritually, civilizationally, and aesthetically superior to the racial others throughout the known world.

The beliefs needed to support and sustain those in power and the populations who served the state in various capacities evolved first within religious categories that were meaningful for Christendom, and later through natural or biological categories that explained the "naturalness" of the emerging inequality between the European Christians of whatever background and the racial others who were marginalized through historically specific forms of domination and hegemony.

The best historical overview of how religion and biology reinforced the material shift from feudalism to capitalism in the context of modernity is provided by George M. Fredrickson in his book *Racism* (2002), which I will present to conclude this section:

> The term "racism" is often used in a loose and unreflective way to describe the hostile or negative feelings of one ethnic group or "people" toward another and the actions resulting from such attitudes. But sometimes the antipathy of one group toward another is expressed and acted upon with a single-mindedness and brutality that go far beyond the group-centered prejudice and snobbery that seem to constitute an almost universal human failing. . . .
>
> It is when differences that might otherwise be considered ethnocultural are regarded as innate, indelible, and unchangeable that a racist attitude or ideology can be said to exist. It finds its clearest expression when the kind of ethnic differences that are firmly rooted in language, customs, and kinship are overridden in the name of an imagined collectivity based on pigmentation, as in white supremacy, or on a linguistically based myth of remote descent from a superior race, as in Aryanism. But racism as I conceive it is not merely an attitude or set of beliefs; it also expresses itself in the practices, institutions, and structures that a sense of deep differences justifies or validates. Racism, therefore, is more than theorizing about human differences or thinking badly of a group over which one has no control. It either directly sustains or proposes to establish a *racial order,* a permanent group hierarchy that is believed to reflect the laws of nature or the decrees of God. Racism in this sense is neither a given of human existence, a universal "consciousness of kind," nor simply a modern theory that biology determines history and culture. Like the modern scientific racism that is one expression of it, it has a historical trajectory and is mainly, if not exclusively, a product of the West. But it originated in at least a prototypical form in the fourteenth and fifteenth centuries rather than in the eighteenth or nineteenth (as is sometimes maintained) and was originally articulated in the idioms of religion more than in those of natural science.
>
> (Fredrickson, 2002, pp. 1, 5–6)

It is important to acknowledge that even though racism can be defined abstractly and analytically—as we shall see shortly—it cannot be understood a-historically. The empirical study of racism is always historically and contextually located in a specific society, with a specific set of institutions, and a unique racial hierarchy that cannot be understood properly unless grounded in its specific history.

The Relationship between Prejudice and Racism

Most popular and media-based discussions or exposés on the topic of racism almost without exception focus on individual or group behavior that demonstrates or documents prejudice, stereotypical beliefs, everyday racist behavior in familiar environments such as work settings, shopping, buying automobiles, renting apartments, media content or coverage, and forms of discrimination that seemingly derive from such biased attitudes, negative emotions, ethnocentric social or group orientations, and apparent double standards that are usually denied by individuals when confronted after the fact by media representatives or journalists who have secretly videotaped the conduct in question.

There is in fact a strong voyeuristic fascination in this age of "hidden videos," "undercover investigations," "secret footage," and "shocking exposés," with revealing deviant behavior, catching people in morally compromising situations, bringing the mighty and powerful down, and using techniques of tabloid journalism and "reality TV" to blur the line between public conduct and the personal or private sphere that many people are willing to violate for money, fame, or short-term publicity. Thus the recognition of what racism is in popular or everyday discourse usually begins with news of representations derived from any of the following familiar topics:

- Public expression of racial slurs.

- Celebrity, politician, or public figure expresses stereotyped, racist, or "politically incorrect" sentiment, not knowing a microphone was "on."

- Minority group individual provides personal or anecdotal accounts "proving" that he or she is subject to "racist behavior" because the individual is [fill in the racial group].

- Extremist groups or their individual members verbally or physically target minority individuals or groups.

- Sudden appearance of racist graffiti on cars, neighborhood homes of minority group members, or on synagogues, churches, or mosques.

- **Profiling** or targeting of minority group members by law enforcement agencies.

- The existence of racist or hate-based publications, music, hotlines, websites, or behavior influenced by such sources.

- **Hate crimes** and **scapegoating** (usually condemned by all, and labeled as "regrettable but isolated incidents" by "lone and/or sick" individuals).

I am not arguing that the media *only cover* racism as manifested by prejudice, stereotyping, or ideology, nor am I claiming that institutional racism and collective organizational or bureaucratic forms of racism *are not covered.*

My point is that it is far easier to define racism as thought, feelings, and behavior that can be located in *specific* or *known individuals* who can be held accountable for morally or legally violating sacred social norms of fairness, inclusion, equality, and justice—and who can be isolated for censure, moral condemnation, punishment, and/or rehabilitation, education, or racial awareness training.

In addition to this emphasis on racism as prejudice and stereotyping, the role of the family, education, and religion as the key institutional sources of primary socialization for children and teenagers is recognized as the critical arenas for the transmission and communication of positive, fundamental, and appropriate values and behavior that reproduce the desired self-consciousness of social and political elites at the individual and group level.

The core values in American society are held to be the moral compass that must be continually reproduced throughout society if moral, ethical, and legal definitions of accountability, responsibility, and right conduct are to be the basis for social and self-control at the level of individual and social conduct.

The functionalist and elitist analysis of racism is provided to describe and explain why the United States has become so preoccupied and obsessed with programs for prejudice reduction; education on racial and ethnic diversity; sensitivity about gender and sexism; tolerance and celebration of differences; multiculturalism; awareness of sexual orientation; and diversity throughout the educational system to eradicate ignorance, teach multiracial knowledge, and build positive values and self-esteem for all students.

This orientation toward racism can and should be applauded by people of goodwill throughout American society. Presumably it reflects the hard lessons that Americans have learned about their actual history and heritage in the post–World War II era, which has encompassed the May 17, 1954, *Brown v. Board of Education* case; the African American struggle for civil rights and equal justice; the equally strident demands for inclusion represented by the actions of Chicanos, Latinos, Indians, and Asians; and new efforts to forge racial, ethnic, gender, and sexual identities based on militant ideologies of nationalism, community empowerment and control, consciousness raising, and particularistic identity politics.

I would argue, however, that the understanding of racism that most Americans now claim is, in fact, not predicated on having truly internalized hard lessons about our racist history and heritage, let alone having grasped or dealt with the post–World War II movements for civil rights, social inclusion, feminism, sexual liberation, peace, or ecology. Whatever the popular consensus *is* about the nature and meaning of racism in America, scholarly writing and research about racism does not accept the analysis of prejudice and ideology as sufficient for defining the term, explaining its historical origins, or dealing with its institutional manifestations and consequences for contemporary society.

Within the disciplines of ethnic studies, racism is never defined exclusively in terms of prejudice, stereotyping, or ideology. While most scholars and activists recognize and appreciate the significant role that prejudice and ideology must play in any useful discourse about racism, the fact is that no definition of racism—other than those that treat it as *ideology* or as a *belief system*—will *reductively* treat prejudice and ideology either as the *cause* of racism or as the *primary solution* to the problems created by the *existence* of racism.

As I explained in Chapter 4:

Prejudice is not the cause of racism but a consequence and symptom of racism's persistence and continuing reality.

I will explain the basis for this claim in the next section.

Defining Racism

Most experts in race relations draw upon a number of concepts that are synonymous with, or that overlap in meaning with, the concept of racism. Among the terms that identify the diverse components and meanings of racism are:

- **White privilege**
- **Systematic discrimination**
- **Institutionalized inequality**
- **Racialized exclusion**
- State-based laws, court decisions, and government policies
- **Genocide**
- **Holocaust**
- **Ethnic cleansing**
- **Annihilation**
- **Extermination**
- **White supremacy**
- Cultural superiority
- Ideological rationalizations, justifications, and endorsement of any or all of the above practices

- **Prejudice**

- **Stereotyping**

- **Ethnocentrism**

Although they are obviously related to each other, I argue that prejudice and racism are not the same.

Prejudice as a Component of Racism

Benjamin P. Bowser and Raymond G. Hunt (1996) provide the following definition of racism:

> Racism results from the transformation of *race prejudice* and/or *ethnocentrism* through the *exercise* of power against a racial group defined as *inferior,* by *individuals* and *institutions* with the *intentional* or *unintentional support* of the *entire culture.*
>
> (Italics added)

The key to this definition of racism is the phrase "racism results from the *transformation* of race prejudice and/or ethnocentrism . . ." Racism involves a relationship and interaction between:

1) Exercise of *power.*

2) *Ideology* of racial inferiority consciously or unconsciously applied to a racial group.

3) *Prejudice* or *ethnocentrism* at the individual or group level.

4) *Institutional* racism.

5) A *societal culture* that *intentionally* or *unintentionally* supports racial prejudice and racist institutional arrangements.

Bowser and Hunt have provided a *comprehensive definition* of racism and a macro and micro *interactive description* of the abstracted social components that one must look for historically and empirically among existing social structures to identify the presence of racism. If the culture, institutions, and group or individual versions of ideology do not act upon or transform prejudiced or ethnocentric individuals or groups, racism cannot fully operate in a society.

Another definition of racism that stresses the dominant society's power to *act* against *racialized subordinate populations* is Paula S. Rothenberg's meaning of the term:

> Racism involves the *subordination* of *people of color* by *white people*. While an *individual* person of color may *discriminate against* white people or even *hate them,* his or her *behavior* or *attitude cannot be* called *"racist."* He or she may be considered *prejudiced* against whites and we may all agree that the *person acts unfairly* or *unjustly,* but *racism* requires something *more* than *anger, hatred,* or *prejudice;* at the very least, it requires *prejudice plus power.* The history of the world provides us with a long record of *white people holding power* and using it to *maintain* that *power* and *privilege over people of color,* not the reverse.
>
> (Rothenberg, 1987, p. 89; italics added)

Rothenberg's definition is controversial. She states that only White people in modern world (**Eurocentric**) history have socially, culturally, and institutionally been able to exercise power over people of color. Her implication is that social dominance and White privilege have resulted in racism against the world's indigenous, African, and Asian peoples. She views the attitudes, prejudices, and emotional reactions of oppressed people against Whites as *regrettable, unfair,* and *unjust,* but *not racist* because such populations cannot *collectively rise up* or *take control of* the *institutions* of society in order to *oppress* or *seek revenge* against Whites for their *real* or *imagined* wrongs to people of color.

Based on the work of Bowser and Hunt and Rothenberg, the concept of racism is centered around *dominant-group power* and *not upon dominant* or *minority group prejudices,* which by themselves are insufficient to create racism. Bowser and Hunt say that dominant-group prejudice must be transformed by dominant power to constitute racism. Paula Rothenberg insists that because the racially oppressed *lack power,* they *cannot be racist* in spite of proof that they are *prejudiced, hateful, unfair,* or *unjust* toward Whites.

These two authors have discussed prejudice as a *component* in their definitions of racism, but neither is willing to *equate prejudice with racism* or to *reduce racism* to the *various manifestations of prejudice* operating *independently* of *dominant social* or *group power.*

Racism as Ideology

The most basic definitions of racism begin by articulating the strict *ideological* meaning of the term. But even the abstract description of **racist ideology** cannot be fully appreciated without knowing the historical evolution of the concept of race in relation to the structural and institutional production of inequality between dominant elites and members within the national or colonial stratification system and the processes by which racialized others are excluded, marginalized, or permanently inferiorized. We shall find that most multicomponent or compound definitions of racism include specific reference to the role of ideology for sustaining, rationalizing, or justifying racist practices over time.

Joe R. Feagin places ideology in a larger historical context in his book *Racist America: Roots, Current Realities, and Future Reparations:*

> The expansion of Europe from the 1400s to the early 1900s eventually brought colonial exploitation to more than 80 percent of the globe. The resulting savagery, exploitation, and resource inequalities were global, and they stemmed, as W. E. B. DuBois has noted, from letting a "single tradition of culture suddenly have thrust into its hands the power to bleed the world of its brawn and wealth, and the willingness to do this." For the colonizing Europeans it was not enough to bleed the world of its labor and resources. The colonizers were not content to exploit indigenous peoples and view their exploitation simply as "might makes right." Instead, they vigorously justified what they had done for themselves and their descendents. Gradually, a broad racist ideology rationalized the oppression and thereby reduced its apparent moral cost for Europeans.
>
> (Feagin, 2001, p. 69)

By understanding that ideology develops and evolves *with* European expansion, exercise of power, and the institutionalization of oppression, it becomes clear that the *function* of ideology is to unify an entire culture and way of life, and to provide solace, certainty, and the moral comfort through which the members of the dominant society can rationalize, live with, and accommodate long-term brutality as natural and even ultimately humane for those subject to such practices.

This discussion of ideology, additionally, provides the grounds for understanding how social prejudice and stereotypes can come to operate throughout the various sectors of society, even if racism is a by-product of ruling elites whose policies of domination cannot be carried out without the hegemony that produces acceptance and consent within the dominant population, while their diverse roles in oppressing various racial others leads the excluded, marginalized to internalize their own oppression.

The concept of ideology not only explains how dominant elites and members of society can rationalize, as natural, the forms of domination that they create and apply, but it can equally be applied to the dominated and subordinated groups and individuals as a counterhegemonic belief system that raises the consciousness of the conquered and colonized and thus motivates them to organize, revolt, rebel, or engage the system of oppression and its **historical imposition** of violence.

I will only present two definitions of racism as ideology, but they are both sufficient to explain abstractly what historical or contemporary racist ideologies assert in their diverse empirical particulars.

James A. Banks provides the following definition (Banks, 1987, p. 74):

Racism is a *belief* that human groups can be *validly grouped* on the basis of their *biological traits* and that these *identifiable groups inherit* certain *mental, personality,* and *cultural characteristics* that *determine* their *behavior.* A corollary belief is that some biological groups, such as *Caucasians,* have *superior mental* and *behavioral traits* and that others, such as Blacks and Indians, are mentally and culturally inferior.

(Italics added)

The key to understanding the ideology of racism involves the legitimization of a racial hierarchy based on permanent and fixed, genetically determined, and phenotypically expressed markers of difference between dominant and subordinate group members. What distinguishes racism is the belief that permanent biologically distinct external differences are an accurate and valid predictor of valued social and cultural traits such as intelligence, moral character, refinement, taste, civilizational capacity, spirituality, leadership, and ultimately the right to rule over others who are labeled as heathen, savage, pagan, barbaric, uncivilized, and inferior. Racism, therefore, involves the justification of a **racial hierarchy** and its designation of superior and inferior statuses based on race. The dominant group, as the superior creators and bearers of civilizational values, is responsible to rule over, administer, and evaluate the potential of their inferiors for development, progress, freedom, rights, responsibility, and assimilation or political independence. Racism favors the status quo and its social and institutional arrangements, unless or until it is resisted with a counterideological force, what Gandhi and King called "soul force," or even physical force and liberatory violence.

The other definition of racism as an ideology comes from Joe R. Feagin (1984, p. 5):

Although this term has been used loosely, for our purposes we can define racism specifically as an *ideology* which considers a group's *unchangeable physical characteristics* to be *linked* in a direct, *causal way* to *psychological* or *intellectual characteristics,* and which on this basis *distinguishes* between *superior* or *inferior* racial groups.

(Italics added)

I do not need to add much commentary or explanation to what Feagin has stated. The key to racism as an ideology is that dominant groups become dominant by first managing to oppress and subordinate a population that can be differentiated from their own membership in terms of territory, color, appearance, culture, and/or behavior that can be directly correlated with racial difference. I do not believe that groups operating from a position of power, territorial expansion, imposition of their institutions or culture upon others, or internally colonizing racial minorities within their own territory have ever defined themselves as inferior, morally deficient, or as lacking historical or social grounds for behaving as they have.

Racism as Historical Imposition, Institutional Arrangement, and Ideological Justification

Maulana Karenga, who headed the cultural nationalist organization US in the 1960s, developed and popularized the Black celebration of Kwanzaa, and has been a professor of African American studies, has written a complex definition of racism that emphasizes the violent imposition of racism, which he defines as a "specious concept." Karenga places racism in an historical and institutional context, and then elaborates on the nature of racism as an ideology.

Karenga (1988, pp. 395–414) begins by asserting:

"For race is not a scientific concept as I have argued elsewhere, but rather a social category used to establish human worth and social status. It is the fundamental category of racism which is not simply attitudes but a system of denial and deformation of a people's history and humanity and right to freedom, based exclusively or primarily on the specious concept of race.

Next Karenga defines the components of racism and emphasizes the violent nature of racism, its imposition on people so as to deny, distort, and destroy their history, and then to use their labor to build up the oppressor's history as though it alone constitutes a universal history of humanity:

> Racism expresses itself in three fundamental ways as: 1) historical imposition; 2) ideological justification; and 3) institutional arrangement. It is an act of violence against and imposition on a people's history and humanity in racial terms, an interruption and appropriation of their history, and a utilization of their labor—the essential process of history—for the building of another's history.

The final two paragraphs of Karenga's definition treat the notion of ideology.

> Moreover, racism as ideology is "an elaborate system of pseudo-intellectual categories, assumptions, and contentions negative to third world peoples and serving as justification of the imposition and reinforcement of the institutional arrangement."

> Its three ideological forms, which may be termed ideological absurdities, are: 1) religious—claims of divinity, and command and support from God to conquer, rule, and ruin the lives of third world peoples; 2) biological—academic and popular claims of diminished intellectual capacity, unrestrained sexuality and propensities for violence; 3) cultural—claims of genetic superiority based on posing world culture as a white construction instead of the human product it is.

Karenga recognizes that race and racism cannot be scientifically legitimated because they are socially constructed categories that are violently imposed upon others and ideologically rationalized through theological, biological, and cultural arguments through which the dominant society claims a God-given right to "conquer, rule, and ruin" the lives of peoples or races who are defined as inferior through fallacious reasoning drawn from the realms of biology and culture.

Racism as White Privilege and Advantage

A number of scholars emphasize the importance of White advantage and privilege in societies that are stratified by race. These definitions, while not as lengthy as Maulana Karenga's, nevertheless stress the systematic and institutionalized nature of racism, while recognizing that ideology reinforces White supremacy and racial inferiority.

Albert Memmi (2000) briefly defined racism as "the generalized and final assigning of values to real or imaginary differences, to the accuser's benefit and at the victim's expense, in order to justify the former's won privileges or aggression." Memmi is treating the historical privileges and aggression of Whites as the process that leads to the need to ideologically justify the resulting social arrangements as a consequence of the supremacy of the victors and the inferiority of the vanquished.

Mark Chesler (Katz, 1976, pp. 21–77) also defines racism to be manifested by *actions* and *institutional arrangements* that produce or maintain *White privilege* and an *ideological* system to reinforce racial superiority and inferiority:

> In our own use of the term racism, we mean, whatever actions or institutional procedures help create or perpetuate sets of advantages or privileges for whites and exclusion or deprivations for minority groups. This usually requires an ideology of explicit superiority or advantages of one racial group over another, plus the institutional power to implement that ideology in social operations.

Two other definitions in this category focus on the nature of racial stratification, White advantage in the system, and the role of resistance or disidentification from dominant material interest, as necessary for altering or overturning racist practices.

Ian F. Haney Lopez writes as follows:

To the extent that racial ideas and practices support a stratified society, the current distribution of power and prestige depends on racial common sense. All but those at the very bottom continually rediscover that they have some stake in keeping things the way they are, even if in other ways they realize that the status quo harms them. Racial activists must be willing to risk whatever privilege their racial standing gives them. Beyond that, though, proponents of racial change must overcome the determined opposition of those who benefit in some way from racial hierarchy. These beneficiaries will include many people within the very groups the militants seek to help. And then, of course, racial insurgents must enlist significant numbers of whites to work against their own racial advantage. Without white participation, racial change does not occur in the United States.

(Lopez, 2003, p. 130)

Ian F. Haney Lopez describes racism as a stratification system that overwhelmingly favors all in the dominant society with the possible exception of those at the very lowest rungs of the social ladder. Overcoming racism requires conscious activists who can mobilize the masses to resist the status quo. This attempt to create resistance is hindered by the fact that segments of the oppressed have either "sold out" or "assimilated" and aligned themselves with the material interests of the dominant society. Lopez argues that without the support of disaffected Whites and the formation of alliances and coalitions, racial transformation and structural change in the United States is virtually impossible.

Finally, I want to cite sociologist Eduardo Bonilla-Silva, who has written and co-authored several books dealing with post–civil rights era White supremacy and **color-blind racism:**

My basic contention is that racism should be conceptualized in structural terms. I argue that actors in racialized societies, which I formally label *racialized social systems,* participate in race relations as either beneficiaries (members of the dominant race) or subordinates (members of the dominated race or races). Furthermore, I contend that since the races in any racialized social system receive different social rewards (one receives benefits and the other disadvantages), they develop different material interests. Whereas the collective interests of the dominant race (whites in the contemporary United States) lie in preserving the racial status quo, the interests of the subordinate race or races (Blacks and other minorities) lie in attempting to change their position in the system; one group tends to fight to maintain the social, political, economic, and even psychological arrangements that provide them privileges and the other tends to struggle to alter them.

(Bonilla-Silva, 2001, p. 11)

Bonilla-Silva tends to stress the material interests of the racially opposed groups as the basis for identifying with or resisting the status quo. But he acknowledges that the racial interests and alignments in American society are not rigidly fixed. Thus, he has treated racial stratification in essentially the same manner as Ian F. Haney Lopez.

Based upon the definitions of Memmi, Chesler, Lopez, and Bonilla-Silva, it is clear that these researchers view racism in terms of:

- Systematic racial inequality

- Racial hierarchy

- Institutional arrangements

- Differential power

- White supremacy

- Racial inferiority

- White privilege

- Minority "false consciousness" or "selling out"

- Dominant disidentification with class and racial interests

- Change as a product of racial struggle and/or alliances and coalitions

Racism in the Post–Civil Rights Era

As a result of the civil rights movement during the 1950s and 1960s, the United States was forced to come to terms with the legacy of southern-style racism, Jim Crow, de jure segregation, and the uglier and more blatant aspects of White supremacy and overt racial bigotry.

Almost before the ink could dry on the 1964 Civil Rights Act, the 1965 Voting Rights Act, and Fair Housing Legislation in the late 1960s, large segments of the dominant population effectively turned their backs on the struggle for freedom and racial equality in the United States.

They had had enough of Black militancy; racial separatism; minority studies programs; cries for Black, Brown, Red, or Yellow power; "long hot summers"; strident accusations of "White racism"; and the struggle of dealing with "White guilt" and ungrateful activists who seemingly had no end of demands regardless of the establishment's efforts to make concessions.

It was not that Whites hated people of color or did not want to see them succeed under conditions of full citizenship, but rather that Whites did not want to be forced to give in to racial demands; change too quickly; or have the federal government create programs that would force integration; bus their kids or minority kids to each other's schools; and require affirmative action, quotas, set-asides, and racial preferences in the name of compensating Blacks (in particular) for slavery, segregation, discrimination, and racial inequality.

The struggle for racial equality, social justice, and democracy may not yet be complete, but everyone agrees that we will never return to the oppressive practices of the past.

One could, therefore, optimistically proclaim that racism was now dead or increasingly irrelevant for the foreseeable future. Presumably the generation of the 1960s had closed the door on our racist past and created a quantum leap forward in terms of new attitudes about race, acceptance, and tolerance.

I want to close this chapter on racism by discussing two final forms of post–civil rights racism noted by Eduardo Bonilla-Silva.

The New Racism

During the 1970s and beyond, a number of researchers began to acknowledge that American attitudes about race had significantly shifted and softened. Clearly, it was no longer possible to appeal to the blatant racism that helped to sustain the racist practices associated with southern slavery (dominative), debt peonage (dominative aversive), or industrial capitalism (aversive racism).

A new vocabulary of racism has developed since the 1970s. Some refer to post–civil rights racism as *meta-racism,* while others speak of "modern racism and "symbolic racism."

Eduardo Bonilla-Silva speaks of the **"new racism,"** which has developed since the late 1960s and which accounts for the persistence of racial inequality:

> This new racial structure comprises the following elements: (1) the increasingly covert nature of racial discourse and practice; (2) the avoidance of racial terminology and the ever growing claim by whites that they experience "reverse racism"; (3) the elaboration of a racial agenda over political matters that eschews direct racial references; (4) the invisibility of most mechanism to reproduce racial inequality; and finally, (5) the rearticulation of some racial practices characteristic of the Jim Crow period of race relations.
>
> (Bonilla-Silva, 2001, p. 90)

In short, the "new racism," in effect, has had to "go underground" or to blend in with the post 1960s claims in favor of antiracism, tolerance, and support for the multicultural movement in the schools, universities, the mass media, and increasingly throughout private-sector and corporate America.

In the language of Michael Omi and Howard Winant, the impact of the "racial minority movements of the postwar period dramatically reshaped the political and cultural landscape of the nation" (Omi and Winant, 1986, p. 113). The "rearticulation of racial ideology" has become necessary because "in the aftermath of the 1960s, any effective challenge to the egalitarian ideals framed by the minority movements could no longer rely on the racism of the past" (Omi and Winant, 1986, p. 113).

The political right wing in the United States, which in the America of the 1960s first became visible with Barry Goldwater's 1964 presidential run, was decidedly out of touch with the liberal consensus regarding race and the radical demands that forced the racial state to give in to the call for a transformation of U.S. racist practice.

Since the 1970s, Omi and Winant argue that America lost prestige internationally while the emerging neoconservative movement operated in a context of resentment toward liberal and leftist movements:

> In the aftermath of the 1960s, any effective challenge to the egalitarian ideals framed by the minority movements could no longer rely on the racism of the past. Racial equality had to be acknowledged as a desirable goal. But the *meaning* of equality, and the proper means for achieving it, remained matters of considerable debate.
>
> With the exception of some on the far right, the racial reaction which has developed in the last two decades claims to favor racial equality. Its vision is that of a "color-blind" society where racial considerations are never entertained in the selection of leaders, in hiring decisions, and the distribution of goods and services in general. As the right sees it, racial problems today center on the new forms of racial "injustice" which originated in the great transformation . . .
>
> (Omi and Winant, 1986, pp. 113–114)

Racial politics in the United States has been drastically affected by America's move to the right and the belief by many that racism is a problem of the past. The attacks on the federal government by the conservative right have undermined the liberal consensus that grew out of FDR's New Deal and that culminated in LBJ's Great Society, which, for a time, focused national attention on issues of racism and poverty.

The movements of the 1960s have lost their momentum in the last thirty-five years. The right seemingly is the new political consensus and the "new racism" that Bonilla-Silva describes has matured into "color-blind" racism, or what he refers to as "racism without racists."

I will end by discussing how racists no longer define people of color as innately inferior, but rather engage in "blaming the victim," condemning minority culture, and justifying racial inequality while parading themselves as victims of "reverse racism."

Color-Blind Racism

Eduardo Bonilla-Silva has described the meaning, reality, and function of post–civil rights "color-blind" racism in his book *Racism without Racists* (2003). I will summarize Bonilla-Silva's discussion that can be found on pages 1–4:

- Few Whites claim to be racist anymore unless they are defiant White supremacists.

- Whites claim not to see color but only people, and they view discrimination as "ugly" and still a problem, but no longer the determinant of the life-chances of minorities.

- Whites not only claim Martin Luther King's quote that he wishes his children to be "judged not by the color of their skin, but by the content of their character" as their own, but they blame minorities (especially Blacks) for the "race problem" in America.

- "They publicly denounce Blacks for 'playing the race card,' for demanding the maintenance of unnecessary and divisive race-based programs such as affirmative action, and for crying 'racism' whenever they are criticized by whites."

- Whites advise Blacks to work hard, stop complaining, and to forget about the past, so that everyone can "get along."

- Bonilla-Silva provides numerous examples of race-based statistics to demonstrate that Whites are wrong when they claim that race is no longer important in America. "Blacks and dark-skinned racial minorities lag well behind whites in virtually every area of social life . . ."

- Bonilla-Silva then asks several questions:

"How is it possible to have this degree of racial inequality in a country where most whites claim that race is no longer relevant?"

"More important, how do whites explain the apparent contradiction between their professed color-blindness and the United States' color-coded inequality?"

Color-blind racism emerged as a new racial ideology, just as the mechanisms and practices for keeping minorities in their place changed. Bonilla-Silva's analysis of post–civil rights racism is similar to Omi and Winant's discussion of the right's rearticulation of racial ideology:

Compared to Jim Crow racism, the ideology of color blindness seems like "racism lite." Instead of relying on name calling (nigger, spics, chinks), color-blind racism etherizes softly ("these people are human, too"); instead of proclaiming God placed minorities in the world in a servile position, it suggests that they are behind because they do not work hard enough; instead of viewing interracial marriage as wrong on a straight racial basis, it regards it as "problematic" because of concerns over the children, location, or the extra burden it places on couples. Yet this new ideology has become a formidable political tool for the maintenance of the racial order . . .

. . . color-blind racism serves today as the ideological armor for a covert and institutionalized system in the post–civil rights era. And the beauty of this new ideology is that it aids in the maintenance of white privilege without fanfare, without naming those who it subjects and those who it rewards . . .

Thus whites enunciate positions that safeguard their racial interests without sounding "racist." Shielded by color-blindness, whites can express resentment toward minorities, criticize their morality, values, and work ethic; and even claim to be the victims of "reverse racism."

(Bonilla-Silva, 2003, pp. 3–4)

I have covered a lot of ground in this discussion of the nature and meaning of racism.

Because this concept is at the core of ethnic studies, it is important to grasp how it developed historically and how it serves the needs of elites and dominant social groups in multiracial societies. The struggle against racism is the dialectical response from the oppressed who work from internalized racism to identities that affirm their heritage, their traditions, their sense of community, and the goals of full citizenship, social acceptance, and social justice, or independence, sovereignty, national liberation, and revolution.

Conclusion

In a world without racism one would expect to see either an equitable, nonhierarchical social structure or perhaps a stratified, class-based social structure in which racial diversity would exist in the various class fractions more or less equally.

Of course, actual social arrangements are not the product of sociological models or abstract "ideal types." The existence of racism is a reflection of the historical relations between nation-states and indigenous populations.

Just how effectively a society deals with issues of incorporation of race, class, and gender, or to what extent stratification and systematic exclusion and exploitation persist, are important theoretical questions.

In Chapter 6 we will explore the theoretical meanings of assimilation and internal colonialism as important ways to deal with ethnicity and race in American history.

Questions, Exercises, and Topics for Discussion and Debate

1) Explain the meaning and implications of the following statement:

   "prejudice is not the cause of racism but a consequence and symptom of racism's persistence and continuing reality."

   Besides attitudes, emotions, cognitions, and beliefs about race, what are the key components of racism according to the majority of researchers who have provided the diverse definitions of racism cited in Chapter 5?

2) What is institutional racism? Provide historical or contemporary examples that indicate how institutional racism operates.

3) Discuss the concept of "White privilege" and indicate how White or Anglo Americans benefit from the existence of racism even when they may personally harbor no prejudice or ill will toward people of color.

4) Provide historical evidence and argumentation to justify the claim that people of color have collectively suffered more due to racism than ethnic populations have from ethnic discrimination and prejudice. Consider also the notion that ethnic populations have come to the United States voluntarily, while racial groups were conquered, colonized, annexed, enslaved, and subordinated as a result of their physical appearance.

5) What does Maulana Karenga mean when he states that racism is a form of "historical imposition," or as he says:

   "It is . . . a system of denial and deformation of a people's history and humanity and right to freedom, based exclusively or primarily on the specious concept of race."

6) Explain the meaning of post–civil rights era forms of racism. Specifically, what is meant by "the new racism" and "color-blind" racism? Has racism in America significantly declined from the Jim Crow era? Explain your reasoning.

7) Discuss what is meant by "blaming the victim," cultural racism, scapegoating, hate crimes, and profiling.

8) Is there a connection between the various meanings of racism and the terms *holocaust, genocide,* and *ethnic cleansing?* Consider doing some library research on:
   a) The Turkish holocaust against Armenians
   b) The German Nazi Holocaust against European Jews, gypsies, homosexuals, and other groups during the 1930s and 1940s
   c) Genocide against the aboriginal people of North America, Mexico, Central and South America, and the Caribbean
   d) The genocide in Kampuchea in the 1970s by the Khmer Rouge, also known as the Killing Fields
   e) The Rwanda genocide of Hutus by the Tutsis in the early 1990s
   f) The ethnic cleansing in the former Yugoslavia involving Serbians and Croats during the 1980s and 1990s

9) Given what you have learned about the realities of racism, should society emphasize programs promoting antiracist education and curricular reform to fight ignorance, erroneous information, and the dangers of prejudice, or should the emphasis be on eliminating institutional inequality, de facto segregation, poverty, and disproportionate minority unemployment, inadequate housing, and overincarceration in the prison industrial complex? Explain your choice in detail.

Theorizing Ethnicity and Race: Assimilation and Internal Colonialism

Chapter Six

Key Terms

acculturation

the American dream

Americanization of immigrants

Anglo conformity

assimilation

class struggle

classic colonialism

colonization migration

consensus theory

contract labor

core values and institutions

cultural pluralism

displaced persons

ethnic enclaves

ethnicity model

exploitation

forced labor

functional theory

functionally interdependent institutions

host society

ideal-type model

immigrant analogy

integration

internal colonialism

involuntary migration

mechanical solidarity

melting pot theory

migration

multiculturalism

organic solidarity

primordial ethnic values

race relations cycle

racial exclusion

refugees

slave importation

social conflict perspective

social incorporation

social order perspective

value consensus

voluntary migration

Key Lesson

Two fundamental cosmological, philosophical, and scientific questions that have influenced, impacted, and shaped the development of human civilization and in particular Western society are: how did human beings come into being or existence, and how were multiethnic and multiracial societies formed? Explanations of human origins derive from two generic sources: (1) human folk knowledge, revealed traditions, religion, spiritual worldviews, syncretic knowledge, and social variations derived from cosmology; (2) philosophical musings and speculation, humanistic rational explanations, secular reasoning, natural law, modern scientific theory, experimentation, and empiricism.

Briefly, major religions and science offer alternative explanations on human origins and the basis of social differences. In Western Judeo-Christian thought, two rival positions were monogenesis and polygenesis—that is, that God created humanity in one primordial location or that there were multiple creations of human groups who were specially adapted physically to the conditions in which they originally found themselves geographically.

The secular sociological view is that the human differences that we refer to as races evolved on the basis of human adaptation to environmental differences and the transmission of inherited genetic traits that favored the survival of groups as they developed patterns of culture and complex social organization.

How did multiethnic and multiracial societies emerge? Contact between migrating human populations and the splitting off or fragmentation of growing societies was in some way related to ethnic and physically distinct populations competing for land, social space, and dominance or subordination of group members.

One view is that primordial ethnic values or differences were inherent to different groups and could be modified through contact with other migrating groups through warfare, competition, accommodation, cooperation, or the **social incorporation** of **displaced persons** or **refugees.** The voluntary migration of ethnically distinct individuals or groups into a **host society** with dominant numbers, core values, language, and institutions is the basis of the related theories of functionalism, the **consensus theory** or view of society, the **social order perspective,** the **ethnicity model** or paradigm, and the theory of **assimilation.**

The alternative viewpoint begins with the recognition that there are dominant individuals or interest groups within any society that is differentiated beyond gender and age-grades. Also, the incorporation of foreign or physically distinct groups into a society may be accomplished through conquest, colonization, warfare, involuntary incorporation, or the occupation of the people on their own land by a more powerful people with their own culture and institutions. Thus, conflict theory, class struggle within a society of competing interest groups, classic colonialism, settler colonialism, or **internal colonialism** may create relations of domination and subordination that will vary historically and produce complex ethnic and racialized social patterns within or between societies.

In modern historical and sociological theorizing about ethnic and racial differences, social thinkers believed that certain social and technological conditions associated with the transformation of medieval European society and proto-nation-states would eventually eliminate ethnic and even racial differences as the system of nation-states became more integrated as a world market system and as capitalist development brought class differences between the bourgeoisie and the proletariat into the foreground of politics.

Theorists from Durkheim, Weber, and Marx, to Park, Wirth, and Redfield all viewed society as evolving in terms of ideal type differences along various social and cultural continua, such as mechanical to organic solidarity, feudalism to capitalism, rural to urban, agricultural to industrial, traditional to modern, sacred to secular, irrational to rational, particularistic to universalistic, and socially differentiated to socially integrated.

The dominance of assimilation and social order or **functional theory** has been superceded in the late twentieth century by conflict and power-coercion theories that emphasize the power of institutions and interest groups in society to shape ethnic and racial reality. Race is viewed as a social construct and racialized groups are no longer viewed as passive victims of social power but as active creators of their responses under different social and globalized relationships.

The reality of ethnic and racial differences will not disappear any time soon. Thus assimilation theory and internal colonial theory and the dialectic between ethnicity and race will continue to inform social interaction, sociology, and ethnic studies into the foreseeable political future.

Theoretically, the ethnicity paradigm represents the mainstream of the modern sociology of race. The paradigm has passed through three major stages: a pre-1930s stage in which the ethnic group view was an insurgent approach, challenging the biologistic (and at least implicitly racist) view of race which was dominant at that time; a 1930s to 1965 stage during which the paradigm operated as the progressive/liberal "common sense" approach to race, and during which two recurrent themes—assimilationism and cultural pluralism were defined; and a post-1965 phase, in which the paradigm has taken on the defense of conservative (or "neoconservative") egalitarianism against what is perceived as the radical assault of "group rights."

(Omi and Winant, 1986, p. 14)

Ethnicity itself was understood as the result of a group formation process based on culture and descent. "Culture" in this formulation included such diverse factors as religion, language, "customs," nationality and political identification. "Descent" involved heredity and a sense of group origins, thus suggesting that ethnicity was socially "primordial," if not biologically given, in character.

(Omi and Winant, 1986, p. 15)

So, ethnicity theory assigned to blacks and other racial minority groups, the roles which earlier generations of European immigrants had played in the great waves of the "Atlantic migration" of the nineteenth and early twentieth centuries. But racial minorities refused to play their assigned roles, structural barriers continued to render the immigration analogy inappropriate and the trajectory of incorporation did not develop as the ethnicity paradigm had envisioned. Many blacks (and later, many Latinos, Indians and Asia Americans as well) rejected *ethnic* identity in favor of a more radical *racial* identity which demanded group rights and recognition. Given these developments, ethnicity theory found itself increasingly in opposition to the demands of minority movements.

(Omi and Winant, 1986, p. 20)

Robert Blauner's *Racial Oppression in America* is probably the most familiar general discussion of race in the United States written from an internal colonialism perspective, and the one most "tailored" to U.S. conditions.

Blauner effectively employs the distinction between "colonized and immigrant minorities" to criticize the ethnic group paradigm. "Colonized" minorities are those whose presence in the United States was the result of "forced entry," a criterion that serves well in general (though not absolutely) to distinguish between those whose entry was the direct result of processes of colonialism and those (Europeans) who "became ethnic groups and minorities within the United States by the essentially voluntary movements of individuals and families.

(Omi and Winant, 1986, pp. 48–49)

Introduction

Theorizing about the historical processes by which American ethnic and racial diversity came about has resulted in a vast array of lay, popular, folk, and politically normative perspectives about the transition and evolution of feudal and traditional societies to modern industrial capitalist society, as well as academic and social science efforts to understand migration, immigration, and incorporation of racially and culturally distinct populations into nineteenth- and twentieth-century U.S. society.

The difficulty in understanding American ethnic and racial diversity is that popular conceptions and beliefs are themselves historically and contextually inseparable from the cultural and political relations of elite power, dominance, and hegemony within the prevailing relations of class, capital, labor, and gender.

It is possible to describe the demographic and historical transition from European feudal relations to modern post-Enlightenment, capitalistic, industrialized, and mass societies. But the development of theories about the evolution of modern societies; about biological and cultural diversity; and about social incorporation or assimilation versus **racial exclusion** of conquered, colonized, enslaved, or subordinated peoples—often reflected the Eurocentric, White, male biases of the social elites and scholarly pundits operating under specific historical and temporal conditions. The quotes taken from Michael Omi and Howard Winant's important study *Racial Formation in the United States: From the 1960s to the 1980s* (1986) are meant to illustrate the politicized context in which racial and ethnic theorizing occurs.

In the post–civil rights period of the 1980s, Omi and Winant attempted to evaluate American ethnic and racial progress based upon how far the United States had moved away from biological White supremacy and to what extent the model of ethnic assimilation was also being fulfilled for Blacks and other racial minorities.

What they found can be summarized as follows:

- In the 1920s, an insurgent ethnicity perspective began to undermine the biological basis for racial hierarchy, segregation, and innate racial differences.

- By the 1930s to the 1960s, a new liberal consensus emerged that legitimized the notions of assimilation, integration, and a tolerant—but limited—ethnic and racial **cultural pluralism.**

- But by the mid-1960s through the mid-1970s, militant, radical, and leftist movements by racial minorities, white antiwar activists, women, and other representatives of the new left pushed the racial state—almost too far.

- The Great Transformation based on demands for equality, inclusion, and incorporation by 1960s activists, had also split the liberal ethnicity paradigm and the civil rights establishment from radical class paradigms, and nation-based perspectives built around pan-Africanism, cultural nationalism, the "national question" and Marxism, and internal colonialism.

- American hegemony began to decline internationally at the same time that racial ideology was rearticulated by Whites representing the "new right" and the neoconservative movement.

- For the past twenty years, many myths about race have reasserted themselves in conservative, color-blind terms to undercut the political and cultural gains of the 1960s in the guise of family values," "welfare reform," the "underclass" debate, "standards," "the fight against Big Government," "faith-based initiatives," and "immigration."

- Multiculturalism has been attacked as radical, leftist, and divisive—while also being appropriated by the right as "a kinder and gentler pluralism," a celebration of our victorious immigrant origins, and a new version of "the American Dream."

- Ironically, in response to the success of Alex Haley's book *Roots* and the extremely successful television miniseries, many White-assimilated ethnic populations began to reexamine their own "roots" and to develop "neo-ethnicity" and a new ethnic pluralism in response to racial nationalism.

The politics of ethnic studies and its subdisciplines have for many years distanced themselves from the insurgent and liberal meanings of the ethnicity paradigm.

There is a great emphasis by those researching and writing about race to stress the racial formation process; the role of state hegemony in producing and maintaining White supremacy; the racist and exclusionary nature of post-1980s immigration and border policy; the need to document the intersections of race, class, and gender; a critical concern with Eurocentrism, new racial and trans-border social movements, and discourses on popular culture and cultural studies.

The field of ethnic studies, in short, is less concerned about historical immigration; social or cultural assimilation of European immigrants; the need to affirm the dominant White settler colonies in North America or Latin America, the Caribbean, South Africa, Australia, New Zealand, or anywhere else in the world; or the validation of Eurocentric models of **Anglo conformity,** the **melting pot theory,** the salad bowl, the bowl of soup, or the pluralistic model that we are distinct, different, and diverse and yet "Americans All!"

Perhaps in time America's politics and the politics of ethnic studies will find common ground that will reflect the realization of true democracy; the reconciliation with our racist historical past; and the necessity to balance neo-liberal economic globalization (which is polarizing the northern "haves" and the southern "have-nots"), while also increasing social injustice and inequality within the United States.

In this chapter I will focus on the nature of assimilation theory (which I equate with Omi and Winant's "ethnicity" paradigm) and internal colonial theory, which is one of many radical and conflict perspectives that emerged in the activist political climate of the 1960s and became a preferred paradigm of younger academic and minority scholars in many colleges and universities where ethnicity models and assimilation theory were harshly attacked as irrelevant to minority experience.

Sources

Some of the books that provide overviews and background for understanding immigrant and ethnic history have also been listed in Chapter 3. The sources that deal with classic immigration history, U.S. diversity, assimilation, **classic colonialism,** and internal colonial theory are:

Stokely Carmichael and Charles V. Hamilton
Black Power: The Politics of Liberation in America

Stephen Cornell and Douglass Hartmann
Ethnicity and Race: Making Identities in a Changing World

Roger Daniels
Coming to America: A History of Immigration and Ethnicity in American Life

Frantz Fanon
The Wretched of the Earth

Joe R. Feagin
Racial and Ethnic Relations (Second Edition)

Donna R. Gabaccia
Immigration and American Diversity: A Social and Cultural History

Nigel C. Gibson
Fanon: The Postcolonial Imagination

Milton Gordon
Assimilation in American Life: The Role of Race, Religion, and National Origins

Oscar Handlin
The Uprooted: The Epic Story of the Great Migrations That Made the American People

Joseph Hraba
American Ethnicity (Second Edition)

Charles Jaret
Contemporary Racial and Ethnic Relations

Milton Kleg
Hate Prejudice and Racism

James S. Olson
The Ethnic Dimension in American History (Second Edition)

Howard Omi and Michael Winant
Racial Formation in the United States: From the 1960s to the 1980s

David M. Reimers
Still the Golden Door: The Third World Comes to America (Second Edition)

Paul Spickard
Almost All Aliens: Immigration, Race, and Colonialism in American History and Identity

Stephen Steinberg
Turning Back

Stephen Steinberg
The Ethnic Myth: Race, Ethnicity, and Class in America

Timothy Walch (Editor)
Immigrant America: European Ethnicity in the United States

Virginia Yans-McLaughlin (Editor)
Immigration Reconsidered: History, Sociology, and Politics

Social Evolution and Modernity

The historical transition of European feudal society to modernity and industrial capitalism forms the structural foundation for political and social science theorizing about social evolution and change, and reflections about the persistence of ethnic and racial social divisions or the disappearance of diversity based upon assimilation into the emerging class structure of modern mass society.

Prior to the development of modern nation-states and the evolution of the industrial division of labor, international trade, and the interconnected flow of labor, raw materials, and manufactured commodities in an increasingly global market system, Europe had been a hierarchical, caste structure ruled by the power of the Catholic Church and the influence of kings, lords, nobility, and landed gentry over serfs, laborers, and common peasants. People lived in more or less isolated communities with limited opportunities for education, social advancement, or upward mobility.

Social evolutionary theorists in the nineteenth century and classical sociological theorists attempted to describe and understand the transformation from feudalism to capitalism or from rural and predominantly agricultural societies to advanced industrial societies.

The large-scale evolution of society was viewed as a natural process that could be studied methodically and scientifically in order to predict likely social trends and to realign social institutions in terms of self-conscious efforts at social reform or to direct people to understanding the moral necessity of conforming their social behavior to the tenets of natural law.

Within the framework of understanding societal change as a macro historical process, classical sociological theorists developed two traditions of theorizing about society that had implications for interpreting feudalism, modernity, folk society, ethnicity, class, and industrialization.

The functional or consensus view of modern society is reflected in the work of the French sociologist Emile Durkheim, who viewed social evolution as a product of changes in the social division of labor that altered simple societies based upon likeness between people—or what he referred to as **mechanical solidarity**—to modern societies with a highly specialized and complex division of labor predicated on the social interdependence between unique individuals or groups who became integrated into the social whole through **organic solidarity.** For Durkheim, the shift from feudal society to modernity was a reflection of two distinct principles of social organization. The folk societies of the past were based on mechanical solidarity where "likeness of consciousness comes from people doing the same thing, day in and day out, when there is a simple division of labor" (Hraba, 1994, p. 34).

According to Durkheim, specialization in the division of labor and the multiplication of the number of occupations and professions caused individuals to become different from one another as they became aligned with guilds or groups employed in specific lines of economic activity. This transformation of society meant that occupational specialists would have to align themselves with the social whole by acknowledging their functional interdependence. According to Hraba:

> Durkheim believed that occupational specialists would realize their interdependence, appreciate the larger whole of which they are part, and cooperate. A complex division of labor from the start represented a cooperative effort to avoid occupational competition. The larger point is that societal change was to bring about a new type of solidarity, providing conditions that would integrate diverse specialists into a complex society, which according to Durkheim, could be buttressed by state regulation and moral education.
>
> (Hraba, 1994, p. 34)

Since social change was associated with the emergence of city-states, the rise of finance, and other modern practices that occurred beyond the local feudal order of social and provincial caste relationships, folk society would not be able to reproduce its traditional or face-to-face social relationships in the environment of urban culture.

> Folk solidarity could be transplanted to industrial cities only for a time, while migrant groups themselves lived in isolated ghettos and worked the same jobs at the bottom of the new occupational hierarchy. These groups eventually would diffuse into the modern city's complex division of labor, however, and become diversified into what are now called ethclasses, different economic and social classes within ethnic groups. They would disperse in urban space, lose their solidarity, and ultimately disintegrate. Occupational interdependence and other secondary forms of social control would then supplant the lost solidarity of the folk past.
>
> (Hraba, 1994, p. 34)

The Marxist or **social conflict perspective** is the second theoretical formulation that attempted to describe the transition of feudalism to capitalism. Marx believed that all history can be characterized in terms of **class struggle.** His position was that between the medieval feudal era and the nineteenth century, the capitalist class had displaced the feudal nobility as the dominant class in industrialized society.

Marx viewed the labor process and the struggle between capital and labor as the primary motor of social change. Whereas Durkheim viewed social change as compatible with society due to the role of social control and moral education, Marx believed that class struggle could not finally be contained within the existing social structure.

The folk or provincial ethnic divisions in society would not be able to survive under conditions of class struggle. As Hraba summarizes:

> Marx had argued that capitalism would elevate the class consciousness of industrial workers. By becoming conscious, workers would become correspondingly less concerned with family, land, locality, and nationality, which might otherwise divide them. All of these, of course, are particular expressions of ethnicity. Ethnicity would be erased, first as the proletariat mobilized for the class struggle, and finally as the universal fraternity of workers was established in the utopian state. Class consciousness is the modern mentality, Marx argued, and folk sentiments would become obsolete and fade.

(Hraba, 1994, p. 33)

The relevance of theorizing the transition from European feudalism to modern Western capitalism is that the resulting European nation-states would develop internal criteria for citizenship and culturally distinct national identities that would affect the development of the modern competitive social order in which competition for territory, raw materials, slaves, labor, religious converts, and markets would result in a new racialized identity for Europeans as White, civilized, Christian—as well as particular identities, such as Spanish, Portuguese, Dutch, French, and English—which would become the basis of White supremacy and Eurocentrism in all of their national contacts, conquests, and colonial and imperial ventures involving indigenous, African, and Asian others.

All discussions about the incorporations of difference into nation-based societies rest, first of all, with modern, secular, and rational criteria for distinguishing social and individual progress from traditional social relations that are organized around ancient or classical states with particularistic prejudices; beliefs based on magic, superstition, and religion; and emotional or irrational grounds for organization and solidarity.

By distinguishing between dichotomies of sacred versus secular, traditional versus modern, irrational versus rational, rural versus urban, and agricultural versus industrial society, we establish the theoretical **ideal-type models** that will reproduce analytically the very basis of popular and political grounds for stratifying national subjects and citizens as being different and distinct from ethnic immigrants and racialized others.

Social evolutionary theories provided a theoretical description of how social change could also change the personality and mental orientation of individuals as phylogenetic development of society resulted in ontogenetic changes in the members of society.

In twentieth-century anthropology and sociology, theories of assimilation of ethnic or racial populations tended to reproduce the Eurocentric biases of social elites. In addition, when ideological racism was critically attacked by ethnicity and assimilation theorists, they often uncritically allowed cultural differences to become a proxy for innate differences that could be used to re-racialize the poor, racial minorities, and recent immigrants.

The concepts of modernity and the rise of Enlightenment thought were supposed to represent civilizational, cultural, and scientific advances over religious prejudice, emotional irrationality, and provincial worldviews. Yet, ironically, the rise of racial and ethnic prejudice and stereotyping are associated with modernity and the development of racism legitimized the degradation of the nations and peoples of color who were subjected to modern technology, warfare, capitalism, and exploitation.

It is in this sense that I have viewed the classical theorists of society as providing the basis for order and conflict theories of society while equally predicting that ethnic differences would eventually be replaced by class stratification and biological amalgamation of racial distinctions and/or the acculturation of ethnic cultures into the mainstream and dominant institutions of society.

> Social evolutionists envisioned in modern society a transformation of the medieval bonds of blood and place, the basis of peasant life, into individualism and rationally calculated human exchange. Modern people would relate to one another as commodities in marketplaces, each trying to maximize individual profit. The mass-produced consumer goods would be consumed en masse, and once-distinct groups would become indistinguishable by what they wore, ate, and did. Impersonal bureaucracy, one symbol of this change, would replace the communal organization of life. Assimilationists read this legacy as reason for the eventual demise of ethnic groups in American society.
>
> (Hraba, 1994, p. 32)

Overview of Assimilation Theory

The concept of assimilation most basically refers to those processes by which a host society or an institutionally and culturally dominant social structure is able to incorporate individuals or groups who initially do not share the same geographic origin, physical appearance (race), or social and cultural values and practices (ethnicity).

There are many ways to discuss how multiracial and/or multiethnic societies come into existence, stabilize the relations between the dominant society and distinct subordinate groups, and over time absorb or assimilate groups into the **core values and institutions** of the *host society* and its stratification system.

The creation of multiracial or multiethnic societies begins with contact between an established or indigenous people and a migrating people, or between two or more migrant populations moving into a previously unoccupied territory at roughly the same time (Feagin, 1984, p. 23). The basis for understanding migration, according to Charles Tilly, includes:

- The actual migrating units (individual or families)

- The situation at the point of origin

- The situation at the point of destination

- The social and political framework within which the migration occurs

(Feagin, 1984, p. 23)

Finally, Feagin specifies that there are five types of **migration,** which range from completely voluntary to completely **involuntary migration.** This as we shall see is important in determining differences in the degree of assimilation or exclusion of ethnic and racial groups relative to the dominant society.

The types of migration cited by Feagin (pp. 23–24) are:

- **Slave importation**

- Movement of **forced labor**

- **Contract labor** movement

- Movement of displaced persons and refugees

- **Voluntary migration**

Feagin also states that colonizers may *voluntarily migrate* into the territory of an indigenous population in order to control them by imposing their power and culture over them. This is called:

- **Colonization migration**

Depending upon the nature of migration and the types of social contact between diverse social elements, initial social contact can range from:

- Exclusion or genocide

- Egalitarian symbiosis

- A hierarchy or stratification system

(Feagin, 1984, p. 24)

Because this overview is concerned with the meaning of assimilation, I will cite Joseph Hraba's definition and summary of the process:

> According to common usage in the social sciences, assimilation is the process by which diverse ethnic groups come to share a common culture and have equal access to the opportunity structure of society. There are two components of assimilation: acculturation and integration. Acculturation refers to the fusion of groups into a common culture. Different ethnic groups acculturate by becoming similar in their thinking, feeling, and behavior. They share the same basic values and patterns of behavior. To illustrate, members of different groups converge to speak the same language, wear similar clothing, and eat the same foods: this is acculturation. Integration means the inclusion of groups into society rather than their exclusion from it. Because of integration, members of different ethnic groups are not segregated with respect to their residence and social participation, and they experience equal access to education, jobs, and other opportunities in the wider society. Obviously, assimilation comes in degrees.

(Hraba, 1994, p. 31)

I will discuss the assimilation process following an overview of classical colonialism and the internal colony model of society, which highlight processes of conflict and coercion between ethnic and racial populations.

Overview of Colonization and Internal Colonial Theory

If assimilation theory represents the ideal-type model for describing voluntary migration and the process of cultural adaptation and social integration, then the examination of various modes of forced entry and involuntary migration of individuals and families provides the contrasting historical data to understand the role of violence, force, coercion, and oppression for excluding, enslaving, compelling labor, subordinating, exploiting, or stratifying distinct populations either on their own territory (colonization) or on the territory of the dominant independent nation (internal colonialism).

Oppression, domination, and **exploitation** did not originate with European contact or "discovery" of non-European peoples beginning in the mid-1400s. But the association of European territorial expansion, conquest, chattel slavery, and labor exploitation occurred in a context of technological dominance, nationalism, racism, and capitalist exploitation that placed colonization, expropriation, and imperial control into a world market, and ultimately, a global grid of White supremacy.

During the twentieth century, oppressed people around the world began to organize, protest, involve themselves in nationalist and revolutionary movements, and finally, after World War II, they challenged colonial oppressors, gained independence, and fought for civil and human rights.

By the 1960s, scholars and academics began to acknowledge some of the tenets of Eurocentrism, White supremacy, and mainstream theories of ethnicity, assimilation, and social tolerance that were viewed as completely unacceptable and inadequate for understanding third world oppression, racial domination, and exclusion in the United States.

Perspectives were developed that had their origins in Marxist theory and practice, labor organizing and anticapitalist struggles, civil rights protest, and the emergence of theories of social conflict that critiqued American social arrangements and imperialist foreign policies and interventions.

Scholars and activists identified with the dominated and oppressed dark-skinned people of the world, and racial minorities that became far more active and visible within the United States. These colonized and oppressed people from Asia, Africa, the Middle East, Latin America, the Caribbean, and within the United States and other European settler colonies were referred to by Frantz Fanon as "the wretched of the earth," and it was in response to their social and political struggles that Robert Blauner and others developed the internal colony model of society as an alternative to the so-called **immigrant analogy** that viewed racial oppression as compatible with the "ethnicity" and "assimilation" models that were fashionable at that time.

I will discuss classical colonialism and internal colonial theory as an important alternative to the assimilation perspective. While the scope of conflict and stratification theory is very broad, internal colonialism still is a significant framework within ethnic studies.

The Assimilation Model

> Traditional assimilation theories seem preoccupied with the relatively voluntary migration of European immigrants into the English colonies and later into the United States.
>
> (Feagin, 1984, p. 26)

> In the United States, as well as elsewhere, traditional racial and ethnic theorizing has placed an emphasis on assimilation, on the orderly adaptation of a migrating group to the ways and institutions of an established host group.
>
> (Feagin, 1984, p. 26)

The United States, as these quotes suggest, has always been defined as an immigrant society built upon core religious, legal, economic, political, and cultural values, that reflected European Old World evolution and, particularly, British institutions. The subsequent migrations of millions of European immigrants throughout the nineteenth and twentieth centuries and their struggles for acceptance, respect, and successful upward mobility are the basis for all popular and social science theorizing about ethnic diversity, contact with the core values and institutions of the host society, interethnic competition, accommodation, and ultimately assimilation into the culture and structures of mainstream society.

In fact, Robert Park is the twentieth-century sociologist who first proposed his **race relations cycle** as an evolutionary and biosocial theory of how foreign ethnic immigrant groups entering urban America would adjust to one another and eventually move out of their **ethnic enclaves** as a result of education and greater access to the diverse occupational structure, and then become incorporated into the middle class as individuals rather than as the bearers of **primordial ethnic values.**

Joseph Hraba describes Robert Park's race relations cycle and the work of Park's student, Louis Wirth, who applied the race relations cycle to Chicago's Jewish immigrants:

> Park's race relations cycle is an exemplar of the assimilationist view of ethnic change in modern society. The cycle goes through four stages, terminating in the assimilation of ethnic groups. The forces behind the cycle return to the basic ideas of nineteenth-century social evolutionism and historical liberalism. There is an increasingly complex division of labor and expansion of opportunity, growth in individual freedom, impersonal competition of individuals in the laissez-faire marketplace, and the eventual eclipse of bonds of blood and place by vocational or class interests. To this Park added that human cooperation and intergroup intimacy would ultimately succeed competition, even accommodation, and bring about assimilation. At a higher level of abstraction, the race relations cycle represents the effort of society to achieve a new equilibrium and social order.
>
> (Hraba, 1994, pp. 38–39)

Louis Wirth carried out empirical research that resulted in *The Ghetto,* which was published in 1928:

> . . . The Ghetto represents the more specific natural history of Jewish assimilation in Chicago. The history passes through the stages of contact, competition, and accommodation, ending with assimilation. Wirth shared with Park the conviction that social change brings the demise of the ethnic group, in this case Jews. Assimilation of Jews is due to their occupational diversification, residential dispersion, and growing intimacy between Jews and others, all of which is made possible by societal change.
>
> (Hraba, 1994, pp. 40–41)

Perhaps the most important study of race relations in the first half of the twentieth century was Gunnar Myrdal's *An American Dilemma: The Negro Problem and Modern Society,* which came out in 1944. Myrdal was critical of Park's use of a natural history of race relations and attempted to argue from purely sociological and psychological principles. But American racism toward southern Blacks was weakened by his emphasis upon the failure of Whites to consistently live in accordance with the values of the American creed:

> American ideals have always implied racial equality and have historically been supported by high institutional structures in the United States, such as Christianity, English law, and the enlightened doctrine of human rights evident in founding documents such as the Declaration of Independence.
>
> . . . On the other hand, white Americans have been over time prejudicial and discriminatory toward African Americans due to their "specific valuations."
>
> (Hraba, 1994, p. 47)

Gunnar Myrdal believed that, over time, Blacks would be assimilated just as other White ethnic groups had been when dominant group members would reconcile their concrete actions with the institutionalized beliefs about fair play, justice, equality, and democracy that were embodied in the American creed.

Myrdal's belief in the inevitability of assimilation, and its desirability, presupposes that racially oppressed populations also share an identification with the abstract values and concrete practices of the society.

The ultimate and continuing critique of assimilation theory is that all racially distinct and socially visible populations have been treated as if their entry into American society was voluntary and identical, in terms of trajectory, with European ethnic groups.

Because American race relations have from the beginning been framed largely in White and Black, it is perhaps understandable that the normative belief in assimilation and the **Americanization of immigrants** and the failure of dominant elites to recognize their racism and abuse of power would lead to the conclusion that Blacks and other racial minorities fully accept the goal of incorporation into society. From this fallacious assumption, assimilationists implicitly built two other corollaries into their theories:

- Racial minorities are in principle no different from foreign ethnic immigrants.

- Therefore, they will in time also be assimilated and incorporated into the dominant culture and distributed as families and individuals throughout the class stratification system.

Because race was viewed as a special form of ethnicity, and because ethnic groups were able to be integrated into society, the belief and practice of "blaming the victim" became a component of popular prejudice and a reoccurring theme of professional pundits, bureaucrats, and politicians.

Racial minorities that failed to assimilate or—even worse—that rejected dominant-group values and goals in favor of community control, nationalism, racial identity movements, separatism, and revolutionary praxis, were condemned as responsible for their own victimization or were attacked for individual, family, or community pathologies.

I will conclude this discussion of the assimilation model by listing the key assumptions of the theory and briefly exploring three variant readings of assimilation based upon the work of Alfredo Mirandé in *The Chicano Experience: An Alternative Perspective.*

Key Concepts and Assumptions of Assimilation

- Racial and ethnic minorities are viewed as immigrant groups.

- They entered society voluntarily.

- Their ultimate goal is to assimilate into the social melting pot.

- The model is built upon the concepts of assimilation, consensus, cooperation, and **integration.**

- Social scientists have treated racial families and communities as dysfunctional, pathological, and deficient.

- European immigrants began with distinctive values and cultures, but in time they discarded them as they were incorporated into the melting pot.

- For racial minorities to succeed they must be acculturated and assimilated.

- American society is composed of diverse racial-ethnic groups integrated into an orderly, cohesive "melting pot" of diverse interests.

- The entrance of these groups into American society is on an individual and voluntary basis.

- Immigrant groups generally come from less industrialized and less developed nations and lack the skills necessary to compete effectively in modern society.

- Immigrants enter the society at the bottom of the socioeconomic ladder, but their economic position is markedly better than it was in their country of origin.

- New immigrants have an initial disadvantage economically, socially, and politically, but their ultimate destiny is to be assimilated and integrated into the dominant society.

- The keys to gaining parity in the society for recent immigrants are education and **acculturation** to the values and culture of the dominant group and the rejection of parochial or cultural values from their country of origin.

- Groups that do not attain parity are those that have failed to assimilate and to take advantage of the opportunities available to them in the open and pluralistic society.

(Mirandé, 2002, pp. 186–187)

Variants within Assimilation Theory

1) Anglo conformity
   All ethnic or racial minorities *imitate* or *emulate* the dominant Anglo-Saxon Protestant value system that is the basis for America's core social, cultural, political, and religious institutions.

2) The melting pot

According to this version of assimilation theory, American society is not simply made up of transplanted European immigrants living in the United States, but rather diverse immigrants from all over Europe and other nations as well, contributing to a new hybrid society in which many peoples and sets of values all add unique ingredients to a new and emerging societal consensus.

3) Cultural pluralism or equalitarian pluralism

Ethnic and racial minorities do not, and are not required, to completely lose their collective cultural values or their bonds to their community or nation of origin, even while gaining fuller structural access into or acceptance from members of the dominant opportunity system and social institutions.

Ethnic groups hold on to their cultural identity, language, ethnic foods, traditions, and communal practices.

Ethnic groups do over time become integrated into the dominant economic and political institutions.

Americans need not abandon that which is ethnically unique while they strive for social acceptance.

Ethnic and racial minorities should not have to endure, tolerate, or put up with:

- Ignorance
- Bigotry
- Prejudice
- Discrimination
- Scapegoating
- Hate crimes

Contemporary Multiculturalism

Today, the more traditional language associated with assimilation theory has been largely replaced by the term **multiculturalism.** Multiculturalism has emerged as a response to:

- Progressive social science agendas
- The activist civil rights movements
- The rise of ethnic studies disciplines and the struggles for multicultural curricula in the American school system
- Mass media campaigns for racial and ethnic tolerance and a greater social awareness about issues of prejudice, discrimination, racism, and sexism

Multiculturalism recognizes and acknowledges:

- Our nation's racial and ethnic diversity
- The history, heritage, and positive contributions of people from all racial and ethnic backgrounds to American history, culture, and social achievement
- The need to celebrate and embrace differences rather than continuing or perpetuating practices such as racism, discrimination, hatred, scapegoating, or exclusion

Conclusions about Assimilation Theory

While I have deliberately left much out of my discussion of the assimilation model, it is still possible to characterize the process of assimilation as follows:

- Assimilation theory is an ideal-type model with its own theoretical assumptions, ideological viewpoint, and political implications.

- Assimilation theory is most compatible with ethnic reality.

- Society is held together by core values and **functionally interdependent institutions.**

- European ethnic immigrants to the United States did not initially find universal acceptance or instant success.

- European immigrants to the United States had to contend with and overcome:

  - Prejudice

  - Exploitation

  - Intolerance

  - Discrimination

  Because of differences in

  - Culture

  - Language

  - Religion

  - Education

  - National origin

- Within two to three generations of their arrival in the United States, most immigrant groups:

  - Learned to speak English

  - Adopted American values

  - Gave up or minimally held on to Old World traditions and practices

  - Became integrated and incorporated into the political and economic life of the United States

- Advocates of assimilation theory argue that racial minorities should emulate the ethnic immigrant groups from Europe if they want to find:

  - Social acceptance

  - Success

  - Personal fulfillment

  - **The American dream**

  The assimilation model is not a complete theory about U.S. ethnic and racial reality:

- The model alleges a greater degree of homogeneity of American culture, core values, group consensus, and social integration than is actually demonstrable historically or in the present.

- Assimilation theory is oriented toward **value consensus** and the notion that prejudice and racism are problems at the level of the individual.

- Prejudice and intolerance are viewed as carry-overs from the feudal or traditional pre-Enlightenment societies that were based in superstition, ignorance, irrationality, and emotional solidarity.

- Assimilation models are not sufficiently structural and do not address:
  - Power differences
  - Structural conflict
  - Institutional racism
  - Discrimination
  - Economic exploitation

- Assimilation theory is deeply implicated in "blaming the victim" rather than examining historical, sociological, or structural forces that promote or maintain racism and social inequality.

Finally, assimilation theory, which is supposed to highlight ethnic differences within European immigrant groups, has legitimated the notion of White Europeans as distinct through national origins and cultural uniqueness, while defining people of color in generic racial terms with only minimal appreciation of national and cultural terms based on the true meaning of ethnicity.

In other words, European ethnic incorporation and assimilation into the dominant society ironically produced racial Whiteness and White privilege, while culturally distinct minorities are treated as though they are only racial groups. Thus, Africans, Jamaicans, West Indians, Brazilians, and other national or cultural groups may be viewed as racially non-White rather than as ethnically distinct in spite of their dark skin. Native Americans may be viewed in racial but not ethnic or tribal terms. Latinos may be categorized in racial or cultural/ethnic terms depending upon the social or national context. Asians may be viewed ethnically or culturally in their countries of origin but in the United States may be thought of as racially distinct and "foreign" even when they are American citizens who have no cultural or linguistic affiliation with an Asian homeland.

As I indicated in Chapter 3, it is very difficult to theorize ethnicity since its meaning is so dependent upon the historical context in which such distinctions exist.

In the United States, power, dominance, labor exploitation, and the operation of White supremacy have had a tremendous effect on how cultural and perceived biological differences within and between groups have been dealt with during the era of North American colonization, and the need to develop the slave and free labor systems in the agricultural South and the commercial and industrializing North. The legacy of U.S. expansion and the dispossession of Indians, the enslavement of Africans, the annexation of Mexicans and their subordination in the Southwest, and the importation, labor exploitation, segregation, and exclusion of Asians all require a different theoretical model and historical and structural description if we are to understand American racism in terms other than "blaming the victim." It is to the elaboration of the racial theoretical model of internal colonial theory that I now turn.

The Internal Colony Model

Colonialism, traditionally refers to the establishment of domination over a geographically external political unit, most often inhabited by people of a different race and culture, where this domination is political and economic and the colony exists subordinated to and dependent upon the mother country. Typically, the colonizers exploit the land, the raw materials, the labor, and other resources of the colonized nation; a formal recognition is given to the difference in power, autonomy, and political status, and various agencies, are set up to maintain this subordination.

(Blauner, 2001, p. 65)

People of color have never been an integral part of the Anglo-American political community and culture because they did not enter the dominant society in the same way as did the European ethnics. The third world notion points to a basic distinction between immigration and colonization as the two major processes through which new population groups are incorporated into a nation. Immigrant groups enter a new territory or society voluntarily, though they may be pushed out of their old country by dire economic or political oppression. Colonized groups become part of a new society through force or violence; they are conquered, enslaved, or pressured into movement. Thus, the third world formulation is a bold attack on the myth that America is the land of the free, or more specifically, a nation whose population has been built up through successive waves of immigration. The third world perspective returns us to the origins of the American experience, reminding us that this nation owes its very existence to colonialism, and that along with settlers and immigrants there have always been conquered Indians and black slaves, and later defeated Mexicans—that is, colonial subjects on the national soil. Such a reminder is not pleasant to a society that represses those aspects of its history that do not fit the collective self-image of democracy for all men.

(Blauner, 2001, pp. 45–46)

Each third world people has undergone distinctive, indeed cataclysmic, experiences on the American continent that separate its history from the others, as well as from whites. Only Native Americans waged a 300-year war against white encroachment; only they were subject to genocide and removal. Only Chicanos were severed from an ongoing modern nation; only they remain concentrated in the area of their original land base, close to Mexico. Only Blacks went through a 250-year period of slavery. The Chinese were the first people whose presence was interdicted by exclusion acts. The Japanese were the one group declared an internal enemy and rounded up in concentration camps. Though the notion of colonized minorities points to a similarity of situation, it should not imply that black, red, yellow, and brown Americans are all in the same bag. Colonization has taken different forms in the histories of the individual groups. Each people is strikingly heterogeneous, and the variables of time, place, and manner have affected the forms of colonialism, the character of racial domination, and the response of the group.

(Blauner, 2001, pp. 60–61)

I have cited from Bob Blauner's recent book *Still the Big News: Racial Oppression in America* (2001) in order to dramatically indicate the political and ideological divide between adherents of the various schools of though based upon assimilationism and the immigrant model of incorporation and the radical perspectives that stress classical colonialism, third world inequality, and racial oppression in America based upon the notion of internal colonialism.

The historical evolution of European expansionist nation-states is critical if we are to grasp the economic and structural factors that led to modern exploration, conquest, racism, slavery, capitalism, colonization, and the internal colonization of racial groups within the territory of independent former settler colonies.

I have indicated in the previous section that the assimilationist orientation stresses a social order perspective within a discussion of large-scale social evolution in order to explain how a rigid, caste-like feudal society could be transformed—through the increased development of the division of labor and massive migration—into a system of global capitalism in which ethnic differences would increasingly give way to class stratification and opportunities for individual social mobility based not upon caste distinctions but upon individual effort, motivation, and achievement in the capitalist system.

But the assumptions of assimilation theory were based upon Eurocentric values that privileged the White elites and classes of nations such as the United States, and established a normative ideology of incorporation of culturally distinct ethnic groups (for the most part), while virtually excluding, subordinating, or segregating racial minorities from full citizenship rights, legal protections, and residential or economic participation in the dominant group's institutions.

The beliefs and biases of the assimilation model were so fully taken for granted that social scientists were largely unprepared for the racial movements of the 1950s and 1960s. In an article titled "Towards an Understanding of the Internal Colonial Model" by John Liu, this predictive failure of assimilation theory is clearly expressed:

> The civil rights movement, the outbreak of racial violence, and the growth of nationalist and separatist movements among America's racial minorities during the sixties were events social scientists failed to foresee. This was because the dominant model in the area of race relations up to this time was the assimilation/integration model which was based on the proposition that America was willing to extend to her racial minorities the same rights and privileges enjoyed by white Americans. Within the framework of this model, social scientists focused on the barriers to assimilation and proposed strategies nonwhite minorities could adopt in order to facilitate their transition to full political and social equality. The subsequent events of the sixties, however, forced social scientists to reassess this basic proposition.
>
> (Liu, 1976, p. 160)

Liu then compares classical colonialism to internal colonialism based upon an enumeration of the characteristics of the colonial process:

1) The forced entry of nonwhite populations into the colonizer's society

2) The creation of a dual labor market economy

3) The sharing of a single polity by the colonizer and colonized in which the former is totally dominant

4) Racial and cultural oppression, leading to the development of racist rules or norms

(Liu, 1976, p. 160)

Key Concepts and Assumptions of Internal Colonialism

Based upon Alfredo Mirandé's *The Chicano Experience: An Alternative Perspective* (2002) and my own analysis, internal colonial theory can be represented as follows:

- The internal colony model is a response and refutation of assimilation theory's claim that American society has integrated people of color into the so-called melting pot.

- Racial minorities did not initially enter American society voluntarily but through force and violence.

- Just as European powers colonized the peoples of the third world, racial minorities in the United States entered into a forced and dependent relationship with the dominant group.

- Internal colonization took place within the territorial boundaries of the United States.

- The United States is not an orderly or cohesive "melting pot" for diverse racial-ethnic groups, but a society characterized by the subordination of some groups by others who benefit from their subordinate status.

- European immigrants migrated individually and freely but some racial-ethnic minorities came here involuntarily, by force, and en mass.

- Racial minorities in the United States are not from less-advanced underdeveloped nations but in some instances came from older, advanced civilizations that were in many ways superior.

- Those who are internally colonized enter society at the bottom of the socioeconomic and political system and are subordinated by various mechanisms.

- Internally colonized populations make up a dependent and secondary labor force that receives lower wages and few, if any, of the benefits of workers in the more privileged primary labor force.

- Racially internally colonized populations are not only subordinated economically and politically, but also culturally.

- Cultural oppression includes efforts of the dominant group to render minority cultures dependent and to eradicate their languages.

- Racially oppressed groups may be culturally dependent, but their cultures have not been eradicated and they have not been fully assimilated or integrated into the dominant society.

- Internally colonized individuals are allowed a certain amount of upward mobility based upon their closeness to Caucasians in appearance and/or their willingness to adopt the values and culture of the dominant group.

- Acceptance of the assimilated individual is often in proportion to the extent that they are perceived as *not* identifying with or representing the interests of the internally colonized group.

(Mirandé, 2002, pp. 188–189)

Clearly, internal colonialism stresses race, oppression, inequality, cultural identity, and struggle.

Conclusion

Ideal-type theories of society—whether based upon order versus conflict or assimilation versus internal colonialism—inevitably are only partial representations of complex historical and socio-logical processes of group formation and interaction.

The validity of such theories is ultimately determined through historical scholarship and empirical investigation. I should also point out that when models have polemical and controversial assumptions and make radically different substantive assertions about the nature of society, their acceptance or rejection may come down to personal ideology, group identity, or political orientation.

When the disciplines of ethnic studies were emerging out of the activist struggles of the 1960s, society was not only divided in terms of civil rights, the war in Vietnam, counterculture versus tradition, gender, and generation, but the academic world was polarized concerning how ethnicity and race were being conceptualized and discussed. The study of racism, nationalism, revolutionary movements, decolonization, and anti-imperialistic struggles was not only a reflection of the historical moment, but it was the preferred perspective of minority youths who became activists in college and radical intellectuals both inside and outside the academy.

Students in sociology and Black, Chicano, Indian, or Asian studies were often exposed to ethnicity and assimilationist perspectives that represented the prevailing wisdom, only to question or critique such orientations as reactionary, irrelevant, or not in touch with the contemporary movements for social justice and full equality.

While the times have certainly changed since the 1960s and the field of ethnic studies is constantly evolving in relation to external political considerations and disciplinary concerns in the social sciences and humanities, the ideological warfare between the political right and the left is intense just as are the substantive arguments regarding ethnicity and race that we have reviewed in terms of the models of assimilation and internal colonialism.

As we move on to representing discussions about American Indians, African Americans, Chicanos, and Asian Americans, we will see that theories and models mirror the complex processes of inclusion and integration or exclusion, exploitation, and genocide that have shaped America's racial mosaic.

Questions, Exercises, and Topics for Discussion and Debate

1) Explain why many sociologists and social theorists of the nineteenth and twentieth centuries believed and predicted that ethnicity and racial differences would decline or become less significant as modern societies and nation-states evolved.

2) Define the meaning of the following terms and explain their relevance for assimilation theory:
   a) Social incorporation

   b) Acculturation

   c) Integration

   d) Host society

   e) Core values and institutions

   f) Anglo conformity

   g) Melting pot theory

   h) Cultural pluralism

   i) Americanization of immigrants

   j) Voluntary migration

3) Define and explain settler colonialism, classic colonialism, and internal colonialism. How do the various forms of colonization relate to:
   a) Conflict theory

   b) Involuntary migration

   c) Slave importation

   d) Forced labor

   e) Contract labor

   f) Racial exclusion

   g) The racial formation process

4) Why does assimilation theory support a conservative and status-quo orientation? Discuss the consensus and functional theory frameworks, the social order perspective, and the ethnicity model of society. How does Robert Park's race relations cycle explain the assimilation of European immigrant populations, and is his theory relevant as a description of the incorporation of racially distinct groups and people of color?

5) What is meant by the notion of "blaming the victim"? Discuss the argument that is often made by Whites, Anglos, or successful European immigrants toward people of color to the effect that: "If the Irish, the Jews, the Catholics, the Italians, the Greeks, and other immigrants overcame prejudice, stereotypes, and exploitation, then there is no reason that racial minorities cannot also follow their example and realize success, opportunity, and the American Dream." Does the so-called immigrant analogy apply to Blacks, Indians, Chicanos, Asians, and other distinct racially visible populations?

6) In what way do various theories of incorporation or exclusion of differences among ethnic and racial groups contest ideal-type models of historical and sociologically pure processes of interaction and institutional reality?

7) What are the implications of the following theoretical terms in relation to the social growth, development, and evolutions of human societies—particularly in the era of modernity and the European Enlightenment:
   a) Mechanical vs. organic solidarity

   b) Sacred vs. secular society

   c) Traditional vs. modern society

   d) Irrational vs. rational humanity

   e) Rural vs. urban society

   f) Agricultural vs. industrial society

8) Discuss order versus conflict theory, and indicate both the strengths and weaknesses of each perspective for dealing with ethnic and racial integration or separation.

9) Do full citizenship and the realization of civil and human rights require groups to support federal, state, and local government and polices of the dominant society in order to gain collective or community recognition?

10) Discuss your own ethnic and/or racial heritage and what terms, concepts, and theories help you to better understand either your group's collective history in America or your own individual successes and failures in confronting social institutions because of your identity or the response of others to you in various circumstances and situations.

11) What is multiculturalism? Should it be welcomed in schools, public social spaces, the media, the work place, and as an ideal consensus that Americans should value? Is a belief in multiculturalism sufficient to bring about social integration, structural incorporation of excluded and/or poor populations, and a lessening of social inequality? Explain your answer.

12) Is it possible to have a thorough-going cultural pluralism and yet recognize, celebrate, honor, and integrate distinct communities in terms of the realization of social justice and popular democracy? Discuss and debate this issue.

Native Americans

Chapter Seven

Key Terms

aboriginal peoples

aboriginal sovereignty

American Indian movement

Bartolomé de las Casas

Bering Strait theory

blood quantum

creation stories

cultural genocide

Dawes Allotment Act

demography

diversity of Indian societies

doctrine of just wars

economic genocide

educational genocide

encomienda system

European and Old World diseases

forms of genocide

genocide

glacial land bridge

Hernán Cortez

Indian civilizations

Indian removal

Indian Reorganization Act

Indian Territory

Indian worldviews

Indians

indigenous peoples

Indios

Manifest Destiny

Mestizos

Native Americans

religious genocide

relocation

reservations

right of occupancy

self-determination

sovereignty

Spanish conquistadors

termination

treaty rights

United States Indian policy

wards of the federal government

World War II

Key Lesson

The populations of the New World whose occupation of the diverse ecological niches from the Arctic and Canadian North through North America, the Caribbean, Mexico, Central, and South America down to Tierra Del Fuego predated the temporary incursions and partial colonization of the Vikings and other pre-Columbian explorers as well as the more permanent and lasting destructive encounters that commenced with Columbus, Cortez, Pizarro, Coronado, and representative of the French, Portuguese, Dutch, and English.

The peoples known by countless original names in their various tribal or aboriginal languages, who developed their own cultures, forms of social organization, trading networks, spiritual and cosmological systems of knowledge and time-keeping, and whose accounts of their origins, creation stories, myths, and rituals so differed from the Protestant, Catholic, Jewish, and Muslim peoples of the Old World, have come to be known as **Indios, indigenous peoples, Indians, Mestizos** when mixed with Spanish inheritance, mispronounced linguistic representation of their names, derogatory and stereotypical labels, names adopted by Whites from competing or enemy tribes, and later identified by the complex rules of **blood quantum** derived from the federal government and the Bureau of Indian Affairs (BIA)—have in recent decades received the generic, politically correct designation of **Native Americans** with all due appreciation, reverence, and respect (but no semblance of social justice) for five hundred years of genocide, removal, forced conversion and labor in missions, destruction of the traditional rituals and sacred practices that held their lives together, and the wardship of the Reservation System, the federal and BIA boarding schools, the allotment of their lands, the expropriation of their natural resources, the broken promises associated with urban relocation, and the attempt to terminate Indian tribes and their sovereignty.

The Europeans and Americans idealized and romanticized the idyllic and "primitive" ways of the Indians while acknowledging, begrudgingly, the level of advanced civilization they encountered, and yet they viewed the **aboriginal peoples** as degraded, paganistic, savage, inferior, and a violent threat to their own progress, advance, development, and **Manifest Destiny.** To deal with Indian presence and occupation of land they created legalistic and religious justifications for their imperialistic actions. Indians had **aboriginal sovereignty** and the prior **right of occupancy.** But they did not fence their land or believe in private property and development in a market system. The **doctrine of just wars** and the doctrine of discovery along with the international legal system of negotiating **treaty rights** were used for the purpose of legally and militarily extinguishing Indian land claims through land cessions in return for promised annuities and removal. Indian annihilation by disease, removal, warfare, enslavement, fraud, and various **forms of genocide** led to lives of hardship in the Indian Territory, the reservation system, and the near destruction of all Indians by the beginning of the twentieth century in North America.

Then came the anthropologists, social scientists, social workers, demographers, missionaries, do-gooders, bureaucrats, lawyers, energy experts, educators, art lovers, vacationers, tourists, souvenir hunters, Indian lovers, hippies, activists, crystal Indians,

Indian wannabees, and all manner of people who had every conceivable motive and agenda for dealing with, discovering, or trying to understand Indian people.

Between 1928 when the Meriam Report was issued, which demonstrated the depths of poverty, destitution, dependency, and health problems that American Indians suffered from, and the present, Indians were offered tribal councils if they accepted the 1934 **Indian Reorganization Act,** they served in **World War II** as combatants and most famously as "code-talkers," began to gain education, seek civil rights following the horrendous policies of **relocation** and **termination,** and developed urban pan-Indian associations. By the 1960s and 1970s Indian activism led to a vital and publically visible militancy whether called Red Power, the fight for recognition on college or university campuses as American Indians studies, or the efforts of young urban Indian activists in the name of the **American Indian movement** to challenge corrupt police power in major cities and corrupt Indian leadership on reservations while reconnecting with spiritual and traditional elders.

Indians or Native Americans have fought for their civil and human rights both in the halls and courts of the U.S. federal government and the United Nations and the World Court. Many victories have been won but the battle for **sovereignty** and tribal **self-determination** is far from over.

> During the four centuries spanning the time between 1492, when Christopher Columbus first set foot on the "New World" of a Caribbean beach, and 1892, when the U.S. Bureau concluded that there were fewer than a quarter-million indigenous people surviving within the country's claimed boundaries, a hemispheric population estimated to have been as great as 125 million was reduced by something over 90 percent. The people died in their millions of being hacked apart with axes and swords, burned alive and trampled under horses, hunted as game and fed to dogs, shot, beaten, stabbed, scalped for bounty, hanged on meathooks and thrown over the sides of ships at sea, worked to death as slave laborers, intentionally starved and frozen to death during a multitude of forced marches and internments, and in an unknown number of instances, deliberately infected with epidemic diseases.
>
> (Churchill, 1997, p. 1)

> All European colonial powers espoused the same basic goals to justify the exploration and settlement of the New World. The imperialist nation-states mutually agreed that the "cross and crown, gold and glory constituted the legitimating symbols in Europeans' eyes for the invasion and takeover of the Americas." While missionaries were undermining Indigenous civilizations in the name of God, European merchants were accumulating private and public wealth through trade, and the enhancement of national and personal glory through colonization. In fact, the ideals and interests of the missionaries and private profit seekers were one and the same. The missionaries, protecting their own profit spread propaganda to enhance national glory and convinced Europeans to promote the imperial system. At the same time, they were deepening the oppression of the Native population. European documentation from that period is nothing more than fictional messages designed to justify the Europeans' brutal actions. The colonizer claimed his actions were humanitarian and divinely ordained—that was the myth used to camouflage, as well as condone the conquest and oppression of Aboriginal peoples.
>
> (Adams, 1999, p. 22)

White academics, primarily historians and anthropologists, have owned the Indigenous past for too long. Although the military was the initial force that colonized Natives, the continuing psychological process of intellectual and cultural debilitation ensure their subjugated status. Therefore, it is from that base that Aboriginal decolonization must begin. The racist pattern established by the first colonizers will be broken only when the colonized reclaim their history. Third World scholars who are now rewriting their history demonstrate that Aboriginal history can be properly interpreted only by Aboriginals. Other scholars and authors do not have the consciousness and experience to express the authentic socio-political values and cultural orientations of Aboriginal society. Only Aboriginals who have experienced critical colonization can understand the nuances of Native customs, spirituality, and traditions, which include unspoken assumptions and symbolic meanings that permeate Aboriginal communities.

(Adams, 1999, pp. 26–27)

Under Lemkin's definition, genocide was the coordinated and planned annihilation of a national, religious, or racial group by a variety of actions aimed at undermining the foundations essential to the survival of the group as a group. Lemkin conceived of genocide as "a composite of different acts of persecution or destruction." His definition included attacks on political and social institutions, culture, language, national feelings, religion, and the economic existence of the group. Even nonlethal acts that undermined the liberty, dignity, and personal security of members of a group constituted genocide if they contributed to weakening the viability of the group.

(Stannard, 1992, p. 279)

Introduction

In the 1960s and 1970s, as a result of the political and cultural activism of both reservation and urban Indians, the people of the United States were forced to reexamine the myths, fantasies, misconceptions, and stereotypes that were ubiquitous in grade-school teachings about colonial America, Thanksgiving, and Pocahontas; the romantic visions of the California missions; the decades of TV Westerns that portrayed Indians as brutal and pagan savages standing in the way of progress, civilization, Manifest Destiny, and the peopling of the continent; and the belief that Indians were safely secured on **reservations** where they lived a museum-like existence that placed them beyond the pull of history and certainly outside the conscience or consciousness of most Americans.

In the early to mid-1960s, Indian activists and their non-Indian supporters staged Fish-Ins in the Northwest and demanded that their treaty rights be legally upheld. In 1968, in Minneapolis and St. Paul, Minnesota, Chippewa activists established the "Indian patrol" to monitor the activities of the police as they arrested the Indians living in the Twin Cities. Out of this effort, George Mitchell and Dennis Banks organized the American Indian movement, which became the militant voice of young, urban Indians, and a bridge back to the reservations where traditionalists and Indians who were silenced by tribal councils, corrupt leaders, and an ineffective federal Indian bureaucracy in the Bureau of Indian Affairs were able to resist the status quo and business-as-usual across Indian country.

By November of 1969, beginning with the bold actions of Richard Oakes and Adam Norwall, a contingent of Indian students from San Francisco and Bay-area colleges and universities occupied Alcatraz briefly on November 9, followed by a larger takeover on November 20.

The stated goals of the occupation were to convert the island into a Native American cultural center and to unify Indians everywhere for bolder and more effective action. The leaders of the occupation aligned themselves with traditionalists by issuing a ringing defense of Indian culture. A cultural center on Alcatraz, they explained, would help keep alive "the old Indian ways." The center would include an Indian college, training school, religious and spiritual center, museum, and ecology center. . . . The occupation of Alcatraz also was a dramatic assertion of Native American treaty rights and Indian sovereignty.

(Rawls, 1996, p. 123)

Stan Steiner's book *The New Indians* captured the new mood that had been developing in post–World War II Indian country. He discussed the growing urban pan-Indian movement, the rise of Indian radical students, and the so-called Red Power movement. Two other books that were tremendously influential on college campuses and around the country were Dee Brown's *Bury My Heart at Wounded Knee* (1981) and Vine Deloria's *Custer Died for Your Sins: An Indian Manifesto* (1988).

I provide this limited overview of the consciousness of **Indian civilizations** and their great impact during the late 1960s and 1970s to demonstrate that the radicalism of the 1960s was not limited to Black nationalists, White opponents of the war in Vietnam and racism and poverty in America, or Chicano and Asian American militants. American Indian studies courses and programs were established on many college campuses, and their impact on non-Indian students as well as upon a growing number of Native students was truly transformative.

It is important that Native American studies or Indian studies should continue to grow both as a specialty in ethnic studies, as autonomous academic units exercising their own sovereignty and Indian-generated perspectives, and as a field of study developed for Native people living on reservations or attending Native American colleges throughout Indian country.

In this chapter, I do not intend to represent the vast historical and contemporary literature pertaining to American Indian nations and their experience with the U.S. government, agencies of social control, dominant institutions, or individual citizens.

But I do want to provide useful sources that will help the interested reader to gain an understanding of Indian history and experience, and I will clarify what I think are crucial political and ideological issues that must be addressed by scholars, researchers, and activists in ethnic studies.

Sources about American Indians

This list of books on American Indians is by no means exhaustive, but I have attempted to provide coverage on:

- Indian origins, history, and tribal life

- Pre- and post-Columbian experience

- Colonial and American history of American tribes

- Warfare and the frontier period

- Twentieth-century Indian history and experience

- Indian rights, law, and sovereignty

- The Red Power movement, American Indian movement, and Indian activism

- Conquest, colonization, and genocide

Rather than list the sources by topic, I have chosen to list them alphabetically by author and title.

1) David Wallace Adams

   Education for Extinction: American Indians and the Boarding School Experience, 1875–1928

2) Howard Adams

Tortured People: The Politics of Colonization

3) J. M. Adovasio with Jake Page

The First Americans: In Pursuit of Archaeology's Greatest Mystery

4) Ralph Andrist

The Long Death: The Last Days of the Plains Indian

5) Dennis Banks with Richard Erdoes

Ojibwa Warrior: Dennis Banks and the Rise of the American Indian Movement

6) Ward Churchill

Perversions of Justice: Indigenous Peoples and Anglo American Law

7) Ward Churchill

A Little Matter of Genocide: Holocaust and Denial in the Americas 1492 to the Present

8) Angie Debo

A History of the Indians of the United States

9) Vine Deloria, Jr.

Custer Died for Your Sins: An Indian Manifesto

10) M. Annette Jaimes, Editor

The State of Native America: Genocide, Colonization, and Resistance

11) Francis Jennings

The Founders of America: From the Earliest Migrations to the Present

12) Wayne Moquin, Editor, with Charles Van Doren

Great Documents in American Indian History

13) Judith Nies

Native American History: A Chronology of the Vast Achievements of a Culture and Their Links to World Events

14) Jack Norton

When Our Worlds Cried: Genocide in Northwestern California

15) Jake Page

In the Hands of the Great Spirit: The 20,000 Year History of American Indians

16) Stephen L. Pevar

The Rights of Indians and Tribes

17) Kirkpatrick Sale

The Conquest of Paradise: Christopher Columbus and the Columbian Legacy

18) Patricia Seed

American Pentimento: The Invention of Indians and the Pursuit of Riches

19) Richard Slotkin

The Fatal Environment: The Myth of the Frontier in the Age of Industrialization, 1800–1890

20) Paul Chaat Smith and Robert Allen Warrior

Like a Hurricane: The Indian Movement from Alcatraz to Wounded Knee

21) David E. Stannard

American Holocaust: Columbus and the Conquest of the New World

22) Stan Steiner

The New Indians

23) Kenneth S. Stern

Loud Hawk: The United States versus the American Indian Movement

24) Robert M. Utley

The Indian Frontier of the American West 1846–1890

25) Jack Utter

American Indians: Answers to Today's Questions

26) Paul VanDevelder

Coyote Warrior: One Man, Three Tribes, and the Trial That Forged a Nation

27) Rex Weyler

Blood of the Land: The Government and Corporate War Against First Nations

28) James Wilson

The Earth Shall Weep: A History of Native America

29) Ronald Wright

Stolen Continents: The Americas Through Indian Eyes Since 1492

30) John R. Wunder

"Retained by the People": A History of American Indians and the Bill of Rights

Controversies in Native American Studies

Indian Origins and Spirituality

The issues of **Indian worldviews, creation stories,** origins, and spirituality are fundamental to understanding the conquest, colonization, and conflict that has characterized the relationship between all peoples indigenous to the western hemisphere and those who came out of Europe with a variety of purposes, agendas, and prejudices related to their own worldviews and epistemologies.

Vine Deloria, Jr., has developed a strong critique of Eurocentric religious and scientific claims about the nature of knowledge and assertions about reality. In *Red Earth, White Lies: Native Americans and the Myth of Scientific Fact,* he writes:

As Western civilization grew and took dominance over the world, it failed to resolve basic issues. A view of the natural world as primarily physical matter with little spiritual content took hold and became the practical metaphysics for human affairs. During the European

Middle Ages, a basic split in perspective occurred with *reason* and *revelation,* the twin paths for finding truth in the minds of Western thinkers, were divided into sacred and secular and became equivalent but independent bodies of knowledge. Once reason became independent, its only referent point was the human mind and in particular the middle-class educated European mind. Every society needs educated people, but the primary responsibility of educated people is to bring wisdom back into the community and make it available to others so that the lives they are leading make sense.

(Deloria, Jr., 1995, pp. 16–17)

Whether one views Deloria's point in terms of a conflict between:

- materialism versus spirituality,

- materialism versus idealism,

- reason versus emotion,

- enlightenment versus superstition,

- rationality versus irrationality,

- christianity versus paganism, or

- progress versus tradition,

the key point is that Indians were subjected to two European forms of domination. One was European technology, which almost guaranteed Native American defeat, and the other was a violation of indigenous spirituality and lifestyle that undermined their cultures and their ability to maintain their sovereignty.

Vine Deloria, Jr., articulates the connection between material domination and spiritual loss as follows:

When Europeans arrived on these shores they brought with them a powerful technology. For much of the first four hundred years of contact, technology dealt Indians the hardest blows. Mechanical devises from the musket to the iron kettle to the railroad made it a certainty that Indians would lose the military battle to maintain their independence. Technology made it certain that no tribe would be able to maintain its beliefs in the spiritual world when it was apparent that whites had breached certain fundamental ways of living in that spiritual world and in this breach had foreclosed even the wisest of their people from understanding the larger arena in which human destiny was being played out.

(Deloria, Jr., 1995, p. 16)

There is tremendous irony in the way that indigenous people were spiritually and culturally undermined because of the technological capabilities of Europeans to overcome virtually any type of resistance by Native people in the course of the first four hundred years of contact with the Spanish, Portuguese, Dutch, French, English, and Americans.

Whether it was the Taino people on Hispaniola; the Mexica of Tenochtitlán; the Incas in Peru; or the diverse nations of the various cultural and ecological niches from the Arctic, Subarctic, and Northwest coast; to the Plateau, the Great Basin, and California; to the Southwest; or California, the northern and southern plains, the Woodlands, the Great Lakes, or the Southeast and Florida— all Indian peoples had to deal with an arrogant Western form of Christian White supremacy that was associated with military, material, and economic forces that saw the imperial and colonial forces of Western progress and advance as very much synonymous with Indian extinction, annihilation, removal, containment, control or forced assimilation into a dominant culture that rejected their sovereignty, independence, tribal identities, and their spiritual worldviews.

The paradox of U.S. contact with Indians is that a society so steeped in the tenets of Christianity could act so maliciously and violently in the pursuit of what sociologist Max Weber called "the protestant ethic and the spirit of capitalism." Weber argued that spiritually minded Puritans with an uncertainty about their state of salvation sought external signs of God's grace in the visible realm of behaviors—such as frugality, hard work, honesty, and commitment to systematically build economic enterprises that ultimately resulted in a capitalistic ethos that would become self-sustaining and independent of the original Protestant values that produced it.

Thus, Western Christians created a set of material structures that were intended to validate their psychological need for certainty over their spiritual values, which had the material consequence of destroying the spiritual and cultural beliefs of Indians while forcing them into an alienated and decidedly intolerant and uncharitable society that Weber called an "iron cage."

> Max Weber defined the consequences of the protestant ethic as follows: The Puritan wanted to work in a calling; we are forced to do so. For when asceticism was carried out of monastic cells into everyday life, and began to dominate worldly morality, it did its part in building the tremendous cosmos of the modern economic order. This order is now bound to the technical and economic conditions of machine production which to-day determine the lives of all individuals who are born into this mechanism, not only those directly concerned with economic acquisition, with irresistible force. Perhaps it will so determine them until the last ton of fossilized coal is burnt. In Baxter's view the care for external goods should only lie on the shoulders of the "saint like a light cloak, which can be thrown aside at any moment." But fate decreed that the cloak should become an iron cage.
>
> (Weber, 1958, p. 181)

For Indian people, their material life and well-being was dependent upon their beliefs and practices, which White society attempted to surround, isolate, destroy, or assimilate. In John G. Neihardt's world-famous book *Black Elk Speaks,* the Lakota medicine man explained his spiritual vision and the state of Indian people as a result of the massacre at Wounded Knee:

> And so it was all over
>
> I did not know then how much was ended. When I look back now from this high hill of my old age, I can still see the butchered women and children lying heaped and scattered all along the crooked gulch as plain as when I saw them with eyes still young. And I can see that something else died there in the bloody mud, and was buried in the blizzard. A people's dream died there. It was a beautiful dream.
>
> And I, to whom so great a vision was given in my youth – you see me now a pitiful old man who has done nothing, for the nation's hoop is broken and scattered. There is no center any longer, and the sacred tree is dead.
>
> (Neihardt, 1972, p. 230)

I am not qualified to explain American Indian worldviews, creation accounts, sacred teachings, or the stories told to the young by elders to develop their character, socialize them into their culture, or to teach them traditions, morality, and everyday conduct. But the first realization that must be communicated in Indian studies is that what has occurred after 1492 through the material rape of the western hemisphere is nothing less than the **religious** and **cultural genocide**— and colonization of—the Native American mind. Whether we represent that process in terms of the **Spanish conquistadors** who destroyed indigenous temples, monuments, codices, and forced the Indios to convert to Catholicism and labor as slaves in the missions or the **encomienda system,** or whether we deal with syncretism or hybrid Indian-Catholic/Protestant worldviews, or the complete assimilation of Indians to Christianity—the result has been a by-product of Western violence, material dispossession, and the colonization of Indian consciousness. In the prologue to Jon E. Lewis's edited book *The Mammoth Book of Native Americans,* the author explains:

> The seeming diversity of Amerindian Creation myths not withstanding, they have much universality about them. In almost all of them, the Maker—the Great Spirit, Wakan Tanka, however named—spiritually binds the people to all the remainder of his works. Put another way, Indians and Nature are one, indivisible, made so by God. When the earth is cut, the Indian weeps. This spiritual, near mystical, union with the land is the heart of Indian religion, aesthetics, morality; improper conduct throws the connection out of kilter, bringing harm to the tribe; reverence, beautiful art, correct deeds harmonize the tribe and their land.
>
> The sacred interconnectedness of the Indian to his environment was beyond the ken of the whites when they came in AD 1492; five hundred years of tragedy was the result. They "sicken and died" said Geronimo of the Apache when they were moved off their land. Exactly the same could be said of all other Indians in post-Columbian America.
>
> (Lewis, 2004, pp. 4–5)

For further discussion of American Indian spirituality, myths, legends, and stories, the reader can consult Appendix V: "Myths and Tales of the Native American (pages 458–567) in the *The Mammoth Book of Native Americans,* or the book *American Indian Myths and Legends,* selected and edited by Richard Erdoes and Alfonso Ortiz.

I will close this section with the words of Black Elk, and then discuss Western theories of Indian origins, population, and what science has to say about how long Indians have been in the western hemisphere. Black Elk's concern was not about his original visions, but that Indian people should continue to live and find life:

> To the center of the world you have taken me and showed the goodness and the beauty and the strangeness of the greening earth, the only mother—and there the spirit shapes of things, as they should be, you have shown to me and I have seen. At the center of this sacred hoop you have said that I should make the tree bloom.
>
> With tears running, O Great Spirit, Great Spirit, my Grandfather – with running tears I must say now that the tree has never bloomed . . . Here at the center of the world, where you took me when I was young and taught me; here, old, I stand, and the tree is withered, Grandfather, my Grandfather!
>
> Again, and maybe the last time on this earth, I recall the great vision you sent me. It may be that some little root of the sacred tree still lives. Nourish it then, that it may leaf and bloom and fill with singing birds. Hear me, not for myself, but for my people; I am old. Hear me that they may once more go back into the sacred hoop and find the good red road, the shielding tree!
>
> (Neihardt, 1972, p. 233)

Indian Origins and the Bering Strait Theory

Because Native Americans throughout the western hemisphere have collectively suffered so extensively following the post-Columbian "discovery" of the New World by Europeans—an event that many Indians refer to as "an invasion," "a holocaust," "a little matter of genocide," or in the words of John Trudell, "the coming of predator," the issue of Indian origins continues to provoke controversy despite the fact that most Western academics, anthropologists, archaeologists, paleontologists, and other experts claim virtually unanimous scientific support for the belief that the distant ancestors of today's Indian populations had their geographic origins in ancestral homelands in northeastern Asia.

The argument of David E. Stannard in *American Holocaust: Columbus and the Conquest of the New World,* which is a hard-hitting and well-documented exploration of the conquest and genocide of Indians, is that where the first humans in the Americas came from and how they got to

North, Central, and South America is "now probably the least controversial of these age-old questions" (Stannard, 1992, p. 8). Stannard summarizes the basic argument for a **glacial land bridge** that connected the continents of Asia and North America across the Bering and Chukchi seas:

> During most, and perhaps all of the time from about 80,000 B.C. to about 10,000 B.C. (the geologic era known as the Wisconsin glaciation), at least part of the shallow floor of the Bering and Chukchi seas, like most of the world's continental shelves, was well above sea level due to the capture of so much of the earth's ocean water by the enormous continent-wide glaciers of this Ice Age epoch. The effect of this was, for all practical purposes, the complete fusion of Asia and North America into a single land mass whose place of connection was a huge chunk of earth actually a subcontinent—hundreds of thousands of square miles in size now called by geographers Berengia.

Jake Page discusses the larger context of Native American origins to capture questions that have fueled the controversy for several hundred years. In his book *In The Hands of The Great Spirit,* he writes:

> Just who these first American humans were and when they arrived is one of the great, and most controversial, questions that confront the modern archaeologist (not to mention the Indian descendents of these pioneers), and has confronted people of such mind for hundreds of years. Were the Indians encountered here the progeny of the lost tribes of Israel? or, it has been asked in more recent times, could some of them at least have arrived in boats made out of straw, drifting across the ocean from Phoenicia on accommodating currents? or from Europe? or the South Seas? Could the Negroid features of the monumental heads of the Olmecs mean that Africans visited here anciently? Such questions tantalize, fascinate, and make headlines, as does any sign that humanity may have been here for longer than previously or currently supposed. Some Indian people today—Sioux political scientist Vine Deloria Jr. among them—say that humanity arose here, in this hemisphere, in the first place and spread around the world.

(Page, 2003, p. 22)

I am not so concerned with the framing a definitive opinion about the **Bering Strait theory** or the possible origin of contemporary Indian distant ancestors as I am interested in indicating why the controversy must be examined as a political and ideological debate that may pit academicians—with their Eurocentric assumptions about the validity of science—against native people, upholding their tribal traditions and spirituality, in the continuing battle against U.S. hegemony and racist denial of atrocities against Indians; while demanding that tribes embrace the American system, bail-out bankrupt or economically challenged states with gaming money, or give up their sovereignty and Indian identities.

The other political question that the Indian origins controversy suggests has to do with the Anglo ideological assertion that "we're all just immigrants" to America. Given the way that Europeans used their emerging system of international law to mediate conflicts between nation-states while each colonizing power used pseudo-legal arguments and Christian theology to force their authority and culture upon Indian people, it is not surprising that many Native Americans reject being described as perhaps the earliest in a long list of migrating populations to end up in the New World. Indians have always had a spiritual and moral claim to their land and their way of life, which came from the Creator and their long-standing traditions.

Because Europeans granted to Indians the right of occupancy of their lands by aboriginal sovereignty, which they quickly over-rode using the doctrine of discovery and the doctrine of just wars, they were able to convince themselves of the legality of their abuses of Indians. If Indians are to successfully assert their rights as original sovereign nations, then, despite how they have been dispossessed, they must appeal to moral principles that cannot be denied them within U.S. legal jurisprudence.

Ultimately, the claims of Indians about their origins and the assertion of non-Indian academic experts—based on glaciers and animal–human continental migrations, or whether Kennewick Man is defined as genetically Caucasian or as Indian due to the alleged age of the skeleton and its presence on aboriginal land—the real issue at stake is social justice for Indian peoples and the preservation of Native culture, tradition, language, and identity that Indian people themselves are able to determine and work out.

For discussions about Indian origins, pre-Columbian history, tribal diversity, and more recent colonization and experience, see the books: *The Founders of America* by Francis Jennings; *American Holocaust* by David E. Stannard; Jake Page's *In the Hands of the Great Spirit;* and J. M. Adovasio and Jake Page's *The First Americans: In pursuit of Archaeology's Greatest Mystery.*

Population Figures, Demography, and Genocide

The study of population figures for New World Indians prior to and after 1492 has been an important arena of controversy for a number of reasons. The field of **demography** involves the methodological and scientific study of populations. Like any other science, the establishment of this discipline relies upon a range of estimation techniques that may include anecdotal data; biological and archaeological procedures to determine the carrying capacity of the land or a particular environmental niche; and sociological analysis of lifestyle, levels of technology, social density, and social complexity as determined by specialization, the nature of the division of labor, and degree of stratification within or between societies.

Over the past century or more, the study of population has become very sophisticated due to the advances in statistics, the evolution of theory, and greater substantive understanding of the complex influences that affect population dynamics.

A critical debate in Indian studies has to do with efforts to establish the pre- and post-1492 populations for Indians in the western hemisphere as a whole and the Native population of the region north of the Central Valley of Mexico that existed in the territory that would eventually make up the United States.

By the end of the nineteenth century, most experts on Indian affairs—including famous ethnographers like James Mooney and the twentieth-century anthropologist Alfred Kroeber—had concluded that the North American Indian population at the time of first contact with Europeans may have been about one million or slightly higher. By the period between 1890 and 1900, the Indian population in the continental United States was about 250,000. Later demographic analysis has suggested a range for the United States of anywhere from 5 million to 12 million or even 18 million or more. Estimates for the western hemisphere as a whole are included in the following quote from David E. Stannard:

> Similarly dramatic developments have characterized scholarly estimates of the size of the pre-Columbian population of the Americas. In the 1940s and 1950s, conventional wisdom held that the population of the entire hemisphere in 1492 was little more than 8,000,000—with fewer than 1,000,000 people living in the region north of present day Mexico. Today, few serious students of the subject would put the hemispheric figure at less than 75,000,000 to 100,000,000 (with approximately 8,000,000 to 12,000,000 north of Mexico), while one of the most well-regarded specialists in the field recently has suggested that a more accurate estimate would be around 145,000,000 for the hemisphere as a whole and about 18,000,000 for the area north of Mexico.

> (Stannard, 1992, pp. 10–11)

Because of the post-Columbian devastation of Native Americans due to the impact of **European and Old World diseases,** warfare, removal, loss of land, alterations in lifestyle, enslavement, exploitation, and countless other factors, the rate of population decline over four hundred years becomes an indication of the possible extent of genocide against Indians throughout the Caribbean, Mexico, Central and South America, and particularly in the United States.

If the initial size of the Indian population was about one million in the territorial United States, then the level of population decline over four hundred years was around 25 percent. This is a damning statistic given the size of the European immigrant population and the growth of the U.S. population from colonial times to 1900. But if the Indian population of North America was substantially higher than one million, then the cumulative effect of genocidal policies and practices becomes considerably more serious—both morally and legally.

Because my analysis of Indian history is rooted in an understanding of the genocidal policies of the U.S. government and the expansionist ideology of Manifest Destiny that fueled westward movement of Euro-Americans (and the vast land cessions and **Indian removals** that accompanied American policy, treaties, and laws and court decisions), I would encourage the reader to examine David E. Stannard's *American Holocaust;* Ward Churchill's *A Little Matter of Genocide;* and Russell Thornton's study *American Indian Holocaust and Survival: A Population History since 1492.*

When Did Indians Occupy the New World?

If one accepts the proposition that human beings were not created in the New World but evolved somewhere else and migrated and adapted to new physical and ecological niches, then it is important to establish how long Indians have lived and moved about on the land. If Indian occupancy of their land was fairly recent, some might argue that their claim to the land would have less standing with newer immigrants who might displace them due to superior cultural, technological, or spiritual claims. On the other hand, if Amerindian occupancy can be established as far earlier and the cultural accomplishments as technically and spirituality equal to or greater than those of comparable Old World societies, then arguments based on White supremacy and ethnocentrism are not only invalidated but the civilizational claims of Indians would be strengthened just because of the time that Indian societies had evolved and created viable traditions and lifestyles.

David E. Stannard is worth quoting regarding how long Indian cultures have been present in the Americas:

> Until the 1940s, for example, it commonly was believed that the earliest human inhabitants of the Americas had migrated from the Alaskan portion of Berengia down into North and then South America no more than 6000 years ago. It is now recognized as beyond doubt, however, that numerous complex human communities existed in South America at least 13,000 years ago and in North America at least 6000 years before that. These are absolute minimums. Very recent and compelling archaeological evidence puts the date for earliest human habitation in Chile at 32,000 B.C. or earlier and North American habitation at around 40,000 B.C., while some highly respected scholars contend that the actual first date of human entry into the hemisphere may have been closer to 70,000 B.C.
>
> (Stannard, 1992, p. 10)

From my perspective, the length of Indian occupancy is important for a number of reasons. First, indigenous peoples have made significant discoveries that matter in the context of world history and civilization. Second, Indians have created civilizations that rivaled the greatest Old World societies in terms of architecture, pyramid construction, concentration of people, and knowledge of measurement, engineering, astronomy, and time-keeping.

The archaeological investigations of the oldest New World societies clearly verify that the spiritual insights and technological accomplishments of the inhabitants of pre-Columbian cultures were amazing. It is important to acknowledge the achievements of Native Americans because of the racist, Eurocentric stereotypes that the colonizers of the Americas perpetrated as they degraded and demonized those who stood in their way.

As important as it is to discuss the controversies in Native American studies that have grown out of Western racism, stereotyping, and denigration of Indian peoples, it is even more important to expose racism in the post-1492 era and to demonstrate the strength of Indian culture, traditions, and tribal self-determination in overcoming historical amnesia, erroneous beliefs, and dangerous misconceptions.

Diversity of Indian Societies

Whether one seeks to understand the Indians of the New World in a generic manner by grouping societies on the basic language, economic practices, political organization, or ecological environment; or whether one seeks to treat each nation, society, or tribe as distinctive and unique, it is universally acknowledged that Indian peoples—at the time of first contact with Europeans—constituted a vast number of groups living in an extremely large and diverse geographical environment that represented a large range of cultural adaptations to the available land and resources.

All accounts of the state of the Americas at the time of first contact indicate the diversity of the aboriginal nations and their cultural and linguistic variety. James Wilson writes about Indian societies in his book *The Earth Shall Weep: A History of Native Americans:*

> Trying to recreate America in 1492 is extremely difficult. No Native Americans north of Mexico had written records, and many of their cultures—including most of those that bore the brunt of the first contacts along the Atlantic coast—are now extinct. But using a mixture of ethnographic and archaeological evidence, European accounts and tiny fragments of Indian oral history, it is possible to build up at least a tentative general picture which both academics and native people themselves would accept as broadly accurate.
>
> Perhaps the most striking feature of it is the enormous cultural and social variety of Native America. At the end of the fifteenth century there were probably more than six hundred autonomous societies in what is now the United States and Canada, each following its own way of life. Some gauge of this diversity is provided by language: in contrast, say, to Europe, where most languages can be traced back to a single Indo-European source, scientists believe that in North America north of Mexico there were perhaps twelve quite distinct and apparently unrelated linguistic groups, in some cases more dissimilar than English and Chinese.
>
> (Wilson, 1998, pp. 20–21)

Most authors discuss cultural diversity by enumerating the geographical areas in which Indians lived. Joe R. Feagin lists the geographical areas as:

> (1) the societies of the East, who hunted, farmed, and fished, and whose first encounters with whites were with English settlers; (2) the Great Plains hunters and agriculturalists, whose first encounters were with the Spaniards; (3) the fishing societies in the Northwest; (4) the seed gatherers of California and neighboring areas; (5) the Navajo shepherds and Pueblo farmers in the Arizona-New Mexico area; (6) the desert societies of Southern Arizona and New Mexico; and (7) the Alaskan groups including the Eskimos.
>
> (Feagin, 1984, p. 177)

A very detailed source for understanding the full range of Indian diversity and culture, as well as pre- and post-contact history, is Arrell Morgan Gibson's *The American Indian: Prehistory to the Present.* I will conclude this section by quoting Gibson's overview of Native American economic practices, since he demonstrates Indian variety, adaptation to the environment, and the importance of culture for survival:

> The character of the Native American economy, the manner in which the Indians supported themselves, was strongly influenced by environmental conditions. And in turn, their particular economies determined the social models, religions, and political systems adopted by each tribe. Whenever environmental conditions permitted, Native Americans practiced agriculture, although they were never entirely dependent upon it for subsistence, mixing crop production with hunting, fishing, gathering, and trade. When agriculture was impractical, they sustained themselves in the style of Archaic-intensive exploitation of the environment through hunting, fishing, and gathering. Certain staples dominated the economy of various tribal territories. In the humid, well-watered East corn was supreme.

Tribes in the Great Lakes area gathered wild rice. For the Great Plains hunters the buffalo was the staple. Corn, produced by irrigated agriculture, sustained the economy of the desert southwest. The acorn supported a surprisingly large population in California. Salmon was the mainstay for the tribes of the Pacific Northwest, both on the coast and in the interior plateau. And sea mammals and salmon were the principal staples of the Indians and Meso-Indians in Alaska.

(Gibson, 1980, p. 46)

The remainder of this chapter will be devoted to what must amount to a cursory attempt to organize Native American history and experience with non-Indians around an examination of U.S. policies toward Indians and the characterization of Indian experience as consistent with the meaning of the concept of genocide—as developed by Raphael Lemkin during World War II and modified by the United Nations General Assembly and unanimously adopted without abstentions in 1948 as the United Nations Convention on the Prevention and Punishment of the Crime of Genocide (Stannard, 1992, pp. 279–281).

Overview of U.S. Policy toward Indians

Colonial America was basically a competition between the European nation-states of England, France, and Holland for control over the land, raw materials, resources, labor, and people of North America and the Africans who would be imported as slaves following the short period of White indentured servitude in the 1600s.

Because of the efforts of the English and the Dutch along the Eastern seaboard, and the French in Canada and the interior of the continent—from the Great Lakes to Louisiana—Indian nations were forced to deal with Europeans, and through trading, military, and political alliances they became allies or opponents in Europe's colonial struggles.

While many Indian nations were not initially affected by White encroachment upon their lands or in colonial warfare, there were indirect influences that would only intensify during the colonial era and following White American expansion after the Revolutionary War and throughout the nineteenth century.

- Indians helped the starving colonists in Jamestown and the Plymouth colony of the Pilgrims.

- Europeans and Indians traded with each other, particularly the pelts of animals obtained by Indians in exchange for various European commodities and useful utensils.

- Many Indians overhunted the fur-bearing animals, which inevitably affected the ability of all Indians to feed themselves.

- Indians would increasingly encroach on one another's territory, which increased the likelihood of misunderstanding and conflict.

- The colonists came into conflict with Indians over land, their aggressive and hostile racism toward Indians, and incompatible worldviews about religion and land use.

- Through alliances, agreements, and treaties, Indians found themselves fighting other Indians on behalf of the French, Dutch, or British.

- The spread of European diseases in countless epidemics and even deliberate infection of Indians by Whites caused decimation of tribal populations—even when the Indians had no contact or knowledge of European presence in North America.

- Increased trade with Europeans and their efforts to purchase, take, or acquire Indian lands often forced tribal people into altered social and even military relationships with one another.

- All of these relationships would only become more complicated during the colonial period due to increased migration of Europeans to North America; White encroachment and expansion into frontier areas despite the efforts of the British to restrict such movement; and the cumulative impact of European diseases, warfare, broken treaties, White prejudice and discrimination against Indians, and the new realignments of Indians with or against one another

By the time the United States was created and became the dominant power in North America—despite the continuing presence of the British and French, along with the Spanish in Florida and throughout the Southwest—the pattern was already laid out regarding how White Americans and Indians would relate to each other regardless of specific policies or variations in how Indians were dealt with.

Martin N. Marger quotes Stephen Cornell to summarize the three aspects of the "Indian problem" for Europeans from the time of settlement down to the present:

Economic—how best to secure Indian resources, especially land; cultural—how best to assimilate Indians into the dominant, non-Indian culture; and political—how best to control Indians so as to bring about solutions to the first two problems.

(Marger, 2000, p. 154)

There was also a "Euro-American problem" for Indians, according to Cornell:

In its essence . . . this problem seems to have been tribal survival: the maintenance of particular sets of social relations, more or less distinct cultural orders and some measures of political autonomy in the face of invasion, conquest, and loss of power.

(Marger, 2000, p. 154)

Marger argues that from the time of European settlement until the end of the eighteenth century, Indian–White relations "centered primarily on the fur trade" (p. 154). The impact of trading with Europeans meant that "Indians were integrated into the emergent North American economy, and as a result, their forms of social organization and cultural institutions were radically changed" (Marger, p. 154).

By the nineteenth century, **United States Indian policy** ran along two parallel tracks, but headed in the same direction. The goal of Indian policy was "a confrontation in which the insatiable quest of white settlers for land led to ever-greater efforts to dispossess Indians of lands they were occupying" (Marger, p. 154).

The goal of Indian policy was to separate Indians from their lands "either through assimilation, that is, by encouraging them to abandon their communal patterns of landholding in favor of private property, or through removal, that is, relocating Indians through negotiated purchase of land or through conquest" (Marger, p. 154).

Whether through the aggressive and often violent methods of the settlers—in concert with the government, politicians, capitalist land speculators, and the military—or in the seemingly supportive and humanitarian efforts of the East Coast reformers to "civilize" the Indians, the solution to America's Indian problem always revolved around getting their land and getting rid of their identities as Indian peoples.

I have always argued that American policy toward Indians has vacillated between the two extremes of:

- Removal, genocide, and extermination

- Assimilation, loss of Indian identity, and forced conformity to Anglo values and cultural standards

No American policy toward Indians has ever produced an entirely just or humane outcome for Indians in terms of moral or legal requirements. Robert Berkhofer provides the final point about Indian policy:

From the founding of the nation until recent times, and some would include today as well, United States policy makers placed two considerations above all others in the nation's relations with Native Americans as Indians: the extinction of native title in favor of White exploitation of native lands and resources and the transformation of native lifestyles into copies of approved White models.

(Berkhofer in Marger, p. 155)

The Meaning of Genocide

Rafael Lemkin coined the term *genocide* in his 1944 book *Axis Rule in Occupied Europe.* Based upon Stannard (1992, p. 279):

Genocide is the coordinated and planned annihilation of a national, religious or racial group by a variety of actions aimed at undermining the foundations essential to the survival of the group as a group . . .

Lemkin's definition includes:

Attacks on public and social institutions, culture, language, national feelings, religion, and the economic existence of the group.

Even non-lethal acts that undermined the liberty, dignity, and personal security of members, of a group constituted genocide if they contributed to weakening the variability of the group . . .

Forms of Genocide

The comprehensive meaning of **genocide** was initially meant to cover the result of fascism and Nazism in World War II. It has also been applied to many other twentieth-century atrocities such as the Armenian genocide, the "Killing Fields" of the Khmer Rouge in Cambodia, the Rwanda genocide in Africa involving Hutus and Tutsis, and the terrible ethnic cleansing that occurred following the collapse of Yugoslavia in the Balkans during the 1990s.

But few people who are cognizant of the treatment that all Native peoples have been subjected to throughout the Caribbean, Mexico, Central and South America, Canada, and the United States for over five hundred years would ever hesitate from using the word *genocide* to stand in as a proxy for all of the collective and individual attitudes, stereotypes, prejudice, racism, exclusion, discrimination, institutional inequality, and destruction of Native culture, religion, and identity that Indian people have been subjected to.

Unfortunately, many people do not accept the term *genocide,* or the United Nations itself, as a legitimate or useful political or institutional framework for dealing with world conflict resolution. Genocide is considered a loaded and divisive term that is all too easily applied to circumstances for political effect rather than even-handedly across the board.

The meaning of genocide in the twentieth century, retrospectively, must be allowable as a description of what occurred in general as well as specifically during American history, where Indians are concerned, if the concept is to have any moral or consensual validity.

Before providing a list of the forms of genocide that I think reflects how Indian lives, cultures, societies, and nations have been systematically undermined, I want to provide one last reference to what David E. Stannard concludes:

However, the Convention's [United Nations statement on genocide] definition remains the most widely used definition of genocide throughout the world—and indeed, in all the world there probably is no other word, in any language, whose definition has been more carefully discussed or more universally accepted. In light of the U.N. language—even putting aside some of its looser constructions—it is impossible to know what transpired in the Americas during the sixteenth, seventeenth, eighteenth, and nineteenth centuries and not conclude that it was genocide.

(Stannard, 1992, p. 281)

Below are listed seven forms of genocide and notations about generic or specific ways that they served to undermine Indian communal life and identity. These conceptual forms are not exhaustive, nor are they mutually exclusive from one another, but they are adequate if considered in relation to Lemkin's definition of genocide.

1) European transmission of Old World diseases or pathogens—whether unintentionally or on purpose

   • Indians lacked immunity to the major diseases such as smallpox, measles, mumps, typhus, influenza, diphtheria, or scarlet fever.

   • Sir Jeffrey Amherst (1763) deliberately used smallpox-infected blankets as a weapon against Indians.

   • "Could it not be contrived to send the smallpox among these disaffected tribes of Indians? We must on this occasion use every stratagem in our power to reduce them."

   • Blankets were taken from recent smallpox victims and given to healthy Indians, thus spreading the fatal epidemic.

   (Nies, 1996, pp. 190–192)

2) Military technology, tactics, organization, and manpower

   • Use of horses, guns, weapons, and technology

   • Manpower, style of warfare, organization, and fortifications

   • See sources on nineteenth-century frontier warfare, Indian wars, and military and civilian massacres against Indians

   • Representative cases such as Andrew Jackson against the Creeks and Seminoles; John Chivington at Sand Creek; Phillip Sheridan: "the only good Indians I ever saw were dead"; George Custer and other Indian fighters; the massacre at Wounded Knee

   • Indians were exceptional fighters who used horses, rifles, bows and arrows, spears and lances, and guerrilla tactics most effectively but ultimately to no avail against the power of the U.S. government.

3) Legal, illegal, and immoral methods of land acquisition

   • Negotiated land cessions in exchange for yearly annuities, provisions, education, and medicine as specified in treaties

   • Introduction of alcohol and deception into trading and treaty negotiations

   • Corrupt politicians, BIA officials, Indian agents, and private individuals contributed to the loss of Indian land and resources.

   • Indians were removed forcefully from their lands and sacred places to the **Indian Territory** in the nineteenth century.

   • The Cherokees and "The Trail of Tears"

   • When reservations were created, Indians were often put on arid and nonproductive land or they were subject to reduction in their holdings through legislation such as the General Allotment Act of 1887.

   • Federal legislation and court decisions have been used to undermine Indians.

   • The operation of various federal agencies, organizations, and bureaus—including the BIA, the Department of Interior, and energy interests (both governmental and private)

4) Religious genocide

- The Spanish mission system in the Southwest and especially in California

- The efforts of the Puritans and various Protestant denominations working among Indians

- Religious instruction associated with reservation schools and off-reservation boarding schools

- The suppression of Indian spirituality, religious and ceremonial practices, the banning of the Sun Dance, the Ghost Dance, and the use of substances such as peyote

- Court cases that have undermined Indian spirituality or failed to support Native American religious freedom when it conflicted with overriding U.S. or government/economic interests

- The struggle of incarcerated Indians for the right to uphold spiritual and religious practices in prison

- The violation of Indian burial grounds; the theft of Indian bones, sacred objects, and personal property for museums and private collections until the passage of the Native American Graves Protection and Repatriation Act (NAGRA)

5) **Educational genocide**

- BIA schools on reservations

- The off-reservation boarding schools

- Policies of Americanization, forced assimilation, and kidnapping Indian children from their families, elders, and tribes

- Punishing children for speaking Indian languages and trying to preserve tribal culture or beliefs

- Undermining Indian identity and self-esteem through racist curriculum, perpetuation of stereotypes, distorted and false representations of Indians in books, erroneous academic claims about Indians, and media representations in television or movies

6) **Economic genocide**

- Removal of Indians from their land

- Destruction of Indian land or the exploitation of resources, raw materials, and sources of energy without payment, compensation, or return of benefits to Indian nations

- Unsafe ecological and environmental practices on Indian land such as the strip mining of coal, exposing Indians to the radioactive tailings from uranium mining, and not protecting Indians during the twentieth century

- Using Indian land for nuclear waste sites or sacrifice areas

- The practices of the Indian Claims Commission in denying Indians economic justice for lands that were unjustly taken or stolen

- The full impact and meaning of internal colonization of Native Americans on their own lands throughout Indian history

7) Cultural genocide

- Many tribes and indigenous peoples have been literally wiped out or became extinct.

- Indian groups were physically exterminated.

- The culture, languages, and way of life of still-existing tribes has been either destroyed, undermined, diluted, or drastically changed as a result of Euro-American contact and destruction of the Indian land base and sacred religious sites.

- Indian languages are becoming extinct at an alarming rate in the United States and around the world because many tribes do not have sufficient numbers of Native speakers or a community in which to practice and preserve their life-ways.

- Indian young people are in danger of losing their heritage as Indians due to being assimilated and socialized in the modern Western technological culture and society.

It is important to recognize what has happened to Indian people historically, especially in fields like ethnic studies and Native American studies, where critical political consciousness is important in linking theoretical and substantive concerns with praxis, which may require working with and learning from the racial and ethnic communities and people one is being trained to understand.

On the positive side, Indian people, society, and communities are not static or frozen in time outside the contemporary world. The persistence of the **diversity of Indian societies** is a testimony to their cultural strength, their determination to remain sovereign, and their commitment to adapt to modern conditions and to aspire to the best opportunities that they can, in order to live up to their full potential.

Summary of American Policy in History

Because of the focus of my analysis, it is not possible to provide an in-depth presentation of American Indian history and experience. The many books I have cited throughout this chapter provide coverage of the full panorama of Indian experience in the New World from the earliest times to the present.

The overview of American epochs and policy toward Indians that I am including comes from notes that I utilize in discussing these issues during class lectures. Because of the amount of material covered, I have to generalize, summarize, and simplify issues that are fully deserving of in-depth analysis in separate courses.

Two sources that provide good insights about American Indian policy and detailed analysis of nineteenth-century history are James A. Banks's *Teaching Strategies for Ethnic Studies* (Fourth Edition) and Robert M. Ultley's *The Indian Frontier of the American West 1846–1890*.

1) 1607–1820

    The colonial era and early years of the Republic

    - First contacts with Indians

    - Alliances, trading, and treaties

    - Conflicts, warfare, coveting Indian land by Anglos, destructive stereotypes such as the Indian as heathen, savage, violent

2) 1820–1840

    Indian Removal during the Market Revolution

    - Removal of the five civilized tribes of the Southeast to the Indian Territory after the passage of the Indian Removal Act of 1830 and efforts at legal resistance by the Cherokees

    - Besides the removal of the Cherokees, Choctaws, Chickasaws, Creeks, and Seminoles, members of other Eastern tribes such as the Delawares also were compelled to leave their lands.

- The Cherokee Removal is particularly tragic and is remembered as "The Trail of Tears," in which over 4,000 of the 16,000 Cherokees died during the forced removal that occurred in the winter of 1838 under military supervision.

- From 1830 to 1844, 70,000 Indians were removed, of whom about one-third died.

3) 1840–1890

Manifest Destiny and U.S. Westward Expansion

- Annexation of the Southwest from Mexico after 1848 and the Treaty of Guadalupe Hidalgo and the Gadsden Purchase of 1853

- California Gold Rush of 1849

- Manifest Destiny articulated during the 1840s

- Rapid American expansion onto, and across, the Plains and the expansion of the frontier

4) 1846–1870s

The Epoch of Frontier Warfare

- "The only good Indian is a dead Indian." What Philip Sheridan actually said after a Comanche chief had referred to himself as a good Indian was: "The only good Indians I ever saw were dead."

- "The Iron Horse in the West"—expansion of the railroads, splitting the Plains, the growth and development of White towns, Indians forced off land or put on reservations

- The massive destruction of the buffalo herds on the plains—especially after the 1870s

(abridged from Thornton, 1990, p. 52)

Buffalo Populations		
1800	-	40 million
1850	-	20 million
1865	-	15 million
1870	-	14 million
1875	-	1 million
1880	-	395 thousand
1885	-	20 thousand
1895	-	< 1 thousand
1983	-	50 thousand

Figure 7.1

5) 1871

Conclusion of Treaty-Making with Indians

- Provision included in an appropriations act as a rider ended Indian treaties with the federal government, but Congress could make agreements that served the same purpose.

- Indians were no longer defined as domestic sovereign nations.

- They became **wards of the federal government.**

- America made 371 treaties with various tribes and nations and broke all of them in whole or in part.

6) 1840s–1880s

Creation of the Reservation System

- Reservations came in the aftermath of Indian removal.

- The government wanted to "scientifically manage Indians."

- Following the Civil War, president Grant pursued a "peace policy" with the tribes of the Plains.

- Progress and civilization were bringing an end to the frontier, and without reservations Whites would be threatened and Indians could be subject to extermination.

- Whites must save Indians from wholesale slaughter by "managing" and "controlling" them.

- Reservations were created to speed up the process by which Indians could make the transition from sovereignty and independence to civilization and assimilation.

7) 1887

The **Dawes Allotment Act**

- This legislation led to the breaking up of reservations as Indian tribes increasingly lost collective sovereignty.

- In 1877 Indians held 138,000,000 acres of land, but by 1900 they only held 78,000,000 acres of land due to the allotment and transfer of their holdings to non-Indians.

- The purpose of the Dawes Allotment Act was to undermine the tribal system and to assimilate Indians as individuals in nuclear families into White economic practices such as farming.

8) 1934

The Indian Reorganization Act

- The 1887 Allotment Act had clearly been a failure, given the findings of the Meriam Report of 1928, which documented the demoralization of Indian people.

- The 1934 Indian Reorganization Act was meant to return some sovereignty to Indian tribes through the creation of tribal councils, and to allow Indians to have limited input into federal and BIA policy.

- Tribal councils created internal tribal divisions between traditional elders and younger, BIA-educated Indians.

- In fact, tribal councils operated almost like corporate boards through which outside interest groups could gain legal access to reservation lands in order to exploit and develop Indian resources such as: 1) coal, 2) oil, 3) natural gas, 4) timber, 5) hydro-electric power, and 6) uranium.

9) 1940s

World War II

- Indians served in the armed forces during World War II.

- The Navajo code-talkers used their Diné language to transmit military intelligence in the war in the Pacific, and the Japanese never broke the code.

- After World War II, Indians began leaving the reservations in greater numbers to live in cities and get education.

10) 1950s

Post–World War II policies

- The policy of termination was another attempt to end tribal sovereignty and to place Indian tribes under state jurisdiction—which would break up Indian tribes once and for all.

- Termination policy was a failure in the cases where it was implemented, but it led to strong resistance by Indians across the country.

- Relocation policy attempted to draw Indians off the reservations where unemployment was extremely high and to encourage them to move into urban areas.

- Indians were promised help in relocating and learning the skills needed for urban living, but the policy was a further effort to assimilate Indians into American society.

11) Late 1950s and 1960s

Emergence of Indian Activism and the Red Power Movement

- Young, post–World War II Indians formed a nucleus of assertive, urban, and increasingly educated activists.

- A new generation of urban, pan-Indian people began to seek Indian identities and empowerment.

- By the 1960s, Indian activists began to struggle for rights and recognition in response to civil rights and poverty programs.

12) 1960s to the Present

Indian Movement Activism and Contemporary Issues

- 1964—beginning of the Fish-Ins by the tribes of the Pacific Northwest under the leadership of Hank Adams

- 1969–1970—occupation of Alcatraz by Indian activists

- February 1972—Raymond Yellow Thunder murdered in Gordon, Nebraska

- American Indian movement activism after 1968

- November 1972—the Trail of Broken Treaties and the occupation of the Bureau of Indian Affairs building

- 1973—Wounded Knee siege on the Pine Ridge Reservation

- 1970s—the repression against the American Indian movement and other radical movements by the FBI and the federal government

- 1970s—Leonard Peltier convicted of killing two FBI agents during the confrontation at the Jumping Bull compound after a very controversial and politically racist trial

- early 1970s—controversy over the Peabody Coal Company and the strip mining of Black Mesa on the Hopi reservation, which illustrated corporate greed versus the emerging ecology and environmental movements

- 1978—Indian Religious Freedom Act and efforts to promote Indian spirituality

- 1990—passage of the Native American Graves Protection and Repatriation Act, which attempts to rectify past and present injustices regarding the recovery of stolen ceremonial objects and bones from museums and the proper burial of individuals

- Indian environmental issues

- Indian education issues

- Indian sovereignty issues for the First Nations and tribal self-determination

- Indian economic development on reservations

- Indian gaming on reservations as a means to increase tribal income and serve the community

Conclusion

Native American people have endured in the United States despite the genocidal policies of the U.S. government and a long history of racist treatment and ignorance that have manifested themselves throughout Indian country, when Whites defined Indians as the "vanishing Americans" during the nineteenth century and expected them to die off because they were not believed to be capable of advancing civilizationally or competing in mainstream society. Indians continue to survive both on reservations and increasingly in major American cities.

Indians have chosen to promote Indian identities and traditional values while fighting for social, economic, educational, and political justice and equality. Indian people will no longer accept second-class treatment, media stereotypes, or social invisibility.

The fields of ethnic studies and Native American studies can contribute to Indian employment in the field of higher education and outreach and support of Indian people in surrounding areas and on reservations.

There is a critical need to promote Indians in higher education and to increase the numbers of Indians in graduate school, law school, medical school, and other professional endeavors. Universities must be sensitive to the needs of Indian students and the need to hire Native American faculty. It is also important that educators, politicians, and other bureaucrats stop exploiting Indians or charging Indian gaming tribes of "ripping off" state governments. Whatever benefits that may accrue to gaming tribes, it is not, in itself, a solution to past injustices against Indians, nor a guarantee of future success or preservation of Indian traditions and values.

There are many issues that Indian people will continue to face in the future. This is partly the legacy of past injustice, but also because Indians will continue to work out their own identities and relationships to each other and to members and institutions of the dominant society.

Questions, Exercises, and Topics for Discussion and Debate

1) In terms of the history of New World peoples and societies, the period from 1492 forward constitutes the era of ongoing contact, conquest, and colonization of Indians by various European nations. Based on material from the chapter and examination of bibliographic sources, discuss the controversies surrounding the conquest of the Caribbean and Latin America by Columbus and the major conquistadors. Briefly consider the following issues:

   a) What factors contributed to the diversity of Indian societies?

   b) Provide a sense of Indian worldviews, creation stories, Indian origins, and spirituality.

   c) How did the Spanish conquistadors and representatives of the Catholic faith view indigenous spirituality, ceremonial practices, and beliefs?

   d) Who was **Bartolomé de las Casas,** and what impact did his eyewitness testimony of the conquest by Columbus and other conquistadors have upon subsequent Spanish-Indian relations?

   e) Who was **Hernán Cortez?** Discuss the conquest of Tenochtitlán and the Aztec or Mexica society. Who was Dona Marina or Malinche, and what is her significance in Mexican history?

2) Various legal doctrines were developed by Europeans and international legal authorities to justify and rationalize the civilizational right to conquer, subdue, and dispossess Indians of their land and/or labor. Define the following terms:

   a) Aboriginal sovereignty

   b) Right of occupancy

   c) Doctrine of discovery

   d) Doctrine of just wars

   e) Requirement of Requerimiento

   f) Encomienda system

3) Discuss the terms *discovery* and *invasion* as different ways of describing the encounter between Europeans and Indians. How do these perspectives create the political grounds for ongoing controversies regarding the celebration of Columbus Day or Indigenous Peoples Day?

4) There is still controversy between Indian people and academic paleontologists, archaeologists, anthropologists, and scientists regarding the alleged migration of the ancestors of today's Indians to the New World and the notion that Indians are themselves "immigrants," no different ultimately than the later-arriving Europeans.
   a) What is the Bering Strait theory, and why do Indians object to its claims?

   b) What does Vine Deloria, Jr., argue in response to claims about a glacial land bridge between Asia and North America?

   c) What do you think troubles Indians about the claim that "we're all just immigrants"?

5) In U.S. history, Indians figure prominently from the earliest efforts of the British to settle in Jamestown and in tribal alliances, competition, and conflict with the British, French, Dutch, and Americans after the Revolutionary War. American expansion and the removal, dispossession, and betrayal of Indian people was referred to by Helen Hunt Jackson toward the end of the 1880s as "A Century of Dishonor." Discuss the following terms:
   a) Treaty rights
   b) Indian removal
   c) Indian tribes as domestic sovereign nations
   d) Manifest Destiny
   e) Old World diseases and epidemics
   f) Frontier warfare
   g) Indian territory
   h) Indian reservations
   i) Friends of the Indians
   j) The Dawes Act
   k) The Ghost Dance
   l) The Wounded Knee Massacre

Questions, Exercises, and Topics for Discussion and Debate (continued)

6) Based on material from Raphael Lemkin (quoted in David E. Stannard) or from Ward Churchill's comprehensive work *A Little Matter of Genocide,* explain the concept of genocide and justify why the term is or is not an accurate description of U.S. policy and behavior toward its Indian peoples.

7) Explain as many methods as you can think of to indicate the diverse ways that Indian people lost their lands, resources, and sovereignty during the nineteenth and twentieth centuries.

8) Discuss the meaning and impact of religious genocide, educational genocide, economic genocide, and cultural genocide for American Indians.

9) Has the United States upheld the 371 treaties that it entered into with Indians? Research and discuss the relationships between the United States and Indians with respect to the following:
   a) The U.S. Constitution and Indians

   b) The War Department

   c) The trust relations between the federal government and Indians

   d) The Department of the Interior

   e) The Bureau of Indian Affairs

   f) The Supreme Court and Indians

   g) The Indian Claims Commission and Indians

10) Review the following policies and their impact on Indians:
   a) Federal wardship in the twentieth century

   b) The Meriam Report

   c) The Indian Reorganization Act

   d) Urban relocation

   e) Termination

11) Discuss the nature of post–World War II Native American protest, activism, and radicalism. Some issues for you to consider are:
   a) Urban relocation and the pan-Indian movement
   b) Resistance to termination
   c) The meaning of Red Power
   d) The Fish-Ins
   e) The American Indian movement
   f) The occupation of Alcatraz
   g) The Trail of Broken Treaties
   h) Wounded Knee II
   i) The Leonard Peletier case

12) Debate the proposition that Indians are still a colonized people whose rights to sovereignty and tribal self-determination are being violated, versus the alternative view, that Indians should not be recognized as collective tribal groups or separate nations, but rather, should be assimilated into the mainstream as individuals like every other immigrant group.

African Americans

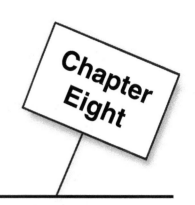

Chapter Eight

Key Terms

affirmative action

African civilizations

Afrocentrism

Albany, Georgia

anti-apartheid struggle

Birmingham, Alabama

Black accommodation

Black history

Black migration

Black nationalism

Black Panther Party

Black Power movement

Black pride

Black separatism

Black studies

Bobby Seale

Booker T. Washington

Brown v. Board of Education

Civil Rights Act of 1964

civil rights movement

COINTELPRO

"color-blind" racism

cultural and political nationalism

debt peonage

desegregation of the U.S. Armed Forces

diaspora

Elijah Mohammad

Eve hypothesis

Fanny Lou Hamer

Frederick Douglass

freedom rides

Freedom Summer

Harlem Renaissance

Huey Newton

Jackie Robinson joins the Brooklyn Dodgers

James Meredith

Ku Klux Klan

"long hot summers"

lynching

lynching of Emmett Till

Malcolm X

March on Washington

Marcus Garvey

Martin Luther King, Jr.

Maulana Karenga

Medgar Evers

the Middle Passage

Mississippi Freedom Democratic Party

NAACP

Nation of Islam

Niagra Movement

Plessy v. Ferguson

prison industrial complex

racial backlash

racial profiling

racial segregation

Reconstruction period

resistance to slavery

Rosa Parks

Selma, Alabama

sharecropping

sit-in movement

slavery

Southern Christian Leadership

Conference

Stockley Carmichael

Student Nonviolent Coordinating
 Committee

UNIA

Urban League

US

Voting Rights Act of 1965

W. E. B. DuBois

Key Lesson

The emergence of the **civil rights movement** following the landmark Supreme Court decision of *Brown v. Board of Education* in 1954, and the post-1960s militancy of Black people or Afro-Americans that led to movements stressing **Black pride,** Black Power, **cultural and political nationalism,** and **Black** studies in the universities and colleges around the country, helped to bring the history and collective social experience of Africans and diasporic Blacks to heightened visibility in a time of radical social transformation that has been called the Second Reconstruction.

The wealth of knowledge, research, cultural production, political activism, and teaching that accompanied the era of civil rights, the **Black Power Movement,** and 1960s radicalism led to the recognition that Black people would no longer remain silent or passive victims of racism, oppression, prejudice, or invidious stereotypes derived from images of sambo, Aunt Jemima, D. W. Griffith's "The Birth of a Nation," images of Tarzan movies, Amos 'N Andy, or other well-known vices based on criminality, hypersexuality, or violence.

The decolonization of nations in Africa and the rise of revolution throughout the third world fanned hope, optimism, and a new self-confidence that dark-skinned peoples could throw off the yoke of colonialism, underdevelopment, and second-class citizenship that made it so hard to respect oneself or to be deemed worthy of the respect of others.

Black people began to learn about **Black history** and cultural contributions in the United States as well as in **African civilizations** in Egypt, Nubia, Kush, and Ethiopia. Archeology and evolutionary theory recognized Africa as the place where humanity began and where culture and institutions may have first emerged before being spread by migration and diffusion. By the late 1980s, the **Eve hypothesis** established through the study of female mitochondrial DNA that all humanity was genetically linked to an African woman as a common ancestor. The experience of Africans under the brutality of the **Middle Passage, slavery,** the **Reconstruction period,** and Jim Crow segregation began to be told by Blacks as well as researchers who were less open to racist norms in their scholarship. The corrective to racist history, historical amnesia, and the trivialization of Black history and culture led to a renaissance of knowledge and to renewed artistic, literary, musical, and other forms of creative expression.

The themes of Black history through the twentieth century are summarized in order to highlight the reality of de jure racism in the post–Reconstruction era and the rise of **Black accommodation,** reaction, and heightened twentieth-century militancy and organizational struggle.

The likes of key leaders such as **Frederick Douglass, Booker T. Washington, W. E. B. DuBois,** Monroe Trotter, **Marcus Garvey,** and others who could be mentioned such as Harriet Tubman, Sojourner Truth, Ida B. Wells-Barnett, various nineteenth-century nationalists, and other twentieth-century leaders in law, education, journalism, and other fields, all have contributed to the freedom struggle and the quest for dignity and full citizenship prior to the modern civil rights movement.

The dynamic of the Depression, the beginnings of what would become the welfare state, and the fight of Black people for double victory against racism abroad and racism at home during World War II contributed to the quickening of events in the aftermath of World War II that began to shake the foundations of Jim Crow segregation in the South and so-called de facto segregation throughout the rest of the nation.

The story of the modern civil rights movement that emerged in the South following the *Brown* decision, the tragic **lynching of Emmett Till** in Money, Mississippi, and the emergence of the leadership of **Martin Luther King, Jr.,** in the aftermath of **Rosa Parks's** arrest for failing to yield to a White bus rider in Montgomery, Alabama, resulted in the events that most people are by now familiar with, such as the Little Rock Nine, the **sit-in movement** and **freedom rides,** the killing of **Medgar Evers,** the integration of Ole Miss by **James Meredith,** the **March on Washington,** the killing of the four Black girls in Birmingham and the subsequent struggles between integrationists using nonviolence, and the tactics of nationalists, separatists, and revolutionaries who advocated "freedom by any means necessary." The conflict for civil rights, equality, and true liberation continues to be debated, fought for, and contested in American society, whether in terms of affirmative action, educational curricula, law, policy, and politically progressive or reactionary **racial backlash** agendas.

Afrocentrists, multiculturalists, neoconservatists, neo-Nazis, White supremacists, Bell-Curve eugenicists, right-wing Christians, and who knows how many other frames of thought and policy are represented in the U.S. twenty-first century struggles for the hearts and minds of American people when it comes to freedom and the rights of Black people in the era of **"color-blind" racism.**

The continuing reality of race and racism in the United States is difficult for many Americans to accept, but African Americans face **racial profiling** under circumstances where non-Blacks do not, and they are disproportionately overrepresented throughout the **prison industrial complex.** The politics of racial inequality has once again become a hotly debated topic in the United States as a result of the devastation along the Gulf Coast and in New Orleans following the feeble initial efforts of the Bush administration, FEMA, and state and some local officials to respond the Hurricane Katrina. Regardless of the realities of race and class, and despite some upward social mobility, Black people recognize that racism is still alive and well in America.

> It is important that African people look beyond the image of Africa which was created for them and the world by Europeans. It is also most important to remember that Africans were the only immigrants who came to America against their will. They were stripped of their history, and had no humanity that their slavemasters were willing to recognize. Their sole purpose for being was to provide free labor for the economic development of the country.
>
> (Browder, 2004, p. 27)

> The rescue and reconstruction of African history is also important because it offers us models to emulate. The sister before me was talking about the heroines of African history. There are heroines and heroes of African history that gave us models of African and human possibility. When you look at the world today, it is often depressing. You can be disillusioned because what is now is so temporary, so contingent. But history offers us models of human struggle and human possibility that we need in order to make a new history. When we read the history of Mary McLoud Bethune or Harriet Tubman, or W. E. B. DuBois, or Kwame Nkrumah, or Sekou Toure, or Martin Luther King, or Queen Nzinga, or Amy Ashwood Garvey, or Amy Jacques Garvey: when we read the history of Anna Julia Cooper or Hatshepsut, or Nat Turner or Malcolm X, we are given clear models of human possibility. And what we see is what Garvey said, i.e. we see the basic principle of "what humans have done, humans can do". And we are inspired, even compelled to ask some important questions. If we raised pyramids above the Nile, do we have any business being satisfied with rundown projects and tenements? If we introduced the basic disciplines of human knowledge, do we have any business allowing Europeans to claim unchallenged that they're the only ones who can learn and contribute to the forward flow of history? Do we accept Hegel's racist division of the world into historical and non-historical people, or do we raise images of Black men and women who dared take their destiny and daily lives in their own hands and shape it in their own image and interest?
>
> (Karenga in Addai-Sebo and Wong, 1988, pp. 24–25)

> Any time you have to rely upon your enemies for a job you're in bad shape. When you know he is your enemy all the time. Anyhow, you wouldn't be in this country if some enemy hadn't kidnapped you and brought you here? [Applause]. . . .
>
> (Malcolm X in Chambers, 1969, p. 208)

> To develop a sense of black consciousness and peoplehood does not require that we scorn the white race as a whole. It is not the race per se that we fight but the policies and ideology that leaders of that race have formulated to perpetuate oppression.
>
> (Martin Luther King, Jr., in King, 1987, p. 33)

The Black Man's history—when you refer to him as a Negro, you can only go as far back as the Negro goes. And when you go beyond the shores of America in history looking for the history of the Black man, and you're looking for him under the term *Negro,* you won't find him. He doesn't exist. So you end up thinking that you didn't play any role in history.

But if you want to take the time to do research for yourself, I think you'll find that on the African continent there was always, prior to the discovery of America, there was always a higher level of history, rather a higher level of culture and civilization, than that which existed in Europe at the same time.

(Malcolm X in Pathfinder, 1990, p. 27)

Introduction

Before there ever was a discipline called ethnic studies or a movement promoting multiculturalism, there was always a Black struggle for freedom, dignity, respect, equality, justice, and first-class citizenship. During the years of the civil rights movement, many Americans were forced by the public visibility of Black activism to end Jim Crow racism in the South—and by a rising militant nationalist struggle that stretched from the streets of Black ghettos all the way into the most elite White universities and academic institutions around the nation—to acknowledge the reality of White racism and the need to deal with a three-hundred-year-old racial legacy of hatred and inequality that began with the colonization of the New World, the enslavement of Africans, and the rape of Africans and their cultures on the continent and throughout their **diaspora.**

The beginning of Black studies and the creation of Black history precedes the efforts of Maulana Karenga, Angela Davis, Nathan Hare, Leroi Jones, Jeffalyn Johnson (my Black history teacher in 1969, at Pasadena City College), and countless other individuals both inside and outside of colleges and universities in America. Africans and Africans in the United States have actively struggled against enslavement, oppression, colonialism, segregation, and imperialism despite the efforts of Europeans and White world supremacists to degrade, scapegoat, victimize, and write them out of history while suppressing their true history and civilizational accomplishments.

Blacks in the United States have made history and transmitted their individual and collective experiences down the corridors of time through family socialization, folklore, oral tradition, in Black civil and fraternal organizations, in their music—whether spirituals, gospel, work songs, field hollers, the blues, jazz, rhythm and blues, hip-hop, or rap—in dilapidated single-room schools or in historic Black colleges and universities, and in the segregated but often rich closeness of Black rural and urban communities of this nation.

By the end of the nineteenth and into the twentieth century, great African American leaders—whether publicly recognized by Whites or not—struggled to promote "race pride" and "racial uplift" regardless of obstacles or opposition. Some had been slaves, like Frederick Douglass, Booker T. Washington, and Harriet Tubman; others were prodigious scholars, such as W. E. B DuBois and Carter G. Woodson; while others were activist leaders, among whom Ida B. Wells-Barnett, Marcus Garvey, and William Monroe Trotter can be numbered.

There were Black ministers with varying degrees of courage who promoted faith, extended encouragement to their congregations, and used their churches and pulpits in the cause of organizing and mobilizing Black communities. There were Black geniuses, inventors, and scientists and Black artists, writers, and cultural luminaries from the folk tradition, to the **Harlem Renaissance,** through the Second Reconstruction and beyond.

The point is that the Black experience in America is rich, diverse, and enduring despite the distortions, stereotypes, and racist ways that books, periodicals, and White-dominated media chose to define Black character or lifestyle in different epochs of American history.

The demands by a new generation of Negro, Black, or Afro-American militants for respect and recognition did not simply emerge out of nowhere, though it might have felt that way for members of the dominant society and the controlling elites who did not know or care to know what Blacks were doing—unless of course they were rioting or "getting uppity" in ways that could not be ignored.

Because of the insistence of Black people for freedom and liberty—as Malcolm X said: "by any means necessary"—the civil rights and Black Power movements placed the United States between the jaws of a vice in which Whites had to come to terms with integration of schools, neighborhoods, and workplaces as a result of nonviolent, direct action and legal cases; or they faced calls for separation, nationalism, cultural identity, community control, self-defense, and always the threat, the rhetoric, and the prospect of violence.

As the quotes opening this chapter demonstrate, Black Americans began to forge new identities that many Americans could not understand, since Afro-Americans did not seek White approval or White permission for what they were doing. In fact, many Negro leaders rejected the demands and actions of militant individuals, leaders of **Black separatist** organizations such as **Elijah Muhammad** and **Malcolm X,** or cultural nationalist and revolutionary nationalist movements led by individuals such as **Maulana Karenga, Huey Newton, Bobby Seale,** Eldridge and Kathleen Cleaver, and Amiri Baraka; or **Stockley Carmichael** (Kwame Ture) and H. Rap Brown.

The importance of Black studies and the growth of Black history was also a by-product of what had been happening around the world since World War II. Countries in Asia and Africa were gaining their independence and throwing off the shackles of colonialism. Nations in Latin America—perhaps inspired by the Cuban revolution and the leadership of Fidel Castro and Che Guevara—were struggling against U.S. imperialism and right-wing U.S.-backed dictatorships that left indigenous and landless peasants poor and vulnerable, and the National Liberation struggles of the Vietnamese and Algerian people against the French and the United States were proving—to the satisfaction of third world people—that liberation from oppression and neocolonialism was possible using the tactics of revolution and guerrilla warfare.

In addition, the civil rights movement in the United States had inspired South African Blacks in their own **anti-apartheid struggle** and had brought United Nations pressure and sanctions against the White South African government.

The activism against racism at home and around the world and the self-conscious need for African Americans to create positive identities helped Blacks to seek a visible presence in American higher education, where they would make an impact in demanding Black studies, calling upon administrators for faculty that came from and/or represented the Black community, and challenging what most Whites thought was the sacred goal of the civil rights movement—by pushing for exclusively separate Black student unions and for the funding of cultural support and services and financial aid for Black students and even for free admission to college.

In this chapter I will provide an overview of Black history that stresses the activist involvement of Black people in seeking freedom and in confronting racism in ways that were available under varying circumstances of structural and legal constraint. I will also discuss the twentieth-century Black experience prior to the civil rights movement and the rise of Black Power. Out of the struggle for inclusion or radical change of society, Black people often succeeded in receiving recognition of their demands but not always getting what they wanted.

The creation of ethnic studies at many universities was often done as a response to the militant programs that Blacks, Chicanos, and Indians and Asians had attempted to institute in the 1960s and 1970s. Whether universities claimed that such programs were too radical, not academically legitimate, not drawing a sufficient number of students, not supporting the presence of non-minority students in classes, or simply could not be sustained due to budget cutbacks or a failure to recruit qualified faculty, the promotion of ethnic studies and the consolidation of separate programs or classes was viewed by many as the beginning of the end for Black and Chicano-Indian studies due to weakening and diluting course content or forcing racial and ethnic groups into a competitive physical and social space where activists would sooner or later undermine each other's political and academic agendas.

The positive result of ethnic studies is that the radical effort to institutionalize anti-Eurocentric and antiracist perspectives has allowed the discipline to evolve and to be transformed for new generations of students and for new faculty who are themselves products of race and gender studies that continued to develop despite the conservative backlash against the movements of the 1960s.

Sources about African Americans

The African American experience in the New World, and particularly in the history of the United States, is now extensively documented. In the list of sources that follows, I have dealt with a variety of topics that are germane to Black studies, Black history, and Black experience:

- African history
- Afrocentrism
- Black or African American history
- Black studies as a discipline
- Black nationalism and Black Power
- Black diaspora
- Slavery in world history and the United States
- Segregation and Jim Crow
- Lynching
- Black representations in film
- Black leaders and intellectuals
- Civil rights movement
- The Ku Klux Klan
- The trans-Atlantic slave trade

I have listed the sources in alphabetical order by author, rather than by topic.

1) Abdul Alkalimat and Associates

    Introduction to Afro-American Studies: A Peoples College Primer

2) Akyaaba Addai-Sebo and Ansel Wong (Editors)

    Our Story: A Handbook of African History and Contemporary Issues

3) Talmadge Anderson

    Introduction to African American Studies

4) Lerone Bennett, Jr.

    Before the Mayflower: *A History of Black America*

5) Mary Francis Berry and John W. Blassingame

    Long Memory: The Black Experience in America

6) John W. Blassingame

The Slave Community: Plantation Life in the Antebellum South

7) Donald Bogle

Toms, Coons, Mulattoes, Mammies, and Bucks: An Interpretive History of Blacks in American Films

8) Anthony T. Browder

Nile Valley Contributions to Civilization

9) Seth Cagin and Philip Dray

We Are Not Afraid

10) James H. Cone

Martin & Malcolm & America: A Dream or a Nightmare

11) Philip Dray

At the Hands of Persons Unknown: The Lynching of Black America

12) Nigel C. Gibson

Fanon: The Postcolonial Imagination

13) Harry Harmer

The Longman Companion to Slavery, Emancipation and Civil Rights

14) Joseph E. Harris

Africans and Their History

15) James Oliver Horton and Lois E. Horton

Hard Road to Freedom: The Story of African America

16) Stephen Howe

Afrocentrism: Mythical Pasts and Imagined Homes

17) John G. Jackson

Introduction to African Civilizations

18) Maulana Karenga

Introduction to Black Studies

19) Peter Kolchin

American Slavery 1619–1877

20) Rupert Charles Lewis

Walter Rodney's Intellectual and Political Thought

21) Rupert Lewis and Patrick Bryan (Editors)

Garvey: His Work and Impact

22) Leon F. Litwack

Trouble in Mind: Black Southerners in the Age of Jim Crow

23) Ali A. Mazrui

The Africans: A Triple Heritage

24) John T. McCartney

Black Power Ideologies: An Essay in African-American Political Thought

25) Milton Meltzer

Slavery: A World History

26) Wilson Jeremiah Moses (Editor)

Classical Black Nationalism: From the American Revolution to Marcus Garvey

27) Kofi Natambu

The Life and Work of Malcolm X

28) Stephen B. Oates

Let the Trumpet Sound: The Life of Martin Luther King, Jr.

29) Kenneth O'Reilly

"Racial Matters": The FBI's Secret File on Black America, 1960–1972

30) Jerrold M. Packard

American Nightmare: The History of Jim Crow

31) Edward Reynolds

Stand the Storm: A History of the Atlantic Slave Trade

32) Walter Rodney

How Europe Underdeveloped Africa

33) Daryl Michael Scott

Contempt and Pity: Social Policy and the Image of the Damaged Black Psyche, 1880–1996

34) Ronald Segal

The Black Diaspora: Five Centuries of the Black Experience Outside Africa

35) William van Deburg

Modern Black Nationalism: From Marcus Garvey to Louis Farrakhan

36) William L. van Deburg

New Day in Babylon: The Black Power Movement and American Culture, 1965–1975

37) Wyn Craig Wade

The Fiery Cross: The Ku Klux Klan in America

38) Robert Weisbrot

Freedom Bound: A History of America's Civil Rights Movement

39) Chancellor Williams

The Destruction of Black Civilization: Great Issues of a Race from 4500 B.C. to 2000 A.D.

40) Juan Williams

   Eyes on the Prize: America's Civil Rights Years, 1954–1965

41) Richard Wormser

   The Rise and Fall of Jim Crow

In addition to these sources, there are countless excellent biographies and autobiographies of African Americans who have lived incredibly rich and full lives despite racism and inequality. These accounts and narratives can only deepen one's appreciation of Black struggle and contributions made in the service of the Black community and to humanity.

Overview of Black History

For generations in the United States, African history and the Black experience in America were virtually ignored throughout the mainstream educational system from elementary school through the university. Most students who were exposed to Black history prior to the 1960s or 1970s usually were taught about slavery, the Civil War, and perhaps about the Reconstruction era.

If presented, Black history was very likely taught as a footnote to American history with strong influences of Eurocentrism, White supremacy, stereotypes, distortions, and inaccuracies.

The lack of Black equality with Whites throughout colonial and American history is a fact whose truth has either been ignored, suppressed, distorted, or forgotten. C. Eric Lincoln acknowledged the separate, unequal, and yet parallel paths of development that affected White freedom and Black subjugation in his popular book. *The Negro Pilgrimage in America:*

> The Europeans who came to America came in search of a new and more complete freedom; the Africans came because the last vestige of their freedom had been taken away. The Europeans came in search of new ways to exploit the full potential of their humanity; the Africans came under conditions which denied even their basic humanity. The children of West Africa and the sons and daughters of Europe were destined for separate roles in the making of America. For the white Europeans, America was to be a land of the free where the self-evident truths of human equality were to be sufficient ground for individual liberty and universal justice. For the black African, America was to mean two hundred and fifty years of slavery. After that would come the belated discovery that even with freedom there were social and moral factors which would qualify that freedom for yet another hundred years and more.
>
> (Lincoln, 1967, p. 2)

Just as Blacks were to suffer material deprivation, so too they were forced to be deprived of their true history in the pages of American textbooks. James and Lois Horton express how people react when they first learn about history that has been excluded or distorted, in their book *Hard Road to Freedom: The Story of African America:*

> People are often surprised, fascinated, even shocked when they first learn about the history of African Americans. Some times outraged, they demand to know why they haven't heard this story before. Why did their textbooks ignore the dramatic tales of the black experience? Why has no one told this story? It is true that until recently, general American history textbooks and courses have paid little attention to this aspect of the country's development, save for a few references to slavery, usually discussed in connection with the period just before the Civil War. But it is not true that the story of black America has not been told.
>
> (Horton and Horton, 2001, p. 1)

The impact of communicating racist history to African Americans has been well documented in the autobiographies of countless individuals. Likewise, generations of minority children have endured racism not only in terms of what they were taught, but also in their interactions with teachers and counselors who undercut their self-esteem, crushed their innermost hopes and ambitions, and steered them away from thoughts of college or professional careers with the common-sense White supremacist notion that such dreams were unrealistic or beyond realization. Malcolm X's English teacher, Mr. Ostrowski, advised him that a career as a lawyer was unrealistic for a "nigger," and this had far-reaching consequences for Malcolm, who not only attended a predominantly White school in Mason, Michigan, but was acknowledged to be an outstanding student.

The purpose of Black studies and of Black history from the beginning was always intimately connected to not only correcting White racist and Eurocentric representations of the Black experience in America, but also to promote Black pride and a personal sense of dignity.

- The task of Black history is to challenge, confront, and correct the distortions, stereotypes, and biases of Euro-American versions of Black experience.

- The goal of Black history is to rediscover, recover, and reconstruct the ancient and modern Black experience.

- Whatever form Black history takes, it is meant to weaken racism by placing African and diasporic Blacks on an intellectual and political equal footing with other ethnic and racial groups.

- Whether for African American or non–African American students, Black history has been established to accomplish multiple goals:

  - Dispel ignorance

  - Reduce White prejudice

  - Promote Black pride and dignity

  - Demonstrate that Black people are worthy and capable

  - Cultivate Black liberation and emancipation that is, mental decolonization and community control and self-determination

Many scholars and activists, both formally trained and self-taught, as well as Black and non-Black, have contributed to the emergence and recognition of Black history and Black studies. There has also been a long list of Black activist and **Black nationalist** leaders that have had their impact on shaping Black consciousness and thought across the generations of the Black struggle. The dominant elites and the status quo within mainstream academic institutions are often disappointed or even scandalized by the claims and assertions of so-called "street scholars"; non-academic, organic intellectuals; Afrocentrists; and non-Black supporters of attacks against traditional Western knowledge, Eurocentric versions of classical and ancient civilizations, and revisionist scholars who help to undermine hegemonic values and worldviews.

Some individuals who have contributed to Black studies and Black history or African history are:

- W. E. B. DuBois

- Carter G. Woodson

- Herbert Aptheker

- John Henrik Clark

- Benjamin Quarles

- John Hope Franklin

- Maulana Karenga

- Molefe Kete Asante

- John Jackson
- Chancellor Williams
- Basil Davidson
- Cheikh Anta Diop
- Yossef ben-Jochanan
- Ivan van Sertima
- Anthony Browder
- George G. M. James
- C. L. R. James
- J. C. deGraft-Johnson
- Walter Rodney
- Martin Bernal
- Marcus Garvey
- Malcolm X
- Lerone Bennett, Jr.
- Asa G. Hillard
- J. A. Rogers

Themes in Black History

The political and ideological implications of Black history are as important as the substantive claims about the experience of Africans on the continent or throughout the diaspora.

Only in a society that built its own history by violently suppressing and denying—to those it conquered and enslaved—their own history and contributions to human civilization is it necessary to rediscover, recover, or reconstruct the story of African and African American people in order to expose, diagnose, and heal the spiritual, mental, physical, and social wounds caused by cultural, institutional, and individual manifestations of racism.

It is a truism of Black studies that a people must know and identify with their past and their collective history to know where they are and where they are headed. Without a sense of conscious identification with a heritage worthy of humanity, African Americans have been forced to accept the definitions of who they are that have been provided by their enemies who have written them out of history only to replace the historical void, so created, with racist fantasies, offensive stereotypes, perverted imaginings about Black character and personality, and degraded possibilities for the present and the future.

It is ironic that the critiques that were leveled against the original Black studies movement or the subsequent rise of Afrocentric theory—that were based on typical Eurocentric demands for objectivity, empirical data, and universal criteria for explaining reality—have always taken precedence over the lived history of the oppressed.

Among the themes associated with Black history are the following:

- The origin and/or creation of *Homosapiens* on the African continent
  From the pioneering archaeological work of the Leakeys at Olduvai Gorge to the analysis of the female mitochondrial DNA and the Eve hypothesis, all evidence points to Africa as the place where humanity emerged, and from where all subsequent population migrations and racial variation would have begun to occur in the distant past.

- Africa as the cradle of civilization
  If humanity emerged in Africa, then biocultural evolution and societal institutional development and adaptation would have had their oldest beginnings where European and White supremacist "experts" claimed there was no culture or civilization unless it had been introduced by White or non-African people.

- Given the impact of African society and culture on the development of Egyptian civilization, which is assumed to be one of the oldest and most philosophically and technologically advanced societies in the ancient world, it is accepted in Black studies that even older indigenous African societies of the interior—such as Ethiopia, Nubia, and Kush—influenced Egypt, and through Egyptian impact on the Greeks, the Western world as well.

- Prior to the rise of European economic dominance in the world in the sixteenth through the nineteenth centuries, which resulted in the underdevelopment of Africa, there existed great African societies, kingdoms, civilizations, and interconnected trading networks that rivaled or surpassed those social relations in European society at a comparable period of time.

- African people have been actively involved in the history and cultural development of every society in which they have participated to the degree that they could resist or overcome existing forms of oppression.

- Black studies is, according to Maulana Karenga, "both an investigative and applied discipline" in which "activist self-knowledge . . . leads to positive social change (Karenga, 1993, p. 19) Karenga argues further that ". . . it is a discipline dedicated not only to understanding self, society and the world but also to changing them in a positive developmental way in the interest of human history and advancement. In this quest, it challenges the false detachment of traditional white studies which contradicts reality and obscures clarity" (Karenga, 1993, p. 19).

The importance of Black studies and Black history (as a core field in the knowledge structure of Black studies) can best be articulated as the creation of non-Eurocentric paradigms that attempt to slow down, halt, or even reverse what Karenga has called ". . . a vital contribution to the critique, resistance and reversal of the progressive Europeanization of human consciousness and culture which is one of the major problems of our times" (Karenga, 1993, p. 20).

The role of Black history in Black studies can be replicated in all fields of ethnic studies to create a multivocal conversation rather that a Eurocentric monologue. To quote Maulana Karenga once again:

> . . . Black studies joins with other ethnic studies scholars in creating and posing paradigms for multicultural discourse and exchange and possibilities of a just and good society. This, of course, presupposes and necessitates respect for each people's right and responsibility not only to exist but also to speak their own special cultural truth and make their own contribution to the forward flow of society and human history.
>
> (Karenga, 1993, p. 21)

Important Issues in Black History

Rather than providing a full account of African and African American history and experience (which is impossible to accomplish in a limited number of pages), I will list themes that also represent topics about which full-length books are readily available.

In this way I will have space to discuss the late nineteenth- and twentieth-century Black experience, the civil rights movement, the Black Power Movement, and the contemporary post–civil rights climate that is dominated by "color-blind" racism and neoconservative thinking on a variety of social, political, and moral topics.

The themes I use as an overview of Black history are the following:

1) The role of Africa as the cradle of civilization

2) The European degradation, distortion, and destruction of African societies, kingdoms, and civilizations

   • the rise of modern racism and Eurocentrism

   • modern capitalism, labor exploitation, colonialism, and imperialism

   • the "development of underdevelopment" and African as well as third world inequality

3) The Atlantic slave trade and the brutality, suffering, and horrors of the Middle passage

4) Racist rationalizations and ideological justifications for the enslavement of Africans and the institution of New World slavery

   • Africans were heathens, living in spiritual darkness, without the light of the Christian gospel.

   • Africans were mentally, intellectually, and morally inferior to Europeans.

   • Africans were like children who required structure, discipline, and direction for their moral development, and their own good.

   • Slavery already existed between African and Arab societies.

   • Before the labor-saving technologies of advanced industrial society became readily available, life was difficult and even tragic for everyone, therefore slavery was a justifiable and necessary hardship for Africans and Blacks in the New World.

   • Slavery might have been brutal and cruel, but it ultimately civilized the Africans and rescued them from heathenism—while exposing them to civilization, progress, and Christianity.

5) New World slavery was a violent and brutal institution that helped to disorganize and undermine African societies that were directly or indirectly impacted by it.

   • Europeans traded for slaves in the beginning.

   • Then came the kidnapping of African men, women, and children.

   • The spread of European fire arms, trade goods, and alcohol brought violence and death to the continent.

   • The institution of slavery was structured around ship building; agricultural and plantation commodities such as tobacco, sugar, rice, indigo, cotton, and other tropical products; the Middle Passage; the auction block; the farm or plantation; the necessity for social control of slaves; and countless interconnected material and nonmaterial cultural and economic practices.

6) The history of slavery and free Africans in the United States

   • Differential treatment of White and Black indentured servants in the 1600s led to changes in the law and customary treatment of Blacks.

   • The structure of southern agriculture revolved around Whites without slaves, small farmers with some slaves, and the diverse needs of the large-scale plantations and the power of the planter class.

   • The slave hierarchy of house slaves; skilled African artisans, craftsmen, and other technical laborers; and field slaves

- Degrees of freedom for slaves depended upon propensities of masters, the ability of slaves to hire themselves out, the opportunity to buy one's freedom or the freedom of loved ones, and escaping to the North or Canada or being manumitted by the master.

- The life of free blacks in the North and the South was usually far from first-class citizenship or social equality with Whites.

7) Resistance to slavery during the nineteenth century

- Slave resistance encompassed:

  - slave revolts and rebellions

  - organized conspiracies

  - sabotage on the plantations

  - work slow-downs

  - feigned ignorance

  - runaway or escaped slaves

  - the creation of Maroon communities

- The Abolitionist movement to end slavery

  - the testimonies and efforts of escaped slaves to stir the abolitionist sentiments in the North and to speak out internationally against slavery (e.g., Frederick Douglass)

  - free Black activists

  - White activists such as William Lloyd Garrison

  - militant activists such as John Brown

  - organized groups such as the Quakers

- Black political protest and agitation

  - petitioning state legislatures

  - militant pamphlets such as David Walker's Appeal of 1828 or Henry Highland Garnet

  - the Negro Convention movement

  - Harriet Tubman and the efforts of the Underground Railroad

8) The end of legalized slavery

- The conflicts and compromises between the North and South regarding the balance of slave and free states

- The Civil War (1861–1865)

- The Emancipation Proclamation (1863)

- The assassination of Abraham Lincoln

9) The Reconstruction period (1865–1877)

- The Radical Republican plans for reconstruction after Lincoln's death

- Passage of the 1866 Civil Rights Act

- Creation of the Freedman's Bureau to help ex-slaves to gain education, land, and the vote

- The failure to redistribute plantation land to ex-slaves

- The initial creation of the **Ku Klux Klan** by former confederate soldiers

- Black political participation in the Reconstruction era at the state and national levels

10) The end of Reconstruction and the rise of racial segregation

- The Tilden-Hayes compromise, which allowed Rutherford B. Hayes to win a contested presidential election and mandated the removal of federal troops from the South

- The terrorism and night-riding by the Ku Klux Klan in order to scare, punish, and intimidate free or activist Blacks and anyone who would support them

- The passage of discriminatory laws called *Black codes* that were used as an extension of the former slave codes to control and coerce blacks by restricting their freedom of movement and severely limiting their economic or employment options

- The creation of the **sharecropping** system, tenant farming, and **debt peonage,** which virtually reinstituted slavery by tying Blacks to the land until they could repay yearly debts or placed them in the penal system, on chain gangs, or as cheap labor to private citizens

- The full implementation of southern Jim Crow or racial segregation evolved in diverse and insidious ways in each southern state—especially following the supreme court decision of *Plessy v. Ferguson* in 1896, which made separate but equal the law that would reinforce, legally and institutionally, what were already practices of habit and custom in **racial segregation**

- The tremendous increase of southern **lynching** of Blacks to keep the Black population from standing up for their rights or "getting out of their place"

Each of these themes clearly covers a wide range of history, social policy, institutional practices, and political and cultural reality in American national growth and development.

The Twentieth-Century Black Experience

The problem of the twentieth-century is the problem of the color line—the relation of the darker to the lighter races of man in Asia and Africa, in America and the islands of the sea.
(DuBois in Newman and Sawyer, 1996, p. 148)

This famous quotation from *The Souls of Black Folk* by W. E. B. DuBois is justifiably an apt description of the state of Black America in the post-Reconstruction era where Jim Crow segregationist practices and southern White supremacy had created the condition that DuBois referred to as life "within the veil" or the experience of "double consciousness"—the realization that one was ". . . an American, a Negro; two souls, two thoughts, two unreconciled strivings; two warring ideals in one dark body, whose dogged strength keeps it from being torn asunder" (Newman and Sawyer, 1996, p. 148).

But Dubois is also describing the racial inequality that already existed between the White colonial powers and the subjugated masses of dark-skinned people throughout the world. At the time that DuBois wrote *The Souls of Black Folk,* African Americans had reached a low point in the decades following emancipation and Reconstruction, and though the United States had begun to welcome the "huddled masses" of Eastern and Southern Europe as a source of unskilled immigrant workers to meet the needs of the corporate capitalist and industrialized society, America was in the process of excluding Asian workers and undermining the life chances of rural southern Blacks as well as Black workers who were being lured North as a result of promises of good jobs, high wages, and an allegedly better quality of life.

From 1882 to 1924, the United States became increasingly closed to non-European immigrants following the passage of the 1882 Chinese Exclusion Act, the 1892 Geary Act, the 1907 Gentleman's Agreement to limit Japanese migration, and the 1924 Immigration Act, which effectively cut off eastern hemispheric migration to the United States, which translated to the exclusion of the Japanese, though the law did not explicitly name them.

The exclusion of Asians was predicated upon their alleged difference racially and their inability or unwillingness to assimilate or to become Americans. Even the massive arrival of millions of Eastern and Southern Europeans to America's shores occurred at the height of the eugenics and social Darwinist crazes in which representatives of elite racism such as Madison Grant and Lothrup Stoddard argued strenuously that the new immigrants were seriously defective and mentally or genetically unfit for American society and culture. American Indians were likewise marginalized on reservations, where they lived demoralized and dependent lives as wards of the federal government. Mexicans throughout the Southwest had been internally colonized and restricted, for the most part, to living in *colonias* and *barrios* and working in secondary labor markets or as seasonal and migrant laborers. Following the Mexican Revolution of 1910, the number of Mexican migrants into the United States increased dramatically—which had major implications for the burgeoning agricultural sectors in California and throughout the Northwest and the Southwest—given the exclusion of Asians or the racism they were subjected to by Anglos.

The plight of African Americans in the South was, by and large, determined by the fact that large numbers of Blacks were poor and segregated in rural communities. But by the first decades of the twentieth-century, large numbers of southern Blacks began to migrate out of states such as Mississippi, Alabama, Georgia, the Carolinas, and Louisiana to the Midwest and the Eastern, urban and industrial centers of production and manufacturing. This movement of southern Blacks, known as the **Black migration,** represented one of the largest internal migrations in the history of the United States. It also was a structural change that would change the urban dynamic between African Americans and ethnic immigrant communities in the context of twentieth-century political economic reality.

Blacks left the South for a number of interconnected reasons:

- The harsh and brutal reality of the Jim Crow system of segregation and the oppression associated with sharecropping and tenant farming pushed Blacks to look elsewhere for a better future.

- The agricultural system throughout the South was often affected by the uncertain effects of weather and infestations of pests, such as the boll weevil, which could ruin the cotton crop and destroy a Black family's hard work and future dreams.

- Into the mix of Black hardship, labor recruiters would enter rural and urban areas to encourage Black laborers to leave the South for northern cities, where they could work in factory labor and on the assembly lines of the automobile industry.

- The North was described in glowing terms as "a promised land" of opportunity, generous wages, and freedom that would make the journey more than worthwhile.

- But the northern promised land, more often than not, turned to a land of failure, frustration, and new forms of suffering.

- Blacks were segregated in urban slums and ghetto neighborhoods.

- They were exploited in menial and dead-end jobs where they were often the last hired and the first fired.

- And yet the Black migration also extended the reach and impact of Black culture in cities such as New York's Harlem, Chicago, Detroit, St. Louis, Kansas City, and so many other areas of the country.

- Musical forms such as ragtime, jazz, blues, gospel, and other innovations developed from the life of Black people in their communities, churches, bars, taverns, brothels, workplaces, chain gangs, and prisons.

- By the 1920s, the flourishing of Black music, literature, art, and social consciousness became known as the Harlem Renaissance, and writer Alain Locke referred to the emerging generation of post-emancipation-born youths as the New Negros who would break the bonds of limitation in their struggle for success and freedom.

Even though Black life after emancipation and Reconstruction was defined by Rayford Logan as "the betrayal of the Negro" in both the farms of the South and in the factories of the North, it cannot be argued that Blacks did nothing, or that they passively and fatalistically accepted the hand that had been dealt to them by a social system that not only did not play by the rules, but had created one set of rules that applied to Whites and another set of rules that virtually guaranteed Black failure in the culture of White supremacy.

The Rise of Black Protest and Struggle, 1890–1930

With the failure of Reconstruction and the removal of northern troops from the South agreed upon in the 1876 election of Rutherford B. Hayes to the presidency, the North seemingly abandoned Blacks by leaving them to the brutalities created by the architects of White supremacy and the supporters of states' rights.

Richard Newman and Marcia Sawyer describe the reality of Black life in the South in their popular book. *Everyone Say Freedom, Everything You Need to Know about African-American History:*

The mid-1890s were probably the most desperate years for African Americans since the end of slavery. Attempts at political and economic Reconstruction were being successfully beaten back by a white South bent on "redeeming" their states from any attempt to construct a democratic society. Murder, arson, rape, looting and intimidation were used without any fear of justice; many blacks were reduced to the economic peonage of tenant farming and sharecropping, institutions hardly different from slavery; and the states enacted without federal hindrance legislation to segregate African Americans into second-class citizenship. A black person was lynched on an average of one every other day.

(Newman and Sawyer, 1996, pp. 154–155)

In 1895 the great African American leader Frederick Douglass died, having left behind a committed life of resistance to slavery, great oratory and writing in the causes of abolitionism and women's suffrage, and a stellar record of reform, militance, and activism that were second to no one. His book *The Narrative of the Life of Frederick Douglass* is one of the best-known slavery narratives of the nineteenth century. His voice on behalf of Black liberation was forceful and strong, but at the time of his passing a political vacuum was created that shaped the alternative and parallel paths of accommodation and struggle that would seemingly coexist in Black politics and organized struggle for generations of African Americans.

The African American freedom struggle has been misrepresented, wrongly portrayed, and distorted by friend and foe alike who, because of their own political values and preferred ideological agendas, have defined the proper path to the destination of freedom as consistent with the landscape, the hindrances, and the opportunities that were identical with the route they had chosen for their own journey.

The dialectic of struggle within a complex sociological totality has been altered from thesis-antithesis-synthesis to a forced march in which all participants must define liberation in terms of the road itself, rather than where it leads. Malcolm X was a committed Black nationalist who recognized the importance of diverse means to the same goal and the impact of divide-and-conquer strategies that had always been employed by slavemasters, White supremacists, and colonizers to prevent Black people from overcoming racism and oppression. In an April 8, 1964, speech sponsored by the Militant Labor Forum, Malcolm X spoke on the topic "The Black Revolution" to an audience that was three-quarters White. He spoke about the goals and objectives of the Black struggle as follows:

> All our people have the same goals, the same objective. That objective is freedom, justice, equality. All of us want recognition and respect as human beings. We don't want to be integrationists. Nor do we want to be separationists. We want to be human beings. Integration is only a method that is used by some groups to obtain freedom, justice, equality, and respect as human beings. Separation is only a method that is used by other groups to obtain freedom, justice, equality or human dignity.

> Our people have made the mistake of confusing the methods with the objectives. As long as we agree on the objectives, we should never fall out with each other just because we believe in different methods or tactics or strategy to reach a common objective.
>
> (Breitman, 1965, p. 51)

Regardless of the state of Black leadership, or the public recognition or disdain that Black leaders may elicit from their own constituencies or from members of the White power structure, it is a fact of history that there are always competing tendencies or possible directions that individuals and groups can pursue in confronting obstacles or seeking their objectives.

In the era following the death of Frederick Douglass, Booker T. Washington was thrust into prominence because of a speech he delivered in Atlanta, Georgia, on September 18, 1895, at the opening of the Cotton States and International Exposition. Washington had gained fame as an educator even though had been born in rural Virginia as a slave.

> At age sixteen Washington walked five hundred miles to Hampton Normal and Agricultural Institute with $1.50 in his pocket. He became a student in this school for blacks founded by the American Missionary Association and headed by Samuel Chapman Armstrong, the first of several white father-figures in Washington's life.
>
> (Newman and Sawyer, 1996, p. 155)

Booker T. Washington became the founding principal of the Tuskegee Normal School for Colored Youth in 1881, and later:

> . . . was called the "Wizard of Tuskegee" because of the power and influence he wielded both within the African-American community and as a power broker between blacks and the white elite who controlled government, education, and philanthropy.
>
> (Newman and Sawyer, 1995, pp. 154–155)

In Atlanta, Washington spoke first of a ship that had been lost at sea and the exchange between its captain and the captain of another ship:

> 'water water; we die of thirst!' . . . 'cast down your bucket where you are'. The ship's captain "at last heeding the injunction cast down his bucket and it came up full of fresh, sparkling water from the mouth of the Amazon River."
>
> (Bennett, Jr., 1988, p. 264)

Washington urged southern blacks to remain in the South and to cultivate friendly relations ". . . with the Southern white man, who is their next-door neighbor" and he advised Whites:

> cast down your bucket . . . among the eight millions of Negroes . . . who have without strikes and labor wars, tilled your fields, cleared your forests, builded your railroads and cities . . . the most patient, faithful, law-abiding, and unresentful people that the world has seen . . .
>
> (Bennett, Jr., 1988, pp. 264–265)

The two areas of Washington's speech that were the most controversial for his opponents and detractors within his own race were his public acknowledgement that Blacks should not protest against racial and social inequality and that the Black community should be satisfied with manual and vocational training rather than with education in the arts or the humanities.

Washington brought the White crowd to their feet when he said:

> In all things that are purely social, we can be as separate as the fingers, yet [he balled the fingers into a fist] one as the hand in all things essential to mutual progress.
>
> (Bennett, Jr., 1998, p. 265)

Washington reassured Whites that "the wisest among my race understand that the agitation of questions of social inequality is the extremist folly, and that progress in the enjoyment of all the privileges that will come to us must be the result of severe and constant struggle rather than of artificial forcing" (Bennett Jr., 1998, p. 265). Washington was presumably a pragmatic realist who wanted to teach Blacks the importance of building sound character and a foundation for economic independence in the segregated communities where they were increasingly forced to live. Many of his quotes have been articulated by Blacks in subsequent generations, whether they represented the opinions of integrationists or those of Black separatists and nationalists.

Washington stated:

> At the bottom of education, at the bottom of politics, even at the bottom of religion, there must be for our race economic independence.
>
> No race can prosper till it learns that there is as much dignity in tilling a field as in writing a poem.
>
> Character not circumstances, makes the man.
>
> (Newman and Sawyer, 1996, p. 157)

Booker T. Washington was attacked in his own time by many Black activists and militants for his stand favoring accommodation to the White status quo. His most severe critic was W. E. B. DuBois, who chastised him in his essay "On Mr. Booker T. Washington and Others," in his 1903 classic *The Souls of Black Folk:*

> So far as Mr. Washington preaches thrift, patience, and industrial training for the masses, we must hold up his hands and strive with him, rejoicing in his honors and glorying in the strength of this Joshua called of God and of man to lead the headless host. But so far as Mr. Washington apologizes for injustices, North or South, does not rightly value the privileges and duty of voting, and opposes the higher training and ambition of our brighter minds,—so far as he, the South, or the nation, does this,—we must unceasingly and firmly oppose him.
>
> (Bennett, Jr., 1988, p. 332)

Dubois was a highly educated and articulate scholar, sociologist, social commentator, and political activist. He did not believe that Black progress could be achieved if people lacked an educated elite, which he referred to as "the talented tenth." DuBois felt that a vanguard of professional, elite, and well-educated people could act as a beacon of leadership who would help the masses by training teachers and professionals to fill needed roles in the Black community and to become politically and culturally aware of their social condition and of the larger society

Thus, even in the aftermath of "the Atlanta Compromise," Black leaders were actively seeking freedom along many different paths. DuBois and William Monroe Trotter and other Blacks met at Niagra, New York, in 1905 to push more militantly for full equality. Though the **Niagra Movement** failed, it was a precursor to the founding of the **NAACP** on February 12, 1909. On

May 31–June 1, 1909, "some three hundred blacks and whites met at the United Charities Building in New York City at the first NAACP Conference" (Bennett, p. 515).

In October 1911, "a group of whites and blacks created the National Urban League, a professional social work agency which concentrated on the socioeconomic problems of urban Blacks" (Bennett, p. 339). The **Urban League** formed at the time that the exodus of southern Blacks was gaining momentum. In fact, as World War I began in 1914, the numbers of European immigrants to America fell dramatically, and urban jobs for Blacks increased.

Black Americans still faced many problems during the first quarter of the twentieth century:

- Lynching of Blacks in the South was a major concern that Ida B. Wells Barnett and others tried to fight through journalistic crusading, calls for federal anti-lynching legislation, and attempts to educate the nation about its unspeakable brutality.

- There were race riots, which usually saw Whites attacking and killing Blacks or damaging their homes and property:

  Atlanta—September 22–24, 1906

  Springfield—August 14–19, 1908

  East St. Louis, Illinois—May 27–30, 1917

  East St. Louis, Illinois—July 1–3, 1917

  Houston—August 23, 1917

  Chester, Pennsylvania—July 25–28, 1917

  Philadelphia, Pennsylvania—July 26–29, 1917

  Charleston, South Carolina—May 10, 1919

  There were twenty-six riots during the "Red Summer" of 1919

  Tulsa, Oklahoma—June 1921

  (Bennett, pp. 514–524)

- The revival of the Ku Klux Klan in Georgia: The modern Klan spread to Alabama and other southern states and reached its height of influence in the 1920s. By 1924 the organization was strong in Oklahoma, Indiana, California, Oregon, and Ohio. At the height of its influence, the organization had an estimated four million members.

- On December 4, 1915, the NAACP led protest demonstrations against showing of the movie "Birth of a Nation."

- On July 28,1917, ten thousand blacks marched down Fifth Avenue, New York City, in silent parade protesting lynching and racial indignities.

- On January 26, 1922, the Dyer anti-lynching bill was passed in the House by a vote of 230 to 119. The bill was killed in the senate by a filibuster.

In 1916, Jamaican-born Marcus Garvey came to the United States to found the Universal Negro Improvement Association or the **UNIA.** Garvey was born in 1887 and had worked as a printer in Jamaica before being employed on a Costa Rican plantation and as a newspaperman in Panama. Before coming to the United States in the hope of meeting Booker T. Washington, whose work on self-reliance and self-help he admired, Garvey had lived in London where he met Duse Mohammed Ali, who was an Egyptian who celebrated African history.

Marcus Garvey was by no means the first Black nationalist leader who promoted a message of racial pride, uplift, and support for African redemption and a physical return to Africa. To understand the life and legacy of Marcus Garvey, I recommend the full-length studies:

Edmund David Cronon
Black Moses: The Story of Marcus Garvey and the Universal Negro Improvement Association

Rupert Lewis and Patrick Bryan (Editors)
Garvey: His Work and Impact

Tony Martin
Race First: The Ideological and Organizational Struggles of Marcus Garvey and the Universal Negro Improvement Association

Garvey's rise to prominence by the 1920s and his problems in fundraising for the Black Star Steamship Line—which led to his conviction for mail fraud, his imprisonment, and his 1927 deportation from the United States—are controversial, but his impact as a speaker and his message of pride in race, heritage, and the destiny of the African continent affected millions of Blacks in the United States, internationally and on the continent of Africa.

> He was an eloquent orator, and his message resonated with working-class black people including returned soldiers who had become enlightened by seeing how differently blacks were treated in Europe. They were disgusted that their participation in World War I on behalf of democracy did not mean an end to segregation and the badge of inferiority at home. Also, African-American civilians had moved North in considerable numbers to take advantage of wartime industrial employment: living in the North and getting higher salaries raised expectations white America had no intention of fulfilling.
>
> (Newman and Sawyer, 1996, pp. 211–212)

Many have viewed Marcus Garvey as a prophet and a leader whose message was very compatible with the phychic needs of African Americans who were so politically, economically, and spiritually oppressed by segregation, White racism, lynching, and American contempt.

Garvey's message of racial pride and the larger-than-life meetings, staged events, and marches of his admiring followers did not resonate with the Black bourgeoisie or with light-skinned leaders such as W. E. B. DuBois, who was very offended by his oratory and tactics.

But Marcus Garvey's influence in terms of twentieth-century nationalism was impressive. Elijah Muhammad, who was the disciple of Wallace D. Fard and the key founder of the **Nation of Islam,** was influenced by the views of Marcus Garvey and other religious and nationalist ideas that were in the air between World War I and the years of the Depression. Malcolm Little—who later joined the Nation of Islam while serving a prison sentence for armed robbery, and changed his name to Malcolm X—was the child of Earl and Louise Little, who were both active followers of Marcus Garvey and the UNIA's program. Through Elijah Muhammad, Malcolm X became the most recognized Black Muslim leader and perhaps the leading theorist of twentieth-century Black nationalist thought following his departure from the Nation of Islam, his acceptance of traditional Islam, his formation of the organization of Afro-American Unity and the Muslim Mosque, Inc., and his own political evolution in support of Black people in America and throughout the world, whom he saw as victims of Americanism and international victims of human rights violations under the U.N. charter.

To conclude my discussion of Black leadership in the era of accommodation and Black struggle—which began with the Washington–DuBois disagreement over Black equality and saw the rise of Black protest organizations and the development of separatist, nationalist, and pan-Africanist movements—I will provide a few representative quotes from Marcus Garvey.

I asked, "where is the black man's government? Where is his kingdom? Where is his president, his country and his ambassador, his army, his navy, his men of big affairs?" I could not find them, and then I declared, "I will help make them."

Black men, you were once great; you shall be great again. Lose not courage, lose not faith, go forward. The thing to do is to get organized; Keep separate and you will be exploited, you will be robbed. You will be killed. Get organized and you will compel the world to respect you.

The only protection against injustice in man is power—physical, financial, and scientific.

And perhaps Garvey's most recognized sayings:

Africa for the Africans, at home and abroad.

Up, you mighty race. You can accomplish what you will!

(Newman and Sawyer, 1996, pp. 212–214)

Marcus Garvey died in London on June 10, 1940. He was seemingly forgotten in almost every part of the world:

Here and there pockets of nationalists stubbornly kept his name alive but their efforts were unnoticed except by a few. It took the Black Power revolution of the 1960s with its revival of Garvey's red, black and green, his race pride, his self-reliance, his separatism, his anti-imperialism and his revolutionary nationalism, to belatedly return to Garvey the recognition he deserves as a major, if not *the* major black figure of the century.

(Martin, 1986, p. 360)

The Harlem Renaissance through World War II

During the 1920s, there was a resurgence of African American culture known as the Harlem Renaissance. It represented a flourishing of Black culture and life by the people Alain Locke collectively referred to as the New Negro. During the period known as "the roaring twenties," Black music, art, and literature were produced and disseminated as never before.

The cultural life of Harlem was a strong draw for Whites and uptown people who wanted to experience the excitement of Black life and culture. The life of the Black community could be a haven for White afficianados of jazz and club life. Some people were interested in "slumming" to see how Blacks lived.

The Harlem Renaissance and the development of Black culture has been in reality a continuous expression of creativity that was magnified in the 1920s due to the literary production of Black poets, writers, and social commentators. Among the literary giants were figures like Claude Mckay, County Cullen, Langston Hughes, James Weldon Johnson, Nella Larson, Jean Toomer, Wallace Thurman, and Jessie Faucet.

Alain Locke wrote that "subtly the conditions that are molding a New Negro are molding a New American attitude" (Newman and Sawyer, 1996, p. 174). Alain Locke summed up the role of Negro artists as follows:

In flavor of language, flow of phrase accent of rhythm in prose, verse and music, color and tone of imagery, idiom and timbre of emotion and symbolism, it is the ambition and promise of Negro artists to make a distinctive contribution.

(Newman and Sawyer, 1996, p. 174)

It is debatable as to how long the Harlem Renaissance lasted. Some claim that it largely ended with the stock market crash of 1929. Yet some writers, such as Langston Hughes and Zora Neale Hurston, were still productive during the Depression.

The Depression was a critical time for American capitalism given the high unemployment for all Americans, the crisis in agriculture, the condition of American production, and the efforts of president Roosevelt to stabilize the economy through the New Deal, which laid the foundations for the modern welfare state and the role of the federal government in what amounted to massive levels of spending and social engineering.

Black life certainly became more precarious during the Depression, as did the lives of other racial minorities. Mexican and Mexican Americans were repatriated in huge numbers back to Mexico. Indians were in the process of being politically reorganized after the passage of the 1934 Howard-Wheeler Act.

One positive development under Franklin Roosevelt was the informal meetings he instituted with a number of Black leaders and experts on various issues that affected Black people around the nation. Blacks benefited from some New Deal programs, but the economic transformation that ultimately turned the nation around was the economic preparation for World War II and U.S. entrance into World War II following the Japanese attack on Pearl Harbor on December 7, 1941.

During World War II, Blacks fought in segregated units, worked in defense plants, continued to fight against racism, and migrated in increasing numbers to California and the Northwest.

Many changes in race relations began to occur at the conclusion of World War II. In 1947 **Jackie Robinson** became the first Black player to break the color barrier in major league baseball when he joined the Brooklyn Dodgers. The daring experiment by Branch Rickey paid off in the long run and led to the further integration of other major league teams. It is also true that the Negro Leagues were decimated as Black stars sought much better contracts with major league baseball.

In 1948, president Harry Truman signed an Executive Order that led to the **desegregation of the U.S. Armed Forces.** This was a prelude to the far greater civil rights activism and movement for social integration that would follow the historic *Brown v. Board of Education* decision delivered on May 17, 1954, overturning the 1896 separate but equal doctrine.

By 1955, with the momentous events that led to the Montgomery Bus Boycott following the refusal of Rosa Parks to give up her seat on the bus to a White man, an unknown young Black minister named Martin Luther King, Jr., was thrust into national prominence and the modern civil rights movement emerged to change U.S. race relations forever.

The Modern Civil Rights Movement, 1954–1965

Rather than write expansively about the civil rights movement, which is abundantly documented in many excellent and readily accessible sources, I will provide an outline and overview of key points, highlights, and important events.

- The civil rights movement can be dated as beginning with the May 17, 1954, *Brown* decision.

- The goals of civil rights movement:

  - end de jure or legalized segregation in the South

  - end second-class citizenship

  - end all forms of racial discrimination

- Civil rights came to impact virtually all areas of public and institutional life in America:

  - education

  - employment

  - housing

  - voting

- public accommodations
- law enforcement, criminal justice, and the legal system

◾ The civil rights movement utilized a variety of means to end segregation and racial injustice:

- the use of legal tactics and the federal courts
- public appeals to morality, conscience, and shared Judeo-Christian values and constitutional principles
- direct action and nonviolent tactics

◾ Among the strategies and tactics used in various local, state, and federal jurisdictions were:

- mass demonstrations
- protest marches
- sit-ins
- court cases
- economic boycotts
- freedom rides
- armed self-defense
- negotiations with power brokers and those with institutional authority
- the media
- the Black church as an arena for organizing and spiritual renewal

Key Events of the Civil Rights Movement

For a more detailed listing of important events and individuals associated with the 1954–1965 years of the civil rights movement, I would encourage the reader to consult the bibliography and the following sources: Lerone Bennett, Jr., *Before the Mayflower: A History of Black America,* pages 551–644; Clayborne Carson, *In Struggle: SNCC and the Black Awakening of the 1960s;* James H. Cone, *Martin & Malcolm & America: A Dream or a Nightmare;* Henry Hampton and Steve Fayer with Sarah Flynn, *Voices of Freedom: An Oral History of the Civil Rights Movement from the 1950s through the 1980s;* Harry Harmer, *The Longman Companion to: Slavery, Emancipation and Civil Rights,* pages 127–133; Robert Weisbrot, *Freedom Bound: A History of America's Civil Rights Movement;* and Juan Williams, *Eyes on the Prize: America's Civil Rights Years, 1954–1965.*

◾ May 17,1954

Brown v. Board of Education decision declared segregation in public schools unconstitutional and overturned the 1896 *Plessy v. Ferguson* doctrine of separate but equal (Harmer, 2001, p. 126).

◾ July 11, 1954

First White Citizens Council organized in Mississippi (Williams, 1988).

◾ May 31, 1955

Supreme Court orders integration "with all deliberate speed," which allowed states to delay implementation of the *Brown* decision (Harmer, 2001, p. 127).

- August 28, 1955

  Emmett Till, age 14, was kidnapped and lynched in Money, Mississippi (Williams, 1988, pp. 37–57).

- December 1, 1955

  Rosa Parks is arrested after refusing to give up her seat in Montgomery, Alabama (Harmer, 2001, p. 127).

- December 5, 1955

  Beginning of the historic Montgomery Bus Boycott at a mass meeting at Holt Baptist Church in which Martin Luther King, Jr., was chosen to be president of the Montgomery Improvement Association. The boycott continued for 381 days (Williams, 1988, pp. 58–59).

- February 1957

  Founding of the **Southern Christian Leadership Conference** and selection of Martin Luther King, Jr., as president (Harmer, 2001, pp. 128).

- August 29, 1957

  Congress passed the Civil Rights Act of 1957 (Harmer, 2001, p. 128).

- September 24, 1957

  President Eisenhower orders federal troops into Little Rock, Arkansas, to prevent local interference with the integration of Central High School (Harmer, 2001, p. 128).

- May 8, 1958

  President Eisenhower orders the removal of federalized National Guard troops from Central High School in Little Rock (Williams, 1988, pp. 90–114).

- May 29, 1958

  Ernest Green graduates from Central High School along with six hundred White classmates (Williams, 1988, p. 118).

- April 25, 1959

  Mack Parker is lynched in Poplarville, Mississippi (Dray, 2002, pp. 436–437).

- February 1, 1960

  Four North Carolina A&T students start the sit-in movement in Greensboro, North Carolina, at a five and dime store, and by February 10, the movement has spread to fifteen southern cities in five states (Harmer, 2001, p. 128).

- April 15–17, 1960

  The **Student Nonviolent Coordinating Committee** (SNCC) is organized by young activists at Shaw University in North Carolina (Bennett, 1988, p. 560).

- October 26–27, 1960

  John F. Kennedy calls Coretta Scott King to express his personal concern following Martin Luther King, Jr.'s imprisonment. Soon King is released on bond from the state prison at Reidsville. This incident was made known to numerous Black churches and increased black voter turnout on behalf of John F. Kennedy's presidential campaign against Richard Nixon (Williams, 1988, pp. 140–143).

▪ May 4, 1961

Thirteen freedom riders begin a bus trip through the South (Williams, 1988, pp. 148).

▪ May 14, 1961

The bus carrying the first contingent of freedom riders was bombed and burned by segregationists outside Anniston, Alabama, and the freedom riders were attacked in Anniston and in Birmingham (Williams, 1988, p. 148).

▪ May 20, 1961

Freedom riders were attacked by a White mob in Montgomery, Alabama (Bennett, 1988, p. 563).

▪ May 24, 1961

Twenty-seven freedom riders are arrested in Jackson, Mississippi. By June 12 it is announced that more than one hundred freedom riders had been arrested (Bennett, 1988, p. 564).

▪ September 22, 1961

The Interstate Commerce Commission issued a decree that prohibited segregation on interstate buses and in bus terminal waiting rooms (Bennett, 1988, p. 564).

▪ November 29–December 2, 1961

In McComb, Mississippi, a mob of Whites attacked freedom riders at the bus station (Bennett, 1988, p. 565).

▪ December 12, 1961

Martin Luther King, Jr., and more than seven hundred demonstrators are arrested in **Albany, Georgia,** in five mass marches on city hall to protest segregation. The unsuccessful Albany Movement continued well into 1962 (Williams, 1988, pp. 162–179).

▪ September 13, 1962

The refusal of Governor Ross R. Barnett of Mississippi to obey a federal government order to admit James H. Meredith to the University of Mississippi at Oxford on the grounds of "interposition" of the state against federal power precipitates the crisis at Ole Miss (Bennett, 1988, p. 568).

▪ September 20–October 1, 1962

Governor Barnett denied James H. Meredith admission to the University of Mississippi, defied court orders three times, and there was massive local resistance to Meredith's admission. President Kennedy federalized the Mississippi National Guard and Ole Miss students, adults, and southerners from other communities rioted on the campus, which resulted in two deaths and over one hundred people wounded. Finally order was restored and Meredith was escorted by federal marshals to register at Ole Miss University (Bennett, 1988, pp. 568–569; Williams, 1988, pp. 213–218).

▪ April 3–May 10, 1963

Martin Luther King, Jr., opened a major campaign to end segregation in **Birmingham, Alabama.** This struggle was immortalized due to the actions of Bull Connor and the police force, which used high pressure fire hoses and vicious dogs to assault Black demonstrators. School-age children also protested, and more than two thousand people were arrested during the demonstrations (Bennett, 1988, p. 570; Williams, 1988, pp. 179–194).

- June 12, 1963

  Medgar W. Evers, the NAACP field secretary in Mississippi, was assassinated in front of his home by a segregationist and racist after returning from a civil rights rally at a church (Bennett, 1988, p. 570; Williams, 1988, pp. 179–194).

- August 28, 1963

  More than 250,000 people participated in the historic March on Washington, where Martin Luther King, Jr., gave his famous "I Have a Dream" speech (Williams, 1988, pp. 198–202).

- September 15, 1963

  Four Black girls were killed in the bombing of the Sixteenth Street Baptist Church in Birmingham, just weeks after the March on Washington (Harmer, 2001, p. 130).

- November 22, 1963

  President John. F. Kennedy assassinated in Dallas, Texas.

- March 12, 1964

  Malcolm X resigned from the Nation of Islam following his silencing by Elijah Muhammad after his controversial remarks made in December 1963 in which he likened the assassination to "chickens coming home to roost" (Cone, 1992, pp. 184–192).

- June 28, 1964

  Malcolm X founded the Organization of Afro-American Unity in New York (Bennett, 1988, p. 573).

- July 2, 1964

  President Lyndon Johnson signs the **1964 Civil Rights Act,** which prohibits racial discrimination in voting, employment, and public accommodations (Harmer, 2001, p. 130).

- August 4, 1964

  The bodies of three missing civil rights workers (Cheney, Goodman, and Schwerner) who were murdered during the **Freedom Summer** effort to register Black voters in Mississippi were discovered near Philadelphia, Mississippi (Williams, 1988, pp. 229–249).

- August 25, 1964

  Despite the fact that Mississippi's democratic delegation to the Democratic National Convention was all White because of racist selection of delegates, the credentials committee seated the delegates while offering a Johnson-negotiated secret compromise to the integrated state of **Mississippi Freedom Democratic Party** of two "delegates-at-large." The MFDP rejected the "peace" motion. **Fannie Lou Hamer** had stunned the nation with her vivid testimony of how she had been beaten in Mississippi due to her efforts to register Blacks to vote. She had concluded: "and if the Freedom Democratic Party is not seated now, I question America." (Bennett, 1988, p. 573; Williams, 1988, pp. 232–249; Cagin and Dray, 1989, pp. 486–509).

- December 10, 1964

  Martin Luther King, Jr., is awarded the Nobel Peace Prize in Oslo, Norway (Harmer, 2001, p. 130).

- January 2, 1965

  A major voter registration drive began in **Selma, Alabama,** under Martin Luther King, Jr.'s leadership (Bennett, 1988, p. 574).

- February 1, 196

  Over seven hundred demonstrators were arrested in Selma.

- February 21, 1965

  Malcolm X is assassinated as he begins a speech at the Audubon Ballroom.

- March 7, 1965

  Alabama State troopers and sheriff's deputies dispersed civil rights demonstrators using tear gas and billy clubs as they attempted to cross the Edmund Petus bridge to March from Selma to Montgomery (Bennett, 1988, p. 575).

- March 9, 1965

  Three White Unitarian ministers were attacked while participating in a Selma civil rights demonstration. James J. Reeb died later in a Birmingham hospital (Bennett, 1988, p. 575).

- March 21, 1965

  Martin Luther King, Jr., led thousands of marchers on the first leg of a five-day Selma-to-Montgomery march. U.S. Army troops and federalized Alabama national guardsmen protected the demonstrators (Bennett, 1988, p. 575).

- March 25, 1965

  Viola Liuzzo, who was a White civil rights worker, was shot to death on U.S. Highway 80 after a rally as she drove other civil rights workers back to Selma from Montgomery. Three Ku Klux Klansmen were convicted and sentenced for violating her civil rights (Bennett, 1988, p. 575).

- August 6, 1965

  President Johnson signed the **Voting Rights Act** into law. It outlawed the poll tax, literacy tests, and other tactics aimed at preventing Blacks in the South from registering to vote (Harmer, 2001, p. 131).

- August 11, 1965

  Beginning of the Watts riot in Los Angeles following the arrest of Marquette Fry. The riot lasted six days and 34 people were killed and over 1,000 injured (Bennett, 1988, p. 576; Harmer, 2001, p. 218).

The civil rights movement of 1954 through 1965 has been accepted by most commentators as the effort by both African Americans and White liberals to fight nonviolently for desegregation of public education, for the integration of public accommodations, and for the removal of all southern tactics that had been used to disfranchise Black voters and to prevent them from freely voting.

It should be evident, however, that there were many tendencies occurring during the civil rights years and that there was a deep and persistent anger as Blacks in the South discovered the hostility and contempt in which they were viewed by southern racists, segregationalists, and even White liberals. In addition, there was a growing militance throughout many of the urban Black communities of the North, where Blacks lived under conditions of de facto segregation, poverty, high unemployment, police brutality, and negative dealings with the criminal justice system and the social welfare bureaucracy.

The mood throughout the 1960s was evolving in the direction of frustration, militance, anger against the war in Vietnam, and either countercultural efforts to promote alternative lifestyles or militant political activism and revolutionary politics.

By 1966, Martin Luther King, Jr., was attempting to confront segregated urban housing and racism throughout the North and West. He was beginning to realize that racism and poverty in the rest of the nation was, perhaps, more of a serious concern than old-style southern racism. King moved to Chicago in order to experience first hand the conditions that Blacks faced in the ghettos of America.

The Watts riot in 1965 seemed to be a response to prophetic statements of Malcolm X in 1964 and 1965 in which he compared the Black community to a racial powder keg that could explode at any time.

In Oakland, California, in October 1966, the **Black Panther Party** was founded by Huey Newton and Bobby Seale. During 1966, racial violence was reported in forty-three cities around the country in which eleven people were killed, more than four hundred were injured, and three thousand were arrested.

On April 13, 1966, Martin Luther King, Jr., denounced the war in Vietnam and on April 4, 1967 (one year prior to his assassination in Memphis, Tennessee), King spoke to a meeting of Clergy and Concerned Laity at the Riverside Church in New York City, where he gave his historic anti–Vietnam War speech: "A Time to Break the Silence."

On May 16, 1966, Stockley Carmichael became the Chairman of the Student Nonviolent Coordinating Committee, and the SNCC evolved in a decidedly more militant and nationalist direction. Carmichael was an activist and a grassroots organizer who became most widely known as one of the key architects of the ideology and philosophy of Black Power, which he and Charles V. Hamilton explained in their book *Black Power: The Politics of Liberation in America*.

The Black Power Movement

The concept of Black Power emerged as a result of the organizing efforts of SNCC workers in the deep South, particularly Lowndes County in Alabama and in the state of Mississippi. On June 6, 1966, James Meredith was shot and injured while marching from Memphis, Tennessee, to Jackson, Mississippi. The assassination attempt on Meredith brought the representative leaders of the SNCC, SCLC, and CORE (Congress of Racial Equality) together at Meredith's bedside. It was decided that Martin Luther King, Jr., Stockely Carmichael, and Floyd McKissick would continue Meredith's "march against fear" in order to challenge the cowardice and racism of the type of individuals who would attack Black people from hiding and ambush.

The march through Mississippi was not without its own drama as conflicts in slogans, tactics, and ideology began to surface between the different civil rights factions involved. The followers of SCLC and King were for nonviolence and integration and shouted or sang "we shall overcome." But the more militant SNCC activists challenged the slogan "we shall overcome" with the more aggressive "we shall overrun." CORE had also taken a strong nationalist orientation.

In Greenwood, Mississippi, the slogan "Black Power" was heard at a grassroots rally where Willie Ricks and Carmichael had primed the crowd and in response to the question "What do you want?" the crowd had shouted "Black Power." The media were present, and almost immediately the Black Power cry became either a rallying point for some or was attacked as violent, irresponsible, and racist by others.

The rise of Black Power is itself rooted in the history of nationalist thought that was an important stream in nineteenth-century Black consciousness. People like Martin Delaney, Alexander Crummell, Edward W. Blyden, and Marcus Garvey (as previously discussed) were forefathers of modern Black nationalism.

The notion of Black Power built upon various nationalist, pan-African, and separatist doctrines, including aspects of DuBois, Elijah Muhammad, and especially the speeches and views of Malcolm X. Stockley Carmichael and Charles V. Hamilton observed that:

Black people must redefine themselves, and only *they* can do that. Throughout this country, vast segments of the black communities are beginning to recognize the need to assert their own definitions, to reclaim their history, their culture, to create their own sense of community and togetherness. . . . Many blacks are now calling themselves African-Americans or black people because that is *our* image of ourselves. . . . This means we will no longer call ourselves lazy, apathetic, dumb, good-timers, shiftless, etc. Those are words used by white America to define us. . . . From now on we shall view ourselves as African-Americans and as black people who are in fact energetic, determined, intelligent, beautiful and peace-loving.

(Carmichael and Hamilton, 1967, p. 38)

Lerone Bennett, Jr. also captures the emergent thrust and meaning of the concept of Black Power that Carmichael and others were pushing after 1966:

Most Black Power advocates denounced the integration orientation of the old civil rights coalition and called for a new strategy based on black control of the organizations, institutions and resources of the black community. Some black-oriented leaders urged the creation of parallel or independent power blocs (black political parties and black unions) outside existing structures. At the other end of the spectrum were nationalists who called for the creation of an independent black state on American soil. Despite different emphases and different strategies, most members of the new Movement stressed black pride, black dignity and self-determination.

(Bennett, Jr., 1988, p. 423)

To summarize the meaning of Black Power, I will highlight points made by Carmichael and Hamilton and Bennett. Black Power denoted:

- rejection of the goal of integration

- rejection of nonviolent tactics

- turning inward and away from White sources of support and leadership

- advocacy of self-determination

- acceptance of the principle of community control

- Black self-defense in the face of White racist attacks or police brutality

- emphasis on Black pride, Black or African cultural symbols, and Black organizational or political unity

- development of cultural nationalism and Black values and artistic production

- development of political nationalism, whether based on separatism, pan-Africanism, or revolutionary internationalism

- notions of religious nationalism, whether derived from the Nation of Islam, traditional Islam, Black liberation theology, or other African-centered spiritual belief systems

Events Associated with Nationalism and Black Power

- The rise of third world nationalist and anticolonial movements following World War II

- The decolonization of most of Africa from the 1950s through the 1970s

- The growth of the Nation of Islam or the Black Muslim movement from the 1930s into the 1950s and 1960s

- The powerful impact of the life and legacy of Malcolm X

- The riots or "long hot summers," which many people viewed as ghetto revolts, rebellions, urban guerrilla warfare, or proto-revolutionary activity, which occurred with increasing regularity from the Harlem riot of 1964, Watts in 1965, Newark and Detroit in 1967, and hundreds of recorded riots that led to the Kerner Commission's 1968 Report on Civil Disorders

- The rise of Black studies nationally, Black militancy on college and university campuses, and the crisis of student radicalism due to opposition to the war in Vietnam and events such as the killing of four Kent State students by national guardsmen

- The emergence of the Black Panther Party and the visible leadership of Huey Newton, Bobby Seale, Eldridge and Kathleen Cleaver, Fred Hampton, and others

- To get a sense of the history and politics of the Black Panther Party, see the books:
  - Gene Marine, *The Black Panthers*
  - Philip S. Foner (Editor), *The Black Panthers Speak*
  - Bobby Seale, *Seize the Time*
  - Eldridge Cleaver, *Soul on Ice*

- The popularity of Black revolutionary leaders such as:
  - Malcolm X
  - Stockley Carmichael
  - Leroi Jones (Amiri Baraka)
  - Jonathan Jackson
  - George Jackson
  - Angela Davis
  - H. Rap Brown

- The influence of Black nationalist organizations and ideologies
  - The Nation of Islam
  - Maulana Karenga's **US** (wherever we are, US is)
  - The Black Panther Party
  - Black liberation theology

- The cult of revolutionary violence
  - Frantz Fanon and *The Wretched of the Earth*
  - Che Guevara and *Guerrilla Warfare*
  - Fidel Castro and the Cuban Revolution
  - Mao Tze Tung and the Long March, the Chinese Revolution, the *Red Book* of the sayings of Mao, and the Cultural Revolution
  - The Mau Mau movement in Kenya and Jomo Kenyatta
  - Ho Chi Minh as the nationalist leader in the years of resistance and struggle against French colonialism and U.S. imperialism
  - The various National Liberation movements in Africa, Asia, and Latin America

The context of Black nationalism, Black Power, pan-Africanism, socialist internationalism, decolonization, revolutionary praxis, and other radical Marxist schemes was well out of traditional or mainstream thought, but these ideals in various permutations and combinations were important in post–World War II politics and throughout the years of the cold war from the 1950s to at least the mid-1970s, when so many of the racial movements of the 1960s began to fade as the United States became more conservative in the aftermath of its failure in Vietnam; the Watergate scandal; the cumulative impact of J. Edgar Hoover's **COINTELPRO** on Black, Chicano, American Indian, and White radical and leftist movements and organizations; and the rise of the various right-wing movements that Sara Diamond evaluates in her book *Roads to Dominion: Right-Wing Movements and Political Power in the United States.*

The Post–Civil Rights Years to the Present

Scholars such as Michael Omi and Howard Winant have argued that the United States began to lose prestige internationally following Vietnam, the increasing economic competitiveness of Japan, and the effect of the cold war with the Soviet Union on American domestic affairs. In *Racial Formation in the United States,* they also discussed the rearticulation of race with reference to the racial state and racial social movements.

In the disciplines of ethnic studies, it is clear that most researchers believe that civil rights have been undermined by state-based ideologies that stress the irrelevance of race, "color-blind" ideology, the importance of character development over the acknowledgement of institutional and structural racism and inequality, and a concern for national standards and meritocracy over **affirmative action** and racial justice.

These points allow me to conclude this chapter with a summary of the development of backlash politics during the 1970s and beyond—which have ensured that the 1960s civil rights movement would either falter, be slowed down, fail, or (in the long run) be reversed and its partial successes become the basis for declaring racism to be over; or a problem that cannot be solved within a context of big government, the welfare state of New Deal and democratic liberals, or within an affirmative action dynamic.

Backlash politics occurred in relation to:

- the anti-busing and neighborhood school concept developed by Whites in Boston and other areas of the nation where de facto segregation prevented school desegregation or residential integration

- negative reactions to Black studies and later efforts to mold a genuine multicultural movement and pedagogy

- the rise and development of neoconservative, grassroots, and populist issue-based movements that in some ways rearticulated direct action, nonviolent, and community organizing efforts in a direction that allowed conservatives to define themselves and their causes as victims of big government, liberal bureaucrats, and a leftist and biased media

- the anti-affirmative action backlash that began with the 1978 *Bakke* decision and continued into the 1990s Ward Connerly era and Proposition 209

- the anti–civil rights policies of the Reagan and Bush Sr. presidencies from 1980 to 1992

- the politics of multiculturalism, the right-wing attack against "political correctness," university "hate speech codes," and concerns about "leftists feminists, Afrocentrists, and tenured radicals" undermining traditional values, Judeo-Christian foundations viewed as essential to our Western heritage, and propagandizing students rather than objectively teaching acceptable knowledge

■ the people who teach, research, and identify with the origins of civil rights movements and with worldwide struggles for human rights view the rise of the political right as having led to:

- anti–civil rights court cases and decisions

- a climate threatening to the movements to end racial discrimination, such as affirmative action

- a host of reactionary propositions and special initiatives—particularly in the state of California—such as Propositions 187, 209, 227, 21, and others

- particularly in the aftermath of the attack on the World Trade Center on September 11, 2001, and the war in Iraq under President George W. Bush, many feel that the nation has been pulled to a far-right position, which is now treated as the political center

African American politics has also changed since the civil rights and Black Power movements. New alignments and coalitions may be necessary in the future now that Latinos of various nationalities have become the nation's largest minority.

1) Discuss the ten themes used to organize and review African and African American history up to the twentieth century.

2) How did European exploration, expansion, and utilization of unfree labor in Black bodies affect the African continent and its civilizations? Explain the nature of the trans-Atlantic slave trade, the Middle Passage, and the establishment of New World chattel slavery in the Caribbean, Latin America, and the United States.

3) Discuss the nature and forms of **resistance to slavery** by enslaved Africans, free Blacks, White individuals, church denominations, and all forms of abolitionism.

4) Why did the Emancipation Proclamation, the Civil War, and Reconstruction measures ultimately fail to liberate African Americans? Consider the following:
   a) The Thirteenth, Fourteenth, and Fifteenth Amendments to the Constitution
   b) The Freedman's Bureau
   c) The failure of the populist movement in the South
   d) The passage of Black codes
   e) The rise of the Ku Klux Klan
   f) Tenant farming
   g) Sharecropping
   h) Dept peonage
   i) Lynching
   j) Grandfather clauses
   k) Literacy tests for voting
   l) *Plessy v. Ferguson*
   m) The institutionalization of Jim Crow

5) Compare and contrast the philosophies and leadership styles of Booker T. Washington and W. E. B. DuBois in the era of Black accommodation.

6) Discuss the efforts of Blacks to organize in the twentieth century—whether toward full and equal citizenship or in terms of Black community autonomy, Black nationalism, separatism, and pan-Africanism. Consider the following organizational efforts:
   a) The Niagra Movement
   b) The NAACP
   c) The Urban League
   d) The UNIA
   e) The Black Church
   f) Historical Black colleges
   g) Pan-African Conferences
   h) The anti-lynching movement

7) Discuss the impact of Black migration on African American life in the post–Reconstruction era and in the early twentieth century.
   a) What was the Great Exodus that began in 1879?

   b) What was the reason that so many Blacks began leaving the South in the twentieth century?

   c) What impact did World War I have on African Americans?

   d) Why did so many working-class Blacks align themselves with the "Back to Africa Program" of Marcus Garvey?

   e) What conditions did African Americans face in the North?

8) Discuss the Harlem Renaissance and Alaine Locke's notion of the New Negro.

Questions, Exercises, and Topics for Discussion and Debate (continued)

9) How did World War II and the early years of the cold war influence efforts of African Americans toward a fuller realization of civil rights and/or Black identity and self-help?

   a) What role did Blacks play in World War II?

   b) What impact did the breaking of the color line in major league baseball have due to the influence of Jackie Robinson?

   c) Discuss the decision of President Truman to integrate the U.S. Armed Forces.

   d) Why was the *Brown v. Board of Education* decision so important as a precedent that undermined the Jim Crow system and ushered in the modern civil rights movement?

   e) Who was Elijah Mohammad and what was the Nation of Islam or the Black Muslim movement?

10) The civil right movement was sparked by a number of important people, events, and organizations in the aftermath of the *Brown* decision. Briefly define the following:

   a) Emmett Till

   b) Rosa Parks

   c) Martin Luther King, Jr.

   d) Southern Christian Leadership Conference

   e) Sit-in movement

   f) Freedom rides

   g) Student Nonviolent Coordinating Committee

   h) Albany, Georgia

   i) Birmingham, Alabama

   j) Killing of Medgar Evers

   k) March on Washington

11) Discuss the role of integration versus separatism during the critical years of the civil rights struggle. Include the following in your discussion:
   a) Martin Luther King, Jr.
   b) Malcolm X
   c) James Meredith and the integration of Ole Miss
   d) Freedom Summer
   e) Goodman, Schwerner, and Cheney
   f) Fanny Lou Hamer
   g) The Mississippi Freedom Democratic Party
   h) Civil Rights Act of 1964
   i) Voting Rights Act of 1965
   j) Urban riots and long hot summers
   k) Black pride
   l) Black nationalism
   m) Maulana Karenga and US
   n) Cultural nationalism
   o) Black Power movement
   p) Stockley Carmichael
   q) Huey Newton and the Black Panthers

12) What was the COINTELPRO, and what role did the FBI have in disrupting, disorganizing, provoking, and undermining the movements of the 1960s and particularly the leaders and organizations of the civil rights movement?

13) The civil rights struggle had effects not only in America but also around the world. But the United States could not allow the movements of the 1960s to fully realize their national and international agendas. Backlash politics and reactions to school busing, affirmative action, and the dismantling of the welfare state have greatly undermined civil rights and President Johnson's war on poverty. Discuss the current state of Black America in terms of:
   a) The state of Black education
   b) The underclass debate
   c) "Color-blind" racism
   d) The role of people of color in the military
   e) Racial profiling
   f) The criminal justice system and Blacks in the prison industrial complex
   g) Black health care and issues of medical coverage

Chicanos

Chapter Nine

Key Terms

Aztecs

Aztlán

Battle of Puebla 1862

Battle of San Jacinto

bilingual education

Bracero Program

Brown Berets

California Gold Rush

Católicos Por La Raza

César Chavez

Chicano

Chicana feminism

Chicano Generation

Chicano movement

Chicano Moratorium

Chicanismo

Chicano studies

Chicano Youth Conference

Christopher Columbus

conquistadors

Cristal City Texas

Crusade for Justice

David Sanchez

Delano to Sacramento March

Dolores Huerta

east L. A. school blow-outs

El Plan de Santa Barbara

English-only movement

exploitation of cheap Mexican laborers

Francisco Coronado

Francisco Pizarro

foreign capital in Mexico

Gadsden Purchase

Hernán Cortez

Hispanic Generation

"I Am Joaquín"

illegal immigration

immigration and the border

Indios

James K. Polk

José Angel Gutiérrez

La Alianza

Latin America

Latino

LULAC

Manifest Destiny

maquiladoras (Border Industrial Program)

MAYO

MEChA

Mestizaje

Mexican American

Mexican–American War 1846–1848

Mexican caste society

Mexican independence from Spain

Mexican Revolution 1910

Mexico

Mexico Lindo Generation

Minute Man Project

Moctezuma

Operation Wetback

Pachucos

Porfirio Díaz

Portugal

Proposition 187

Proposition 209

Proposition 227

racism against Mexican immigrants

Raza Unida Party

Reies Lopez Tijerina

repatriation

requirement

Rodolfo "Corky" Gonzales

Ruben Salázar

sanctuary movement

Santa Barbara Conference

Simpson–Mazzoli Bill

Sleepy Lagoon Case

Spain

Spanish land grants

Texas revolt

the Alamo

the Border Patrol

the Caribbean

the Catholic Church

the conquest

the crown

the Incas

The Mexican American Generation

the Southwest

Treaty of Guadalupe Hidalgo

UMAS

United Farm Workers Union

Westminster v. Mendez

Zoot-Suit Riots

Key Lesson

Most Anglo Americans, and those non-Anglos who have been socialized and assimilated culturally within the United States and its educational system, have consciously or unconsciously been taught that North American history begins with the founding of the Jamestown Colony, the arrival of the Pilgrims to Plymouth, or the settlement of the Puritans in the Massachusetts Bay Colony. The history of the original thirteen colonies, the rivalry with the French and Dutch, and initial concerns over the Spanish in Florida, and hostility toward Indians on lands the Americans coveted presents an image of North American history and civilizational advance that proceeds from the East via Europe to the New World (with the victories of Anglo-Saxons and their traditions and institution-building) as the arrow of progress that penetrated the heart of any existing inferior races or cultures that stood in their way, just as the doctrine of Manifest Destiny suggested and racist White supremacy all but guaranteed.

The prior presence and existence of the peoples Columbus labeled Indios and the early Spanish and Portuguese exploration, occupation, conquest, and colonization of the islands of the Caribbean, the lands of Mexico, Central America, and South America, and the Spanish presence in Florida, the Gulf region, and the southwest of the northern parts of New Spain were minimally acknowledged but usually in the context of U.S. expansion and cultural supremacy over Indians and Catholic Spaniards and later Mexicans in Texas, New Mexico, Arizona, and California.

Within the field of Chicano studies the complex relationship between Old World civilization and the indigenous societies and civilizations of Mexico, Central, and South America begins with the Spanish Catholic reconquest over the Moors under the Spanish **crown** as represented by King Ferdinand and Queen Isabela, the unification of **Spain,** the expulsion of its Jewish and Muslim populations, and its competition with **Portugal** through exploration and colonization for lands, resources, raw materials, labor, and access to the wealth of the Far East during the late 1400s through the nineteenth century. Columbus sailed West in the hope that he could reach Japan, India, and China, while the Portuguese explored the coasts of Africa and reached India in 1497 with Vasco da Gama's voyage. Because of the papal decree of 1494 known as the Treaty of Tordesillas, the Spanish and Portuguese had agreed to a division of the New World based on the line of demarcation set at 370 leagues west of the Cape Verde Islands drawn from pole to pole. The Portuguese had discovered Brazil prior to 1500, but only formally claimed it as a colony following the voyage of Pedro Alvarez Cabral. The Spanish conquest established the incalculable cruelty that would dominate the biological and cultural fusion and hybridization of Spaniard and Indian from the time of Columbus, Cortez, **Pizarro,** Coronado, countless conquistadors, soldiers, encomenderos, settlers, priests, and missionaries. The Mexican-Chicano legacy is a rich but contested and often ambivalent relationship that draws upon indigenous New World beginnings, heritage, and civilization; interrupted and altered by Columbus and the introduction of Spanish language, Catholic faith, new forms of law, the system of the encomienda, the suppression of indigenous traditions and ceremonial practices, and the long-term introduction of new technology, property relations, and cultural variations; and the transformation that occurred after Cortez defeated **Moctezuma** and the **Aztecs** with the help of the much maligned and misunderstood figure of Doña Marina—also known as Malinzin Tenepal or as La Malinche.

The **conquest** of **Mexico** and **Latin America** resulted in the creation of a complex caste system with countless grades of descent from the peninsular-born Spaniards through Criollos, **Indios,** and Africans. The whole notion of Mexican racial relations is known as **Mestizaje** based on the fusion of Spaniard and Indian to create the mestizo through coercion or voluntarily.

Out of conquest and colonization, the wealth of New World gold and silver mines and the cash crops of plantations was transferred via Indian labor to Spain and Portugal. The humanity and worthiness of Indians to receive the word of God, salvation, and the

Sacraments was debated in Spain by men like Sepulveda and Bartolome de las Casas, but the resulting Laws of the Indies were never fully enforced and the decimation of Indio populations led to the tragedy of the trans-shipment and enslavement of millions of indigenous Africans to the Caribbean, Latin America, and North America.

The Spaniards conquered the Aztecs, the Mayans, the **Incas,** and countless lesser known tribal societies. The areas they explored in what became the American **Southwest** would be claimed by Chicanos as **Aztlán** based on the story of the Mexica original homeland prior to their migration into the valley of Mexico and their development of Tenochtitlán. In 1810 the rule of the Spanish was challenged in Mexico following Father Hidalgo and El Grito de Dolores. In 1821 Mexico became independent from Spain but was too weak to effectively govern her northern territories. The Anglo Moses Austin and his son Stephen both received land grants after 1821, but under the condition that they would obey Mexican law, not import slaves, and learn Spanish. Soon Mexicans and the Anglo Tejanos revolted against the government in Mexico City. The Anglos were defeated at **the Alamo** by Santa Anna, but he was in turn defeated at the Battle of San Jacinto six weeks later by Sam Houston.

The establishment of the Lone Star Republic after 1836 lasted until it was annexed and added to the United States as a slave state in 1845. President **James K. Polk,** under the influence of the ideology of **Manifest Destiny,** badly wanted to add California to the United States but Mexico would not negotiate. Polk, in a controversial move, provoked a fight with Mexico based on a disagreement regarding the true border between Texas and Mexico. This resulted in the 1846–1848 **Mexican–American War,** the **Treaty of Guadalupe Hidalgo,** and the annexation of half of Mexico's land and the promise of U.S. citizenship (including Spanish language rights, practice of Catholism, and honoring of Spanish-Mexican land grants) for the 80,000 or so Mexicans who remained on the U.S. side of the border one year following the Treaty of Guadalupe. Following the **California Gold Rush** after 1848 and the **Gadsden Purchase** in 1853, Anglos gained control of California, carved out of its newly gained territories both slave and free states, inherited responsibility to deal with new tribes of Indians, fought a bloody Civil War with the confederacy, expanded across the Plains, dispossessed Indians and relocated them on reservations, and began to build railroads and develop the economy of the Southwest, and to **exploit the cheap labor of Mexicans** and Chinese laborers who had increased in number during the 1850s.

For the remainder of the nineteenth century, Mexicans were swindled out of land grants by crooked lawyers, a corrupt Anglo court system, and by Anglos who engaged in criminal conspiracies, committed gross injustices—as in the case of the hated Texas Rangers—and **overwhelmed and exploited Mexican laborers** in mining, railroad construction, ranching, the development of southwestern agriculture, and through the degradation of Mexican culture and the disfranchisement of raza politically.

In Mexico itself, the French, under Maximillion and Carlotta, tried to establish an empire while the United States was fighting the Civil War. Mexicans won a great victory at the **Battle of Puebla in 1862,** which is the basis for the celebration of Cinco de Mayo. President **Porfirio Díaz** came to power in 1876 and allowed foreigners to invest in order to modernize the country. By 1900 until the 1910 Revolution, Mexicans were being oppressed and subordinated by Anglos and Mexican elites in the Southwest and inside Mexico. The U.S. Southwest was being developed in the age of monopoly capital and the Robber Barons. Thus the use of cheap labor greatly facilitated the profit margins of capital. Anglo laborers not only benefited from the existence of dual wage systems but also by their refusal to allow Mexicans to join their unions. Despite the heroic efforts of Mexican laborers to resist Anglo racism, degrading stereotypes, and countless injustices through their efforts to unionize and to support one another through mutualistas, the plight of raza was desperate on both sides of the border because huge numbers of impoverished Mexicans entered the United States after the Revolution looking for work and hope, only to find poverty and internal colonialism in America.

The U.S. established **the Border Patrol** in 1924, and the politics and economics of migration and immigration, labor, **repatriation, Bracero Programs,** deportations, **Operation Wetback,** union organizing, strikes, boycotts, marches, and political organizing all began in earnest.

From the **Mexico Lindo Generation,** to the **Mexican American Generation,** to the **Pachucos** and Zoot-Suiters, to the **Chicano Generation,** raza struggled and their identities shifted between romanticizing life in Mexico before the Revolution to sublimating their heritage and culture in order to prove themselves Americans first. The children who came of age during World War II joined the armed forces, worked in defense plants, or were caught between their parents's Mexicaness and their inability to be accepted or respected by Anglos who viewed them as dirty, degraded, delinquent, dangerous, violent, or unpatriotic. The Pachucos and Zoot-Suiters are viewed by many as the beginning of what would evolve into the Chicano Generation who brought working-class and Mexican cultural values into their efforts to gain education, political representation, community power, and recognition that their origins in Mexico and their labor in the United States would have to be acknowledged along with the right for equal treatment and first-class citizenship.

The **Chicano movement** produced great leaders, grassroots activists, countless organizations throughout Aztlán, mobilization for social justice, education, and an end to police brutality.

The Chicano movement is at the heart of **Chicano studies;** the activism of **César Chavez, Dolores Huerta, Reies Lopez Tijerina, Rodolfo "Corky" Gonzales,** Bert Corona, **José Angel Gutiérrez,** Luis Valdez, the Madres of East Los Angeles, the Chicanas who challenged sexism and machismo while working on behalf of the community and in support of **Chicana feminism;** and the rank-and-file individuals, workers, and unnamed heroes and heroines of every family and **Chicano** community of occupied Aztlán and around the nation.

Despite the backlash against raza that began in the late 1970s and culminated in the "English only" movement, anti-immigrant legislation and propositions, the Minute Man Project, the exploitation of Mexican women in maquiladoras, the oppression of peasants and Indians in El Salvador and Guatemala that led to the **sanctuary movement,** the uprising in Chiapas, the union-busting of capitalism in the global neo-liberal economy, the overzealous recruiting of Brown bodies for Bush's wars in Iraq and Afghanistan, and the disproportionate incarceration of raza in the prison industrial complex, and despite the newest label of Hispanic Generation—the Chicano movement is not over. The relevance of Chicanos for the twenty-first century is not only the projected size of the population, but the proximity to the border, the role of immigration, the importance of Chicano markets and business, the power of the vote, and the contributions of Mexican-descended families and communities to American life despite rejection, exploitation, and racism.

Notable Quotes

I am Joaquín

Lost in a world of confusion,

Caught up in a whirl of a

    gringo society,

Confused by the rules,

Scorned by attitudes,

Suppressed by manipulations,

And destroyed by modern society.

My fathers

have lost the economic battle

and won

the struggle of cultural survival.

And now!

I must choose

Between the paradox of

Victory of the spirit,

despite physical hunger

    Or

to exist in the grasp

of American social neurosis,

sterilization of the soul

and a full stomach.

Yes,

I have come a long way to nowhere,

Unwillingly dragged by that

monstrous, technical

industrial giant called

    Progress

and Anglo success . . .

I look at myself.

I watch my brothers.

I shed tears of sorrow.

I sow seeds of hate.

I withdraw to the safety within the

circle of life . . .

    MY OWN PEOPLE

(Rodolfo "Corky" Gonzales in Esquibel, 2001, pp. 16–17)

Mexican Americans became an oppressed minority group as a consequence of the expansion of the US Empire in the nineteenth-century, and that fact has had a profound impact on their political and intellectual development. The subjugation of Mexican Americans, beginning with the Texas–Mexico War of 1836 and the US–Mexico War of 1846–1848, has never been considered a moral or constitutional issue by US society or even by liberals. Like the Native American peoples, Mexican Americans were subjected to a process of colonization which, in addition to undermining their culture, relegated the majority of them to a permanent pool of cheap labor for US capital. As a "conquered" and nonwhite people, they were never the beneficiaries of the fruits of capitalist development. Even the once privileged Mexican gentry who welcomed the white colonizers with open arms soon lost their social status and political power with the formation of a new class structure.

(Muñoz, Jr., 1990, p. 19)

On the morning of 3 March 1968, shouts of 'Blow Out!' rang through the halls of Abraham Lincoln High School, a predominantly Mexican American school in East Los Angeles. Over a thousand students walked out of their classes, teacher Sal Castro among them. Waiting for them outside the school grounds were members of UMAS and various community activists. They distributed picket signs listing some of the thirty-six demands that had been developed by a community and student strike committee. The signs protested racist school policies and teachers and called for freedom of speech, the hiring of Mexican American teachers and administrators, and classes on Mexican American history and culture. As might be expected, the signs that caught the attention of the mass media and the police were those reading "Chicano Power!", "Viva La Raza!", and "Viva La Revolución!"

(Muñoz, Jr., 1990, p. 64)

Culturally, the word Chicano, in the past a pejorative and class-bound adjective, has now become the root idea of a new cultural identity for our people. It also reveals a growing solidarity and the development of a common social praxis. The widespread use of the term Chicano today signals a rebirth of pride and confidence, Chicanismo simply embodies an ancient truth: that a person is never closer to his/her true self as when he/she is close to his/her community.

(Rosales, 1997, 364)

Our struggle is not easy. Those who oppose our cause are rich and powerful and they have many allies in high places. We are poor. Our allies are few. But we have something the rich do not own. We have our own bodies and spirits and the justice of our cause as our weapons.

When we are really honest with ourselves we must admit that our lives are all that really belong to us. So it is how we use our lives that determines what kind of men we are. It is my belief that only giving our lives do we find life. I am convinced that the truest act of courage, the strongest act of manliness is to sacrifice ourselves for others in a totally nonviolent struggle for justice.

To be a man is to suffer for others. God help us to be men!

(César Chavez in Valdez and Steiner, 1972, p. 387)

Introduction

The conquest of the New World began in 1492 with the first of the four voyages of **Christopher Columbus,** who sailed under the sponsorship of the Spanish monarchs Ferdinand and Isabela.

Columbus and his men established the patterns that would characterize European contact with indigenous peoples throughout the Caribbean and the Americas. Initial contact was peaceful but inevitably was followed by an assessment of the level of development of the people; the likelihood that they possessed or had access to valuable resources such as gold, silver, jewels, or other wealth; the capture or enslavement of Indios who would either be forcefully taken back to Spain to be displayed like some rare species of plant or animal or sold as servants or slaves; the **requirement** that the colonized population submit to the superior power of the Europeans and accept peaceful obedience to the teachings of the **Catholic Church** and come to worship Jesus Christ and the visible Church hierarchy that were His earthly representatives—or face the threat of harsh punishment from the **conquistadors;** and finally, the creation of new institutions such as the encomienda or colonial forms of domination based upon initial military power and cultural imposition by which the Indian and later African slaves would become a part of the new racial and class hierarchies that were established in the Latin American and Caribbean areas.

Prior to the development of the disciplines of Chicano studies, Indian studies, and ethnic studies, the discovery of the New World by Columbus—and its subsequent colonization—were understood within what has come to be known as the Western triumphalist paradigm of the advance of civilization, Judeo-Christian values, and progress within an Enlightenment framework. But more recent scholarship and writing coupled with the activism of Indian peoples and Chicanos who have aligned themselves with their indigenous roots and heritage has led to strong critiques and revisionist views of the conquest and the genocide that began over five hundred years ago.

In addition to the works by Kirkpatrick Sale on *The Conquest of Paradise* (1990) and David E. Stannard's *American Holocaust* (1992), which I cited in Chapter 7, I would also include the following works that deal with Columbus, the conquest, New World colonization, and racism:

- Jan Carew
  The Rape of Paradise: Columbus and the Birth of Racism in the Americas

- Jan Carew
  Fulcrums of Change: "Columbus and the Birth of Racism in the Americas," pages 3–48

- Felipe Fernández-Armesto
  The Americas: A Hemispheric History

- Hans Koning
  Columbus and His Enterprise: Exploding the Myth

- The special issue of the journal *Race & Class, 33*(3) (January–March 1992): "The Curse of Columbus," pages v–105

- Patricia Seed
  American Pentimento: The Invention of Indians and the Pursuit of Riches

The conquest of the New World is the foundation for understanding all subsequent developments in the field of Latin American studies and for comparing the history and experience of all the Spanish-speaking people and nations of **the Caribbean,** Mexico, and Central and South America as well as those who reside in what became the United States.

In this chapter I do not intend to develop the history of all so-called **Latino** peoples who were created out of the diverse relationships of the Spanish and Portuguese with countless indigenous populations in the western hemisphere and African, Asian, or other Europeans who were implicated in the formation of mixed or mestizo races and Latin American nation-states.

As important as Puerto Ricans, Cubans, Dominicans, Central and South Americans are—both in their own national contexts and in their diasporic relationships with the United States—I only intend to specifically concentrate on the experience of the Mexican and Mexican American populations.

In the southwestern portion of the territory that would eventually be incorporated and annexed by the United States in 1848 under the provisions of the Treaty of Guadalupe Hidalgo, there already had been diverse Indian populations that had experienced both Spanish exploration and attempted occupation of their lands.

Following the Spanish conquest of the Aztecs by **Hernán Cortez** from 1519 to 1521, the colony of New Spain was created. The Spaniards explored and occupied territories from Florida to the Mississippi River and into the Southwest, although their numbers were not sufficient to establish power or permanent settlements beyond Florida and later in the Southwest as a result of the expedition of **Francisco Coronado,** who in 1540 led six hundred men in search of the Seven Cities of Cibola. Coronado failed to find vast riches but he did claim areas he explored for Spain.

It is the history of the people of Mexico and the area of the Southwest that has been called Aztlán by Chicano scholars and activists that I will concern myself with in this chapter.

The meaning of the term *Chicano* is surrounded by controversy, which is understandable. For those Mexican Americans that Carlos Muñoz, Jr., discussed under the term "Mexican-American Generation," the term *Chicano* was not an appropriate label for respectable U.S. citizens of Mexican heritage who did not identify with working-class origins, indigenous roots, or the cultural life of the barrio.

But the people who Muñoz, Jr., called the "Chicano Generation" represented a political shift in consciousness that was generically influenced by the Mexican American realities that grew out of World War II, the Pachuco and Zoot-Suit experience, the Korean War, and the political maturation of raza throughout the Southwest who began to take pride in their heritage and who asserted themselves in the late 1950s and increasingly in the 1960s.

The term *Chicano,* which had been seen as a pejorative put-down that was somewhat analogous to the words "Blacks" or "African" prior to the 1960s, became a word that was appropriated by Mexican American youth, activists, and a new breed of militants who were at the forefront of struggles for recognition, respect, rights, and a new identity.

The Mexican-origin population in the United States still constitutes the largest segment of the Latino community and is by far the most important group throughout the American Southwest. Even given the significant size of other Latino segments in the major Southwest cities such as Los Angeles and San Francisco, the proximity of the Southwest to the Mexican border is a political, social, cultural, and ideological reality guaranteeing that the whole region will continue to maintain a Mexican flavor and influence well into the twenty-first century.

In addition, the politics of **immigration, and the border, bilingual education,** labor force participation, the influence of Mexican and Latino culture, the reality of racist stereotypes in the media, and the denigration to raza as violent, criminally prone, and unpatriotic despite evidence to the contrary all speak of the importance of the Chicano movement, the struggle for Chicano studies, and the ongoing need to protect the political and economic gains of previous generations from the racist assaults and right-wing attacks against Chicano and Mexican communities through the Southwest. Given the different political and national histories of Latinos in the United States, it is important that Chicanos not be swallowed up in pan-ethnic movements that would promise unity or greater political and economic clout without representing the specific values and goals that derive from Chicano experience or a Chicano analysis of specific problems and proposed solutions that ensure the survival and prosperity of the Chicano community.

Sources on Latinos and Chicanos

The focus of this chapter is the Mexicano and Chicano experience in the United States. My emphasis is to provide references on the history of Mexico, the Southwest, and Mexican/Chicano history. I also have highlighted material pertaining to the Chicano movement and issues that are important in current Chicano politics and culture. But I have also provided important sources on Latino and Chicano studies and biographical citations of key movimiento leaders.

The sources on Latino, Mexicano, and Chicano history and experience cover a variety of related and overlapping topics or subject areas, including:

- Latino history

- Latino studies

- Mexican history

- Chicano history

- History of the Southwest

- Chicano studies

- Chicano family

- Immigration and repatriation

- Women, work, and globalization

- Chicano movement

- Politics of language and bilingualism

- Migrant labor

- World War II era, Pachucos, Zoot-Suit riots, and the Sleepy Lagoon case

- Chicano gangs and police relations
- Chicano biography

The field of Chicano studies is an important area and is not limited to the materials that I have provided. There is a vast literature in Chicana feminism and gender, and an ever-growing number of sources in Chicano/a literature, essays, political commentary, and specific topics. Given the diversity among all Latinos and within the Mexicano/Chicano community, this source list is at best minimal and suggestive. The following materials are presented in alphabetical order:

1) Rodolfo Acuña

   Occupied America: A History of Chicanos (Third Edition)

2) Francisco E. Balderrama and Raymond Rodríguez

   Decade of Betrayal: Mexican Repatriation in the 1930s

3) Deborah Barndt

   Tangled Routes: Women, Work, and Globalization on the Tomato Trail

4) Yolanda Broyles-González

   El Teatro Campesino: Theatre in the Chicano Movement

5) Ernesto Chavez

   "Mi Raza Primero!" (My People First) Nationalism, Identity, and Insurgency in the Chicano Movement in Los Angeles, 1968–1978

6) John R. Chavez

   The Lost Land: The Chicano Image of the Southwest

7) James Crawford

   Hold Your Tongue: Bilingualism and the Politics of "English Only"

8) Livie Isauro Duran and H. Russell Bernard

   Introduction to Chicano Studies (Second Edition)

9) Antonio Esquibel (Editor)

   Message to Aztlán: Selected Writings of Rodolfo "Corky" Gonzales

10) Leobardo F. Estrada, F. Chris García, Reynaldo Flores Macías, and Lionel Maldonado

    "Chicanos in the United States: A History of Exploitation and Resistance"

11) Mario T. García

    Memories of Chicano History: The Life and Narrative of Burt Corona

12) Manuel G. Gonzales

    Mexicanos: A History of Mexicans in the United States

13) Gilbert G. Gonzalez and Raul A. Fernandez

    A Century of Chicano History: Empire, Nations, and Migration

14) Juan Gonzalez

    Harvest of Empire: A History of Latinos in America

15) Richard Griswold Del Castillo

   La Familia: Chicano Families in the Urban Southwest, 1848 to the Present

16) Richard Griswold Del Castillo and Richard A. García

   César Chavez: A Triumph of Spirit

17) Camille Guerin-Gonzales

   Mexican Workers and American Dreams: Immigration, Repatriation, and California Farm Labor, 1909–1939

18) José Angel Gutiérrez

   The Making of a Chicano Militant: Lessons from Cristal

19) Thomas D. Hall

   Social Change in the Southwest, 1350–1880

20) Benjamin Keen (Editor)

   Latin American Civilization: History and Society, 1492 to the Present

21) Gary D. Keller, Rafael J. Magallán, and Alma M. Garcia

   Curriculum Resources in Chicano Studies: Undergraduate and Graduate

22) Elizabeth Martinez

   De Colores Means All of Us

23) Mauricio Mazón

   The Zoot-Suit Riots: The Psychology of Symbolic Annihilation

24) Carey McWilliams

   North from Mexico: The Spanish-Speaking People of the United States

25) Alfredo Mirandé

   The Chicano Experience: An Alternative Perspective

26) Alfredo Mirandé

   Gringo Justice

27) Carlos Muñoz, Jr.

   Youth, Identity, Power: The Chicano Movement

28) Armando Navarro

   The Cristal Experiment: A Chicano Struggle for Community Control

29) Armando Navarro

   La Raza Unida Party: A Chicano Challenge to the U.S. Two-party Dictatorship

30) Armando Navarro

   Mexican American Youth Organization: Avante Garde of the Chicano Movement in Texas

31) Himilce Novas

   Everything You Need to Know About Latino History

32) Eduardo Obregón Pagán

   Murder at the Sleepy Lagoon: Zoot-Suits, Race, and Riot in Wartime L.A.

33) Juan F. Perea (Editor)

   Immigrants Out! The New Nativism and the Anti-Immigrant Impulse in the United States

34) Refugio I. Rochín and Dennis N. Valdés

   Voices of a New Chicana/o History

35) Luis Rodriguez

   Always Running: La Vida Loca: Gang Days in L.A.

36) Roberto Rodriguez

   Justice: A Question of Race

37) F. Arturo Rosales

   Chicano! The History of the Mexican American Civil Rights Movement

38) F. Arturo Rosales (Editor)

   Testimonio: A Documentary History of the Mexican American Struggle for Civil Rights

39) Daniel Rothenberg

   With These Hands: The Hidden World of Migrant Farmworkers Today

40) Ramón Eduardo Ruiz

   Triumphs and Tragedy: A History of the Mexican People

41) Julian Samora and Patricia Vandel Simon

   A History of the Mexican-American People

42) Earl Shorris

   Latinos: A Biography of the People

43) Stan Steiner

   La Raza: The Mexican Americans

44) Reies López Tijerina

   They Called Me "King Tiger": My Struggle for the Land and Our Rights

45) Jesús Salvador Treviño

   Eyewitness: A Filmmaker's Memoir of the Chicano Movement

46) Luis Valdez and Stan Steiner

   Aztlán: An Anthology of Mexican American Literature

47) Francisco H. Vázquez and Rodolfo D. Torres

   Latino/a Thought: Culture, Politics, and Society

48) Ernesto B. Vigil

   The Crusade for Justice: Chicano Militancy and the Government's War on Dissent

49) James Diego Vigil

   Barrio Gangs: Street Life and Identity in Southern California

50) James Diego Vigil

   From Indians to Chicanos: The Dynamics of Mexican-American Culture

51) Victor Villaseñor

   Rain of Gold

52) David J. Weber (Editor)

   Foreigners in Their Own Land: Historical Roots of the Mexican Americans

53) Eric Wolf

   Sons of the Shaking Earth

When Does Chicano History Begin?

In order to understand the relationship between the indigenous societies of pre-Columbian Mexico and the territory known in Chicano studies as Aztlán, and the creation of the racial caste system following the conquest of Mexico by Cortez, it is essential to provide a preliminary framework that articulates the basic meaning of the term *Chicano* and a reasoned discussion as to when the dynamic of Chicano history begins.

It is important to state that the meaning of the term *Chicano* and the designation as to what constitutes Chicano history are by no means settled once and for all for Mexicanos in the United States, for professionals in the field of Chicano studies, or for the activists who first self-consciously called themselves—and the communities they struggled for—"Chicano."

There are several possible positions that logically can link the indigenous people of the territory now defined as Mexico and the American Southwest with the invasions, conquest, colonization, and internal colonization by the Spanish and Anglo Protestant populations that interrupted and changed indigenous history after 1492.

- Chicano history begins with the Indio societies that predated the arrival of both the Spanish conquistadors and the Anglo colonizers of North America.

- Chicano history presupposes indigenous societies but does not begin until at least 1492 and, more accurately, following the conquest of Mexico by Cortez from 1519–1521 and subsequent events.

- Chicano history presupposes indigenous societies and the Spanish colonization of Mexico and the Southwest, but does not begin until the Mexican freedom struggle, which began in 1810 and culminated with an independent Mexico after 1821 that increasingly had to deal with the Anglo population that gained permission to enter the northern territory of Mexico.

- Chicano history presupposes the existence of a **Mexican caste society**—composed of elite criollos, a large mestizo population, and Indios—which must defend its land and boundaries from the incursion of Anglos in Texas who lost the battle at the Alamo but won at San Jacinto and created the Lone Star Republic between 1836 and 1845, after which Texas became a part of the United States.

- Many scholars and Chicano activists define the beginning of Chicano history as the period when President James K. Polk provoked an incident with Mexican troops to legitimate his plan to invade Mexico in order to occupy and add Mexican territory to the United States following a war based upon the doctrine of Manifest Destiny. The formal signing of the Treaty of Guadalupe Hidalgo and America's payment of 26.8 million dollars allowed the

United States to control the Southwest and the Mexican population of about 80,000 who chose to remain on the U.S. side of the border and become U.S. citizens.

▪ Some scholars recognize the importance of everything that occurred during and after the Mexican War and the Treaty of Guadalupe Hidalgo, but they choose to emphasize the changed dynamic between the United States and Mexico during and after the reign of Porfirio Diaz, which led to the penetration of **foreign and U.S. capital into Mexico** between 1876 and 1900 or so, followed by the **Mexican Revolution of 1910.** The development of Mexico's political economy led to the dispossession of Mexican peasants from their land at the same time that the American Southwest was being developed and the final Apache wars were coming to an end. The influx of large numbers of dark-skinned mestizos into the Southwest in search of work and security in the aftermath of the Mexican Revolution led to a new dynamic in the twentieth century that pre-figured issues related to:

- the border

- legal and illegal immigration

- subordination of raza throughout the Southwest

- cultural subordination of Mexicanos in terms of denial of language rights, inferiorization of their religious faith, and stereotyping of Mexicans

- political and economic suppression as a result of internal colonization

- denial of education to Mexican children and disruption of the Mexican family due to the necessity to work as migrant and seasonal farmworkers

▪ Some scholars and activists view the beginning of Chicano history as a manifestation of a changing social and political consciousness that began to develop during or after World War II. They argue that Mexican Americans throughout the Southwest have always struggled for rights, dignity, and respect, but that so-called responsible Mexicans tended to be middle-class, assimilationist, and distant from working-class or recent immigrant populations. This was the Mexican American generation that took its social and political cues from the Anglo society. Only during and after World War II and the Korean War did a more vocal Mexican American community begin to show more visible and outward signs of resistance. The Pachucos and Zoot-Suiters were ambivalent about their identification with Mexican culture and their failure to gain acceptance from Anglos who still treated them as inferior.

▪ Some scholars and analysts view Chicano history as the history of the Chicano movement, which has come to be defined as a specific era of Chicano identification, activism, and community struggle that more or less encompasses the late 1950s and early 1960s through the early to mid-1970s. The significant manifestations include:

- early phases of political representation at local or state and federal levels

- César Chavez and the struggle to create the **United Farmworkers Union**

- Reies López Tijerina and the struggle to defend New Mexican **Spanish land grants** under the Treaty of Guadalupe Hidalgo

- Rodolfo "Corky" Gonzales and the **Crusade for Justice** and the **Chicano Youth Conference**

- Chicano student "blow-outs" in East Los Angeles, the activism of raza on college and university campuses, the formation of organizations such as **MAYO, UMAS, MEChA,** and the **Brown Berets**

- The creation of the **Raza Unida Party** and the organizing of José Angel Guitérrez in **Cristal, Texas**

- The Santa Barbara Conference to create a plan for Higher Education which led to El Plan de Santa Barbara, MEChA, Chicano studies, and the framework for Chicanismo

- The radical efforts of Chicano Catholics in groups such as Católicos por la Raza

- The anti-Vietnam protest of August 29, 1970, which led to a police riot and the death of three Chicanos, including the journalist Ruben Salázar

- The rise of Chicana feminism

- Chicano/a arts, murals, literary culture, music, and Brown Pride

- The energy and commitment of youth and the demands for respect, rights, opportunity, and power

This overview of Chicano history is both a summary of important epochs and a framework for the discussion of Mexican and Chicano experience that will follow.

I do not particularly want to force the reader into accepting any one of the versions of what constitutes Chicano history as a preferred doctrinal position, but I will conclude this discussion by insisting that the meaning of the Chicano experience is linked to the conquest and colonization of Mexico; the independence of Mexico from Spain; the Anglo invasion, occupation, and annexation of Mexican land and people; and the internal colonization of raza throughout the Southwest and their historic responses to that process throughout the twentieth century and beyond.

The Nature of Chicano Oppression

Chicano oppression is rooted in the same processes that led to the dispossession of the Indians of Mexico, Central America, and South America. Chicanos identify with the collective reality of Indian people of the western hemisphere, Mexico, and the Southwest. Chicanos view themselves as a product of the brutality and violence of the conquest of Mexico that led to the rape of Indio people and the creation of a racial hierarchy based on Mestizaje that gave them both their "Brown heritage" (often shading into a White European look) and their cultural, linguistic, and religious heritage.

Leobardo Estrada et al. define Mexicans who were dominated by Anglos in the American Southwest as having actively resisted oppression and exploitation:

Mexican resistance to exploitation has taken a great variety of forms since the conquest, contributing to the maintenance and perpetuation of cultural patterns among Mexicans living in the United States. These cultural patterns include: a national identity built around an Indian past; an Indianized Catholicism (La Virgen de Guadalupe); racial miscegenation (Mestizaje—Indian and Spaniard—although almost as many Africans as Spaniards were brought to Middle America during the colonial period); and a regional single language, Spanish. These patterns and practices, which distinguished the Mexican population from other groups, have persisted even among those who left the Southwest for other regions of the United States.

(Estrada, García, Macías, and Maldonado, 1981, p. 103)

Tomás Almaguer views the oppression of Chicanos as intimately bound up with the dialectics of race and class that developed in North America. His view can be summarized in his description of European colonialism:

Since its inception at the turn of the sixteenth-century, European colonization has spelled the domination of people of color throughout the world. Everywhere the Western European or North American has ventured he has sought colonial super-profits through either new markets, new investment outlets, new territories and raw materials, or an exploitable supply of cheap labor. The net result of this colonial expansion and conquest has meant that the economic and social life of the colonized was to be totally disrupted and reorganized to fill the needs of the intruding European metropolis.

(Almaguer, 1974, p. 28)

Almaguer views the Spanish oppression of Indians in Mexico as a part of the same historical dynamic that resulted in the oppression of Chicanos in the American Southwest:

It is the development of both racial and class oppression in the colonial situation of North America that provides us with one of the unifying threads that historically ties the Chicano experience with the Spanish colonization of Mexico in the sixteenth-century. The colonial and class relations that initially oppressed the Indigena in Mexico and those that oppress the Chicano today have shifted from a semi-feudal pre-capitalist colonial base to the monopoly capitalist base found in the United States. These two colonial situations were part of the same historical process that characterized European and North American hegemony in the Americas.

(Almaguer, 1974, p. 29)

It is within the context of European colonial expansion that Mexican and later Chicano oppression occurred. The oppression of Mexico's indigenous population following the downfall of Aztec and other indigenous societies will be briefly discussed in the following section.

Overview of the Spanish Conquest

The indigenous people of Mexico represented a diverse array of historical societies that ranged from the high civilizations of the Maya in Yucatán and the Aztecs in the central valley, to countless tribes that lived in highland and lowland ecological niches and habitats throughout Mexico.

The importance of Indian societies for Chicano studies is that the Spaniards did not colonize an empty land nor did they encounter people without culture, history, civilization, or humanity. There could not be a Chicano people or history if Mexico had simply been occupied without violent or accommodative interactions between the non-Indian Spaniards and the aboriginal peoples. The history of the peoples of Mexico and Guatemala is discussed in Eric Wolf's book *Sons of the Shaking Earth,* and the conquest of the Mexica is analyzed in Mark Cocker's *Rivers of Blood, Rivers of Gold: Europe's Conquest of Indigenous Peoples,* part I: "The Conquest of Mexico," pages 25–112.

Any evaluation of the conquest of Mexico, Central or South America, and the islands of the Caribbean will inevitably discuss first contacts; the differences between the Spanish culture, language, religion, technology, and lifestyle from those of the Indian societies; and the degree of violence, plunder, rape, destruction, and pain that were inflicted during the conquest and colonial periods. It is also necessary to recognize the new institutions, material culture, and technology that were introduced in colonial societies and the extent to which they either undermined, modified, or changed indigenous communities and social structure.

From a Chicano perspective, there has been a hybridization of Spanish and Indian culture that accounts for both the richness of the spiritual and material cultures of raza in Mexico and the United States as well as the ambivalence of the post-conquest love–hate relationship that sometimes influences how raza attempt to reconcile the European heritage with the conquered indigenous part of their psyche or personality.

The colonization of the New World was initially organized around the competition between Spain and Portugal for control of the territories, resources, and peoples they claimed on behalf of their respective sovereigns or monarchs. To prevent or minimize conflict between competing European powers or nation-states in the emerging international legal system that would help to regulate the evolution of mercantilism, there had to be a consensus as to who had the right to colonize which areas of the New World following the discoveries of Columbus and subsequent explorers.

The advent of this European world hegemony was set in motion with the early colonial ventures of the Iberian axis. Symbolically, through a series of Papal bulls, the world was divided in 1493 between Spain and Portugal. Rectified a year later to permit Portugal ownership of Brazil, the treaty of Tordesillas further delineated the partition of the "new world" into spheres: the West going to Spain and the East to Portugal. By the close of the fifteenth-century the Americas had been "discovered" and the turn of the century was to signal a further escalation in the early European scramble for colonial possessions throughout the world.

(Almaguer, 1974, p. 30)

The racial and class system that was developed in New Spain by the Spaniards established a system of social prestige that divided colonial Mexico into a series of classes that reflected the legal and cultural complexities that resulted from racial interactions between Spaniards, Africans, and Indios:

While the organization of the colonial economy was to produce well-defined social classes, the division in its social classes came to closely correspond with the racial differentiation that miscegenation was to produce in the colony. The size and relative position of each of these major groups was, of course, subject to some change as the colonial period progressed. Like the social organization of the society, the organization and division of its labor system came to be largely defined in terms of race, "The peninsulars then appear as the bureaucrats and merchants par excellence, the criollos as the large landowners, the mestizos as the artisans, shopkeepers, and tenants, the mulattoes as urban manual workers, and finally the Indians as community peasants and manpower for different kinds of heavy, unskilled labor."

(Almaguer, 1974, p. 32)

The principle of a class system and a division of labor based upon socially designated racial differences that developed in central Mexico also impacted social life in colonial areas to the north. In Nuevo Mexico, the Indio-mestizo legacy was reflected in the semi-feudal social relations between the patrón and the peón.

A few wealthy families came to wield tight control over the internal affairs of the colonized area. Composed primarily of Spanish criollo origin, the patrones were joined in their control of Nuevo Mexico by Spanish aristocrats, officials, and the influential clergy of the Church. Subservient to this Hispanic elite were the peones—composed primarily of Mestizos and Indios. The economic relations of this village life were organized in such a way as to benefit the light-skinned European and deprive the Indio and Mestizo.

(Almaguer, 1974, p. 33)

Almaguer also indicates that colonial California had a race-class system organized around the mission system and the ranchos:

. . . class stratification in California was again marked by the predominance of a small Spanish criollo elite—the so-called "gente de razón." Like the patrones in Nuevo Mexico, they controlled the lives of the mestizos and indios in the colonial territory. After the secularization of the missions, this ruling elite was estimated to number no more than 48 landowners and it retained a tight-fisted control over the affairs of California.

(Almaguer, 1974, p. 34)

The significance of the Spanish conquest and colonization of Mexico and other parts of the Caribbean and Latin America is that Spain redirected the labor and wealth of her colonies back to Europe. However, the role that Spain played in facilitating the transition of Europe from feudalism to mercantilism was overshadowed by her subsequent decline as a colonial power. The legacy of Spain in the New World was that Indios and mestizos were racially denigrated and relegated to the lowest social class positions in her colonies, despite the wealth that they created for the colonial elites and for European nation-states. When Spain's power declined after the defeat of the Spanish armada in 1588 by the British, the competition for land and wealth in the emerging capitalist system shifted from the Iberian Peninsula to the nations of Holland, France, and England.

These nation-states would build their own colonial systems in North America and throughout the developing world system. In time the English colonies would effectively block Spain's influence in Florida and the territories that constituted Northern New Spain. The emergence of the United States as an independent nation and the struggle of 1810–1821, by which **Mexico gained her independence from Spain,** set the stage for American dispossession and removal of the Indians, the development of the southern system of slavery, the expansion of the nation into the Southwest and to the Pacific based on the ideology of Manifest Destiny, and the penetration and ultimate annexation of one-half of Mexico's territory into the expansionist and (especially into the nineteenth and much of the twentieth century) racist nation.

The elite classes of Tejano society, New Mexico, and California would eventually face social and economic decline as a result of Anglo penetration into their social systems through strategic marriages, legal and political chicanery, and imposition of Anglo institutions and cultural values that would displace the wealthy and elite families or force them to enter into alliances with them.

The independence of Mexico and the expansion of Anglo power did not end the racial subordination of mestizos or Indian people, but rather assured their continued oppression within a framework of internal colonialism of the racial minorities that were annexed or incorporated into the expansionist U.S. political economy.

Chicano history and oppression recognize Spanish and Anglo forms of racism toward populations of color within economic relations based on semi-feudal or more advanced forms of capitalist exploitation.

> The "primitive accumulation" of capital to which Spain contributed conditioned the gradual development of capitalism and the world market economy. Without the massive plunder of the Americas by Spain, and the eventual redirection of this wealth to England, Holland, and France, large-scale capitalist manufacture and industry would not have been brought about so successfully. This massive accumulation of capital was therefore a crucial prerequisite for the development of nascent capitalism and the perpetuation of the colonial exploitation of the non-European world. . . . It is through the historical dialectic of colonial and capitalist development that racial and class oppression have become integrally bound. The establishment of colonial systems of domination (be they either "classic," "neo," or "internal") have dialectically fed into the world development of capitalism from inception to its present monopoly stage, and capitalism has in turn reinforced and perpetuated the colonial situation in all parts of the world.
>
> (Almaguer, 1974, pp. 36–37)

In the following section I will connect the development and expansion of the United States to the events that led to México's annexation and to the subordination of those Mexicans who chose U.S. citizenship following the Mexican–American War. The denial of first-class citizenship to Mexicanos and the injustices they faced and fought against throughout Aztlán form the nineteenth century context in which Chicanos were molded—regardless of the terms they called themselves or the epithets that were hurled at them by racist Anglo-Saxon Protestants or immigrant ethnic groups who were caught up in the capitalist expansion of American society.

Manifest Destiny and U.S. Expansion

Following the successful American Revolution against the British, the United States not only gained independence but also began to develop a republican ideology of self-government and a collective self-consciousness based upon its Puritan heritage and a sense of mission or destiny that would propel the nation's policies and collective actions throughout the nineteenth century.

The concept of Manifest Destiny was first explicitly expressed by John O'Sullivan in the **New York Sun** during 1847 (Rosales, 2000, p. 8). Matt S. Meier and Feliciano Ribera explain the meaning of Manifest Destiny in **Mexican Americans/American Mexicans: From Conquistadors to Chicanos:**

> Manifest Destiny was a peculiarly Anglo American version of the concept of a chosen people. By the beginning of the nineteenth-century North Americans began to believe that their country was destined by divine providence to settle and control the area from the Atlantic seaboard to the Pacific Ocean. Subsequently more extreme exponents of this concept were convinced that the Arctic Circle to the North and the Strait of Magellan in the South were the only logical limits to inevitable Yankee expansion. The country to suffer most in the nineteenth-century as a result of Manifest Destiny was Mexico, since approximately half its territory, about one million square miles, lay between the American Southwestern frontier and the Pacific Ocean.
>
> (Meier and Ribera, 1993, p. 55)

The ideology of Manifest Destiny has been most crucially associated with the Mexican–American War of 1846–1848. President James K. Polk is the person who ordered General Zachary Taylor into Texas to "protect" the U.S. Mexican border, which was in dispute (Acuña, 1988, p. 12). Some argue that Manifest Destiny was the doctrine that Polk and other defenders of the war with Mexico used to justify the aggressive actions of U.S. troops, while others rationalize the results of the outcome as Divine Providence as explained by the popular doctrine.

If the United States had not been so bent on expansion and had more willingly respected the claims of other European sovereigns to North American territories, one could argue that the Chicano people would never have come into existence in the first place.

But the Anglo American belief in Manifest Destiny and the expansion of capitalism during the Industrial Revolution and the market revolution in America guaranteed that the hunger for more land and freedom would never be fully satisfied until the continent was in fact controlled by the ever-expanding U.S. population.

Rodolfo Acuña has provided a more comprehensive explanation of the theological and philosophical meaning of Manifest Destiny in *Occupied America: A History of Chicanos:*

> Manifest Destiny had its roots in Puritan ideas, which continue to influence Anglo-American thought to this day. According to the Puritan ethic, salvation is determined by God. The establishment of the City of God on earth is not only the duty of those chosen people predestined for salvation but it is also the proof of their state of grace. Anglo-Americans believed that God had made them custodians of democracy and that they had a mission—that is, they were predestined to spread its principles. As the young nation survived its infancy, established its power on the defeat of the British in the War of 1812, expanded westward and enjoyed both commercial and industrial success, its sense of mission heightened. Many citizens believed that God had destined them to own and occupy all of the land from ocean to ocean and pole to pole. Their mission, their destiny made manifest, was to spread the principles of democracy and Christianity to the unfortunates of the hemisphere.
>
> (Acuña, 1988, p. 13)

Acuña's discussion of Manifest Destiny is important because it reflects an ideological framework that is remarkably close to Max Weber's thesis concerning the elective affinity between ideas and material conditions as articulated in *The Protestant Ethic and the Spirit of Capitalism.*

The growth and development of American capitalism required a vigilant search for raw materials and resources that could be exploited by the bourgeoisie only through the control of masses of laborers—both slave and free—in an ongoing dialectic with technology and the relations and forces of production. The growth and expansion of capitalism required the acquisition of new territory and the integration of those lands and the people on them into the organized political and economic institutions of the nation.

Manifest Destiny was a master framework by which America's culture makers and elite thinkers could morally legitimate expansion; material prosperity as a sign of God's blessing; the superiority and power of the White race; the paternalistic control of inferior Indians, Blacks, and Mexicans as a mission of redemption and racial uplift; and the integration of regional economies into the Republic as a justification for extra-territorial expansion of American democracy and capitalism into the world's markets by the turn of the twentieth century.

Thus the ideology of Manifest Destiny can be viewed as the moral frosting on the American cake of White supremacy that compelled elites and masses alike to impose their values and practices associated with individualism, private property, Christian civilizational superiority, and the work ethic that fueled capitalism on to the peoples whose land and labor they usurped throughout the nineteenth century.

Before summarizing the process that brought American expansionists into a position to conquer and annex Mexico's northern territories and create Mexican citizens in the American Southwest, I want to reinforce a point concerning the U.S. elite and their role in maintaining and reinforcing the nation's institutions for the masses. The following quote is taken from Ronald Takaki's *Iron Cages: Race and Culture in 19th-Century America:*

> Although their role as culture-makers did not preclude criticism of certain aspects of American capitalism, the men analyzed in this study shared a basic commitment to the system and its values, and participated in its maintenance and advancement in varying degrees and ways. They were what Karl Mannheim described as the "intelligensia": Their special task was to provide an "interpretation of the world" for American society. As intellectuals or interpreters of social reality, most of them were agents or members of a class that owned property used for production, appropriated labor from workers either through enslavement or wages, and possessed an inordinate degree of control over institutions which had the power to disseminate information and ideas, make laws, punish in the courts and use the instruments of state violence. What white men in power thought and did mightily affected what everyone thought and did.

(Takaki, 1989, p. vii–viii)

Tomás Almaguer cites Alonso Aguilar to point out six stages in America's westward expansion that occurred from the Louisiana Purchase in 1803 and culminated with the Gadsden Purchase in 1853:

- 1803—The Louisiana Purchase

  France lost Haiti and much of its North American territory. The United States paid France only 15 million dollars for almost one million square miles of land.

- 1819—Following repeated border incidents and long negotiations, Spain ceded her possessions east of the Mississippi River and renounced any claim to Oregon. The United States paid 5 million dollars to acquire the territory of Florida, which measured 38,700 square miles.

- 1846—England and the United States both claimed the Oregon territory, which consisted of 286,000 square miles, until the United States pressured England to relinquish its claim. That territory includes the states of Oregon, Washington, Idaho, and parts of Wyoming and Montana.

- 1846—The unjust expansionist war with Mexico began.

- 1846–1848—The U.S. gained Texas as a state, which had existed as the Lone Star Republic and after 1848 incorporated 945,000 square miles of Mexican territory, for 26.8 million dollars. This land ultimately included the state of Texas, Arizona, New Mexico, California, Nevada, Utah, and part of Wyoming.

- 1853—The Gadsden Purchase of 45,000 square miles of land in the Mesilla Valley was obtained for only 10 million dollars.

(Aguilar in Almaguer, 1974, pp. 38–39)

Aguilar summarizes America's various land acquisitions as follows:

> To sum up, in the course of half a century, the United States increased its territory tenfold—not including Alaska. This is to say; nearly 2.3 million square miles were acquired by various means for the reasonable price of a little over $50 million.

(Almaguer, 1974, p. 39)

The Southwest: Indian, Spanish, Mexican, and American

What has happened in the territory of North America known as the Southwest can be described almost as an ethnic studies laboratory for historically observing the processes of racial and ethnic accommodation, competition, and conflict that have impacted the diverse peoples and nations that have attempted to live there.

Rather than chart this temporal and geographical history in detail, I will summarize important dates and events with an emphasis upon those concerning Indian, Spanish, Mexican, and Anglo American experiences.

In the following section I will provide a brief survey of the Southwest from the signing of the Treaty of Guadalupe Hidalgo to the beginning of the twentieth century in order to explore how Mexicans were treated following Anglo annexation and the capitalist development of the lands obtained from Mexico.

Chronology of Significant Dates and Events

Date	Events
50,000–10,000 B.C.	Amerindian origins
10,000–8,000 B.C.	Basic human populations of the New World established
<1492 A.D.	Pre-Columbian Indian societies, cultures, nations, and civilizations
1492 A.D.	Columbus and the beginnings of New World exploration, conquest, contact, and genocide of Indian peoples
1519–1521	Hernán Cortez and his soldiers—with Indian allies—conquer the Aztecs and sieze the capital of Tenochtitlán
1528–1541	Spanish exploration of Florida to the Mississippi River, and throughout the Southwest
1598	Juan de Oñate establishes the first Spanish settlement in New Mexico—San Gabriel de los Españoles
1610	Oñate's successor settles Santa Fe de San Francisco to the south
1718	New Spain founds the mission and presidio of San Antonio
1769–1823	Junipero Serra and Gaspar de Portolá establish the first of California's twenty-one missions (1769) at San Diego as well as a presidio
1781	El pueblo de Nuestra Señora, la Reina de los Angeles de Porciúncula is founded by a diverse group of Spaniards, Indians, and Blacks; we know this as Los Angeles

1803	Louisiana Purchase followed by the Lewis and Clarke Expedition
1810–1821	September 16, 1810—El Grito de Dolores by Padre Miguel Hidalgo signals the beginning of Mexico's war of independence against Spanish rule
1819	Spain cedes Florida to the United States
	Foreigners are allowed to settle Mexico's northern territory of Texas
1821	Stephen Austin founds San Felipe de Austin
1829	Mexico abolishes slavery
1830	20,000—mostly Anglo Southerners—have entered Texas along with 2,000 "freed slaves"
1836	Anglo Texans and dissident Mexicans revolt and establish the Lone Star Republic; Santa Anna won a decisive victory at the Alamo but was defeated weeks later by Sam Houston at the Battle of San Jacinto
1845	Texas is annexed from Mexico by a joint resolution of Congress and becomes a state
1846	May 13—the United States declares war against Mexico
1848	Hostilities against Mexico end and on February 2; the Treaty of Guadalupe Hidalgo is signed with important provisions for Mexicans choosing to remain on the American side of the new border
1849	Following the discovery of gold at Sutter's Mill in 1848, the Gold Rush begins and there is a massive movement of Anglos into northern California
1851	Congress establishes the Land Commission to judge the validity of Spanish and Mexican land claims in California
1853	The Gadsden Purchase is negotiated in Mexico City, allowing the United States to obtain 45,000 square miles in the Mesilla Valley; this region was later found to have some of the richest copper mines in the world
1860	Mexico is invaded by the French, who hope to reestablish a colonial presence in the New World
1862	In the Battle of Puebla, Mexicans won an important victory against the French; this victory is commemorated in the celebration of Cinco de Mayo
1876–1910	As the president of Mexico, Porfirio Díaz allows European and American capital to be invested in Mexico in an effort to modernize the country
1848–1900	Mexicans in the annexed American Southwest are systematically dispossessed of land, wealth, and rights and become a cheap and exploited labor force and a reserve army of labor in Texas, New Mexico, Arizona, and California

1850–1900	Mexican resistance to Anglo atrocities, racism, murder, rape, and vigilante attacks throughout the Southwest and especially along the Texas–Mexico border—Mexicans were called bandits, outlaws, and desperados by Anglos, and Mexicans particularly detested the racism and violence committed against them on both sides of the border by the infamous Texas Rangers

Chicano Oppression in the Southwest, 1848–1900

Prior to the Mexican–American war of 1846–1848, Anglos had begun to enter Texas primarily from southern states. Even though Mexico had abolished slavery in 1829, by 1830 there were about 20,000 Anglos in Texas who were accompanied by about 2,000 "freed" slaves who had in reality been forced to sign lifelong contracts with their former owners.

The immigrants to Texas were supposed to sign written pledges agreeing to support the Mexican government, to adopt Catholicism, and to free any slaves they had. But the Anglos circumvented the agreements, which, in any case, were virtually unenforceable given the distance of Texas from the capitol in Mexico City. The Anglos considered themselves to be morally, intellectually, and politically superior to Mexicans and hoped to ultimately create an independent entity with its own sovereign status.

This is the context for the **Texas revolt** in 1836 following the defeat at the Alamo and the victory of Sam Houston at the **Battle of San Jacinto.** The Anglo Texans and dissident Mexicans created the independent Lone Star Republic, which lasted until 1845 even though Mexico did not recognize its legitimacy.

The Lone Star Republic was really a pretext for U.S. territorial expansion and for the extension of southern slavery. The alliance of U.S. imperialists and the proponents for the extension of slavery pushed for the recognition of Texas, and in 1845 it was granted statehood and pushed America that much closer to war with Mexico.

The war was declared on May 13, 1846, and was enthusiastically promoted by U.S. politicians and businessmen who believed Mexico to be weak and torn by internal divisive disputes that had not been resolved since she gained independence from Spain.

The Treaty of Guadalupe Hidalgo

As bitter as the Mexican–American War was for the people of Mexico and other countries in Latin America to accept—given the aggression of the United States toward Mexico—the controversies that surround the conclusion of the war and the Treaty of Guadalupe Hidalgo have affected the relations between the United States and Mexico and the Mexicans who chose to remain on their land within the territory acquired by the United States for the last one hundred and fifty years or so.

Even before the war with Mexico was concluded militarily, negotiations between the government of the United States and that of Mexico under President Santa Anna had begun. But the U.S. State Department, under orders from President Polk, sent a low-ranking chief clerk of its staff to Mexico City to begin the process of negotiating a peace accord that would allow the United States to finalize its inevitable military victory.

Nicolas Trist began peace talks with Santa Anna, but before much real progress could occur, Santa Anna's government fell following General Winfield Scott's entrance into Mexico City. Even though Trist was ordered back to Washington, he refused to return and continued to negotiate with the new government. The peace talks were ongoing from autumn of 1847 to the final signing of the Treaty of Guadalupe Hidalgo on February 2, 1848. Trist may have had good intentions, but the peace that followed hostilities between Mexico and the United States may have been more destructive in the long run for Mexicans on both sides of the new border than the American provocation that led to the war in the first place.

In the nineteenth century, the winning of wars was almost always associated with territorial expansion by the victorious nation. The United States ratified the Treaty of Guadalupe Hidalgo on March 10, 1848, but as Julian Samora and Patricia Vandal Simon argue, "the ratification seems a farce: Only those articles which won the approval of the senators were ratified and the document that remains is a patchwork of deleted paragraphs" (Samora and Simon, 1993, p. 99).

The provisions of the treaty as ratified by the U.S. Senate were different than those agreed to by Mexico under Trist's efforts, but Mexico as a defeated nation had little choice regarding terms in any case.

> By the terms of the treaty, Mexico approved the prior (1845) U.S. annexation of Texas, thus ending twenty years of squabbling and warfare over the future of that territory. Further more, Mexico ceded a vast expanse of territory, long coveted by Americans to the United States. The Mexican Cession fulfilled the goals of Manifest Destiny, including modern California, Arizona, New Mexico, Nevada, Colorado, Utah, and a bit of Wyoming. In return, the United States agreed to assume the war claims of Americans against Mexico and pay Mexico the sum of $15 million. (This was later amended to $10 million, to be paid in two installments of $7 million and $3 million, respectively . . .). Mexico thus lost more than half the territory which had been hers at the time of independence in 1821. Loss of territory was a bitter pill to swallow, made additionally so by the discovery of gold in California and subsequent economic development of the region.

> (Samora and Simon, 1993, p. 99)

The Treaty of Guadalupe Hidalgo also created future problems for Mexicans in the Southwest who became American citizens legally, but in fact were internally colonized throughout the Southwest by Anglo violence, racism, stereotyping, and institutional subordination.

With regard to the Mexican territory that the United States annexed, provisions of the treaty outlined how Mexicans and their rights were to be recognized:

- Mexicans were given one year following ratification to decide if they would move to the Mexican side of the border.

- Mexicans who chose to remain on the U.S. side of the border could either retain the title and rights of Mexican citizens or acquire those of citizens of the United States. ". . . and those who shall remain in the said territories after the expiration of that year without having declared their intention to retain the character of Mexicans shall be considered to have elected to become citizens of the United States" (Samora and Simon, 1993, p. 101).

- The Treaty of Guadalupe Hidalgo promised in the strongest legal language to protect Mexican and Mexican American property rights in the territory incorporated into the United States.

- Mexicans who returned to the Mexican Republic would be able to retain "the property, which they possess in the said territories, or disposing thereof, and removing the proceeds wherever they please without their being subjected, on this account, to any contribution, tax, or charge whatever" (Samora and Simon, p. 101).

- The property that most concerned Mexicans who left the United States, as well as those who remained and those who chose to become citizens, was the land grants that had been established under both the Spanish and Mexican governments whose boundaries and legal title (and, in fact, were questioned by Anglos and disputed—often for years—in American courts under the jurisdiction of the Anglo-American laws governing property and contracts).

> "In the said territories, property, of every kind, now belonging to Mexicans not established there, shall be inviolably respected. The present owners, the heirs of these and

all Mexicans who may hereafter acquire said property by contract shall enjoy with respect to it guarantees equally ample as if the same belonged to citizens of the United States" (Samora and Simon, 1993, p. 101).

▩ The Treaty of Guadalupe Hidalgo also guaranteed Mexican American citizens ". . . some special privileges derived from their previous customs in language, law, and religion" (Lynn I. Perrigo in Acuña, 1993, p. 19).

▩ The Treaty of Guadalupe Hidalgo did not establish a permanent border between Mexico and the United States ". . . but merely provided for a joint Mexican-American commission to undertake the task" (Samora and Simon, p. 102).

▩ Problems associated with the border that was finally established included:

- The unreliable course of the Rio Grande River, which often changed its course—thus affecting the legal boundary between the United States and Mexico.

- The border was virtually impossible to patrol, and Mexicans, Americans, and Indians could easily cross at will over land or river.

- Indians in the Southwest often raided far into Mexican territory, and the United States chose to ignore the Indians they had "inherited for a long time."

- Mexico held the U.S. government responsible for damages inflicted in their territory based on the treaty.

The Gadsden Purchase of 1853

Boundary disputes and a number of unresolved issues surrounding the Treaty of Guadalupe Hidalgo compelled the United States to seek a further strip of Mexican land. Some Americans had argued that the United States should have annexed all of Mexico, and many Americans resented Mexico's unwillingness to share liability with the United States for Indian depredations deep inside Mexico. Also because of the California Gold Rush in 1849, thousands of Americans were competing with Mexicans, Latin Americans, and other foreigners such as the Chinese to get to the gold fields as quickly as possible. Americans from the East Coast would have to journey by foot across the Isthmus of Tehuantepec in southern Mexico and then try to catch ships on the Pacific side headed for California. Anglos in Mexico were either harassed or denied permission to land in Mexico.

The California Gold Rush also encouraged the United States to build railroads that could facilitate quicker cross-county travel to California either across the Plains or through the South-west. One ideal route for a railroad was across land south of the Gila River that still belonged to Mexico.

James Gadsden went to Mexico in 1853 to settle the disputed boundary, resolve other loose ends, and purchase the land in the Mesilla Valley that would fill out the contiguous territory that makes up the lower forty-eight states.

Samora and Simon summarize the significance of the Gadsden Purchase in relation to the Treaty of Guadalupe Hidalgo:

▩ "It was, in essence, a renegotiation of the Treaty of Guadalupe Hidalgo."

▩ It established the right of Americans to cross the Isthmus of Tehuantepec.

▩ It led to the resumption of trade between Mexico and the United States.

▩ It amended the Treaty of Guadalupe Hidalgo by reaffirming the civil rights of the Mexicans who accepted U.S. citizenship and "pledged the United States to guarantee their land titles" (Samora and Simon, p. 105).

- It reduced the payment due to Mexico for its ceded territory from $15 million to $10 million.

- Santa Anna, who had been returned to power, was forced to accept the version of the Gadsden Purchase Agreement that the U.S. Senate ratified with modifications of a few of Gadsden's provisions because Mexico was so in need of money and the risk of another war with the Americans would have been far too costly.

- The United States was able to degrade Mexico to the level of a "conquered, ineffective nation" and to deny its own Mexican citizens full citizenship or their treaty rights under Guadalupe Hidalgo in the context of rapid Anglo penetration and development of the Southwest in the areas of agriculture, ranching, cattle raising, mining and the extraction of minerals and precious metals, railroad construction, and the linking of Mexico's political economy to that of the interests of the Anglo leaders of the Southwest and the nation as a whole.

Results of the Annexation of Mexican Land after 1848

Space limitations prevent me from fully exploring the nature of the Anglo takeover of the Southwest and just how Mexican Americans lost their social, cultural, political, and property rights and became both a numerical minority on land that had been theirs and that the U.S. government had promised to protect from the purveyors of violence, racism, vigilante justice, and other unconstitutional abuses.

For fuller explication of Chicano oppression throughout the Southwest, see part I of Acuña's "The Conquest and Colonization of the Southwest" (pp. 1–133); Samora and Simon, "The New Southwest" (pp. 107–118); Manuel G. Gonzales, "The American Southwest 1848–1900" (pp. 82–112); and John R. Chávez, "The Lost Land" (pp. 43–62). Tomás Almaguer argues that the development and stabilization of American capitalism could not have occurred independently of ". . . the 'annexation' of the land and natural resources of Northern Mexico and the proletarianism of an exploitable Mexican labor force" (Almaguer, 1974, p. 41).

Almaguer makes four principal points about Chicano oppression and capitalist development:

- The use of Chicano labor greatly contributed to the concentration and accumulation of capital needed to transform the Southwest from a relatively undeveloped area into an "agricultural oasis." Chicano surplus-value led to the creation of the "agricultural base that enabled advanced capitalism to grow (p. 41).

- Chicano labor and technical skills provided for the development of the mining and railroad industry. "Both of these sectors were crucial components of the mineral-transport-communications' infrastructural base needed for future industrialization and modernization of the area" (p. 41).

- Chicanos were forced into a largely mobile and seasonal workforce that served as a reserve army of labor. When there was a need for intense labor, Chicanos could be actively recruited to work in agriculture, mining, the livestock industry, or on the railroads. This process of intense manual labor exploitation that helped build monopoly capitalism at the end of the nineteenth century was often reduced in the twentieth century through deportation, repatriation, or large-scale disemployment of the surplus labor force.

- Chicano workers and the Chicano community have played the role of "shock absorber," to use Robert Allen's word, ". . . Any social or economic crisis that this society produces is generally felt most strongly and 'absorbed' by Third World people within the United States" (pp. 41–42).

Porfirio Díaz and Mexico's Political Economy

At the time that the United States was divided by the Civil War (1861–1865), the French intervened in Mexico (1861–1867), which prevented the rapid modernization of Mexico.

In 1876 Profirio Díaz gained power in Mexico. Some modernization had begun to occur prior to the French invasion, and Díaz established policies ". . . which encouraged the industrialization of agriculture, mining, and transportation, which led to the uprooting of the Mexican peasants, many of whom moved northward" (Acuña, p.147). The modernization of Mexico was largely financed by foreign capital investment.

The processes that began to transform the Mexican economy were fueled by demographic shifts, foreign investment, displacement of poor peasants from rural villages to urban areas, and the possibility of linking Mexico's economy to the development of the American Southwest, which needed cheap labor in the late nineteenth century and in the first one-third of the twentieth century.

Rodolfo Acuña documents some of the changes that took place in Mexico:

The importance of the railroads cannot be overemphasized. As in the case of the Southwest, they united the area internally and they linked the country with the United States. Railroads accelerated the nation's industrial and agricultural growth. They stimulated the flow of capital into the economy, increasing the possibility of commerce and exploitation of Mexico's resources. The decline of ruralism and the uprooting of the Mexican peasant would be a prime factor in Mexican migration to the United States.

(Acuña, 1988, p. 147)

Acuña also indicates that peasants were uprooted as a result of industrialization due either to mechanization or because they could move into better paying jobs ". . . on railroad construction crews, in the mines of northern Mexico, or in the nascent urban industries" (Acuña, p. 147).

By the year 1900 and at the time of the 1910 Mexican Revolution, conditions in Mexico were rapidly deteriorating for the poor masses who were most negatively affected by the impact of changes brought about by massive investment of the U.S. and European capital.

According to the Mexican historian Victor Alba, whom Acuña quotes:

. . . U.S. corporations owned three-quarters of mineral holdings in Mexico. . . . by 1910, "U.S. investment amounted to more than $2 billion, more than all the capital in the hands of Mexicans." According to Alba, the Díaz government gave foreign investors preferential treatment.

(Acuña, 1988, p. 147)

The importance of Mexico for the twentieth-century Chicano experience cannot be overemphasized. Modernization, foreign capital investment, economic and social injustices in the mills, mines, and railroads were also evident in the other industries in the countryside.

The masses in Mexico were oppressed by the policies of Díaz and by the practices of foreign or rich Mexican managers, landholders, industrialists, and bosses.

Modernization had improved communication through an increase in newspapers, easier transportation, and concentration of workers in urban areas and company towns. The improved communication network facilitated the spread of knowledge of these injustices throughout urban centers and rural areas.

(Acuña, 1988, p. 149)

It is no wonder, then, that the exploitation of Mexicans inside Mexico and the sense of injustice that led to the 1910 Revolution would come to also radically change the demography of the American Southwest, intensify the process of immigration, create an unrelenting border problem, produce masses of cheap labor for southwestern agribusiness and midwestern farms and factories, and ultimately strengthen Mexican and Mexican American culture, political consciousness, labor organizing and protest, and the resolve of three important groups of Mexicans—the Mexico Lindo Generation, the Mexican American Generation, and the Chicano Generation.

When W. E. B. DuBois prophetically summed up the meaning of the twentieth century for Blacks as "the problem of the color line," he succinctly evaluated the African American struggle to overcome slavery, segregation, and racism.

Perhaps one can paraphrase DuBois to capture the problematic nature of Mexican and Chicano experience in the twentieth century by saying: "the problem of the twentieth century is the problem of the border."

At the time of the Mexican Revolution in 1910, U.S. capitalism and powerful forces in Mexican society had brought about a massive concentration of wealth and had created such disparities of wealth and poverty inside Mexico that massive migration from rural areas to urban areas, from the interior of Mexico to the north, and from the north of Mexico to the U.S. Southwest and beyond, was inevitable.

What began at the time of the Mexican Revolution as the beginning of the expansion of monopoly capitalism and U.S. imperialism into Mexico, Latin America, the Caribbean, and the Pacific, had by the 1980s resulted in a new form of oppression of primarily low-paid Mexicanas under the **Border Industrial Program.** The BIP or, more commonly used, **maquiladora** involves the development of factories along the Mexican side of the U.S. border where foreign countries, or Mexico itself, can establish plants that assemble everything from electronic devices to automobiles.

The problem of the border, immigration, and cheap labor inside Mexico and in the United States itself relates to U.S. capitalism and racism. I want to quote Rudy Acuña, for the impact of capitalism at the time of the Mexican Revolution, and Gilbert G. Gonzalez and Raul A. Fernandez to show the ongoing oppression of Mexican labor in the northern maquilas into the twenty-first century during the era of globalization of capitalism and the impact of the regional domination of the United States over Mexico and Latin America as a result of NAFTA and more recent western hemispheric agreements.

According to Acuña, by 1910:

. . . foreign investors controlled 76 percent of all corporation, 95 percent of mining, 89 percent of industry, 100 percent of oil, and 96 percent of agriculture. The United States owned 38 percent of this investment, Britain 29 percent, and France 27 percent . . . Anglo-Americans alone owned over $100 million in the state of Chihuahua. In contrast, 97.1 percent of families in Guanajuato were without land, 96.2 percent in Jalisco, 99.5 percent in Mexico (state), and 99.3 percent in Puebla.

(Acuña, 1988, pp. 149–150)

In 1900, the official number of Mexican immigrants was 103,000, and Acuña believes that the 1910 figure of 220,000 Mexican immigrants to the United States is far below the figure of 500,000 that some experts estimate to be more realistic (Acuña, p. 150).

The Border Industrial Program began in 1967:

. . . Mexico took a giant step in the complete abdication of its economic sovereignty when it established the Border Industrial Program along its Northern border. This program began the transformation of the entire area into a gigantic assembly operation. . . . Mexico has become dependent on its maquilas, which do not solve its unemployment problems nor allow the country to become self-sufficient, developed, and modern.

The maquiladoras turned Mexico's Northern border into an enclave with few links to the rest of the economy. Into the border area followed duty-free manufacturing inputs to be assembled into final products, using cheap labor for entry into the United States or export to other countries. The Northern tier of Mexico became a direct appendage of U.S. manufacturing, replicating the examples of railroads and mining in the Mexican economy during the early 1900s.

(Gonzalez and Fernandez, 2003, pp. 52–53)

In the nineteenth century the ideology of Manifest Destiny and America's racism toward Indians and Mexicans justified genocide and the incorporation of half of Mexico's territory into the United States. Perhaps 80,000 Mexicans accepted U.S. citizenship and learned that America's promises through the ratification of the Treaty of Guadalupe Hidalgo were just as easily violated as the 371 treaties through which the United States removed and killed Indians as a prelude to the peace policy by which Indians were confined to reservations and subjected to forced assimilation and further loss of land by the politicians and the "friends of the Indians" back East.

By the turn of the twentieth century, Mexicans in the Southwest were internally colonized and had become a part of the capitalist machinery that transformed the industries, agriculture, and economy of the Southwest.

Capitalism profited on both sides of the border and continued to marginalize Chicanos and Mexicans—until by 1910, a violent revolution again pushed thousands of Mexicans into the United States, where their presence as cheap labor would be welcomed in times of shortage, even as they were segregated in colonias and barrios, racially degraded, their children condemned to racist labeling and inferior educations, and countless families relegated to following the crops that needed planting and harvesting for the dinner tables of Anglos who detested Mexicans, but could not live comfortably in America without them.

Throughout the twentieth century, Chicanos have been exploited for their labor, deported and repatriated when they were not wanted, only to be welcomed as braceros, kicked out as wetbacks, condemned as illegal immigrants, and loved and hated for their patriotism, their valor under fire, their hard work, their laziness, their faith in overcoming adversity, their fatalism in accepting adversity, and their lives of virtue and their lives of vice and crime.

The Chicano in the twentieth century has indeed been a victim of the border, of immigration policies, of capitalism, and of racism.

The cycle of oppression that created the mestizo from the Indio and the Chicano from the Mexican, and the Hispanic from the ambiguity of being American or being afraid to be a Chicano in America, continues into the twentieth and twenty-first centuries.

The problem of the twentieth century for Chicanos is the problem of the border. Is it any wonder, in the context of anti-immigrant bashing and taunts by racists who tell raza to "go back where you came from, if you hate this country so much!" that Mexicanos and Chicanos are often heard to say: "We didn't cross the border, the border crossed us!"

The Chicano in the Twentieth Century

Rather than writing a detailed description of the Mexicano-Chicano experience in the twentieth century, I will highlight important dates and key events that are fully documented in the various sources I have cited in this chapter.

Date	Events of Importance
1900–1930	Major U.S. development of the Southwest's agriculture and related industries. Need for cheap agricultural labor. Mexicans also migrated to the Midwest and North to find factory jobs and to follow the crops.
1900–1940	Mexicans-Chicanos were heavily involved in labor organizing, protests, strikes, and mutual aid associations.
1924	United States Border Patrol is established.
1929	LULAC—League of United Latin American Citizens—is formed in Corpus Christi, Texas.
1929–1939	The Great Depression in the United States, era of massive repatriation of Mexican and Mexican-American citizens to Mexico—60 percent were U.S. citizens.

1941–1945	Mexican Americans distinguish themselves in terms of bravery during World War II.
1942	The internment of 110,000 West Coast Japanese Americans in ten concentration camps around the country. The United States and the Mexican government sign the agreement that allows Mexican seasonal farmworkers to enter the country under the Bracero Program.
1942–1943	Anti-Mexican violence and racism occur in two incidents in Southern California: August 1942: the **Sleepy Lagoon Case** (see Eduardo Obregón Pagán) and Spring-June 1943: the **Zoot-Suit Riots**—attacks against Pachucos by racist soldiers and sailors (see Pagán and Mauricio Mazón)
1947	In December, the Bracero Program formally ended, but the United States became concerned about the smuggling of Mexican workers across the border.
1948	The Community Service Organization is founded in Los Angeles. The American G.I. Forum is founded in Texas.
1950s–1970s	Rodolfo "Corky" Gonzales was a Golden Gloves Boxer and a political organizer in Denver, Colorado. He was active in the Viva Kennedy Clubs and in mainstream city politics. He became a militant activist on behalf of youth, students, gang members, and Chicanos in prison. He organized the Crusade for Justice, the first National Chicano Youth Conference in 1968, wrote the Chicano epic poem: **"I Am Joaquin,"** and was active in La Raza Unida Party politics along with Reies Lopez Tijerina and José Angel Gutierrez.
1951	The United States and Mexico jointly accept a Migratory Labor Agreement known as the Public Law 78, which is the basis for the New Bracero Program that remains in place until 1964.
1954	Implementation of Operation Wetback, in which 1,075,000 so-called illegal immigrants were rounded up and sent back to Mexico. The civil rights and human rights of the deportees and their families were callously ignored.
1959	Bert Corona, Eduard Roybal, and Eduardo Quevedo found The Mexican American Political Association (MAPA) in Fresno, California.
1960	The Political Association of Spanish Speaking Organizations (PASSO) is established.
1960s–1975	The modern Chicano movement.
1963	Reies López Tijerina founds **La Alianza** Federal de los Mercedes. He struggles in New Mexico to try to challenge the illegal violation of Spanish and Mexican land grants as protected under the Treaty of Guadalupe Hidalgo. In 1967 the organization's name is changed to La Alianza Federal de Pueblos Libres. During the 1960s, Tijerina's activism includes the occupation of the Kit Carson National Forest and the Courthouse Raid in the town of Tierra Amarillo.
1963–1993	United Farm Workers Organizing Committee.

1965	Congress passes the Immigration Reform Act, which becomes effective in 1968.
1965–1993	César Chavez forms the United Farm Workers organizing committee, which becomes the United Farmworkers Union. He led the Delano to Sacramento March, the Grape and Lettuce Boycotts, and countless other strikes, boycotts, marches, organizing efforts, fasts, and efforts to expose the dangers of pesticides to farmworkers, pregnant women, and babies and children. Dolores Huerta has been involved in these and countless struggles on behalf of farmworkers and labor organizing for decades. Chavéz died on April 23, 1993.
1966	Mexican American Student Association (MASA) founded at East Los Angeles College.
1967	José Angel Guitérrez and Mario Compean found the Mexican American Youth Organization (MAYO). United Mexican American Students (UMAS) is founded out of Loyola University. Brown Berets founded in East L.A.
1968	Beginning of the Chicano **school "blow-outs" in East Los Angeles** to protest racist curriculum, teachers, and treatment. UMAS provides leadership in the high school "blow outs."
	Mexican American Legal Defense and Educational Fund (MALDEF) is founded.
	Mexican American Student Confederation (MASC) is founded.
1969	The University of California, **Santa Barbara Conference** takes place. The event was instrumental in creating a Chicano Plan for Higher Education, strategies for implementing Chicano studies and support for Chicano students on college and university campuses, and the establishment of MEChA (Movimiento Estudiantíl Chicano de Aztlán).
1970	José Angel Gutiérrez founds the Raza Unida Party as an alternative to mainstream politics.
	Catolicos por La Raza is organized to protest abuses and the insensitivity of the Catholic Church in predominantly Mexican American parishes where priests failed to meet the needs of raza.
1970	August 29—The **Chicano Moratorium** against the Vietnam War. At least 20,000 Chicanos come together to hear leaders and activists speak out against the Vietnam War and the disproportionate numbers of Chicanos dying on the front lines or given the most dangerous duty. The peaceful march and protest was turned into a violent police riot that led to the killing of two Chicano Brown Berets, and the journalist Ruben Salázar in the Silver Dollar Bar after the police fired a tear gas canister into the bar and refused to get Salázar prompt treatment or transport to a hospital.

1980s	Issues of **illegal immigration** take center stage along with a right-wing political backlash.
	"English only" movement and opposition to bilingual education. The support of the Reagan–Bush administration of right-wing repression and death squads in Guatemala and El Salvador leads to a major influx of Central American refugees to the United States. Many are labeled "economic refugees" despite the real violence they or their families face. Activists organize to show support and solidarity with the people of Central America, and the sanctuary movement helps to shelter and hide "political refugees" from the INS and Border Patrol who would have them arrested, detained, and deported.
	Strong interest in liberation theology throughout Latin America and the radical educational philosophy of Paulo Freire.
	The 1985 Simson–Mazzoli Bill attempts to halt illegal immigration by imposing civil and criminal penalties on employers.
1990s	Anti-immigrant sentiment—**Proposition 187**
	Anti–bilingual education—**Proposition 227**
	Anti–affirmative action—**Proposition 209**
	Anti–Chicano and minority youth—**Proposition 21**
	Massive building of new prisons, three strikes legislation, and special prosecution of gang members to enhance sentencing in penalty phase of trials—all while the state of California has a major educational crisis. Latino/Hispanic empowerment and greater visibility in mainstream culture. Recognition of Latinos in music, drama, television, and movies, concerns about negative stereotypes about raza due to overemphasis in news and racist websites about immigration, illegal drugs, and the border. The NAFTA issue passes in November 1993 and the Zapatista movement in Chiapas comes to the world's attention on January 1, 1994. The Elian Gonzalez affair receives serious and comedic attention because of the strained relationship between the U.S. Cuban immigrant community in Florida and the dictatorship of Castro.
Present	The election of George W. Bush in 2001, the September 11, 2001, World Trade Center bombing, and the War on Terrorism and against Afghanistan and Iraq still trouble many raza due to issues about the border, U.S. security, vigilantes in Arizona who target undocumented workers, the issue of California driver's licenses for undocumented immigrants, and concerns about Mexicans and Chicanos in the right-wing climate in America.
	The racist and reactionary **Minute Man Project,** which targets "illegal aliens" and predominantly Chicano communities with vigilante tactics while claiming to be helping the Border Patrol to do its job.

Conclusion

I have deliberately and forcefully presented a Chicano perspective on the relationship between Indios in the New World, the conquest and colonization of Mexico and Latin America, the independence of Mexico from Spain, and the history of Anglo Manifest Destiny and expansion into the Southwest and the war with Mexico.

Only by exploring the double dialectic of Mestizaje and class oppression in Mexico before the Mexican–American War and the Anglo racism and capitalist expansion that gave Mexicanos citizenship in an oppressive internal colonist framework following the Treaty of Guadalupe Hidalgo is it possible to relate Mexican experience, and Chicano experience, to the political-economic and cultural realities of the Southwest under Anglo domination and control.

The Chicano worldview does not separate past history from the present conditions of oppression. Chicanos will accept social progress but only in the context of the collective struggles of raza, not in order to achieve individual success to the exclusion of social justice. Colonialism is a reality, as is the need to preserve the integrity of cultural heritage, familia, identity, and the fulfillment of *Chicanismo*. A Chicano perspective incorporates corazón, intellect, and the spirit in a synthesis that balances collective and individual identity, the knowledge of tradition against the needs of the future, and the unity of theory and praxis for the need to grasp and act in the present moment. *Si se puede!* In unity there is strength!

Questions, Exercises, and Topics for Discussion and Debate

1) Briefly discuss the conquest of the Aztecs by Cortez. What type of society did the Spaniards observe? Who was Doña Marina and what role did she play in the conquest? What is meant by the term *Mestizaje,* and what role does this concept play in the Chicano experience? What does the term *Aztlán* mean, and why is it important for Chicanos and in the development of Chicano movement?

2) In 1810 to 1821, Mexico fought for and gained independence from Spain. Explain how Mexico and the United States interacted from the time of Independence through the Mexican–American War of 1846–1848.
   a) What was the Texas revolt?

   b) What was the significance of the victory by Santa Anna at the Alamo and his subsequent defeat by Sam Houston at the Battle of San Jacinto?

   c) What is Manifest Destiny, and how did this belief contribute to U.S. expansion and imperialism against Mexico?

   d) What was the Lone Star Republic?

   e) Why is the 1846–1848 Mexican–American War important in Chicano history?

3) Explain in detail the Treaty of Guadalupe Hidalgo, which was ratified on February 2, 1848.
   a) Why is this treaty important and pivotal for Chicano history?

   b) What were the key provisions of the treaty, and how did they impact Mexicans living on the U.S. side of the border?

   c) Discuss the reasons for and the results of the 1853 Gadsden Purchase.

4) Between 1848 and 1900, Mexican labor became a critical factor in the development of the Southwest, and Mexicans faced oppression and internal colonization.
   a) What role did Mexican labor play in the Southwest?

   b) What impact did the California Gold Rush have with regard to the subordination of Mexicans and racial minorities in California?

   c) Who was Porfiio Díaz, and what impact did his policies in Mexico have upon Mexican peasants, migration of Mexicans into the United States, and capitalist investments in Mexico by foreign countries?

5) Following the 1910 Mexican Revolution, Mexican migration, labor, and the border became critical issues in twentieth century America.
   a) Why did Mexican immigration increase after the Revolution, and why was Mexican labor so essential during World War I?

   b) Discuss the creation of the U.S. Border Patrol.

   c) Did Mexican laborers in the Southwest experience economic and political equality with White workers? Explain.

   d) What were mutual aid societies, and what role did they play in Mexican American communities?

6) There has been a constant tendency in U.S. history under capitalism to welcome cheap or low-cost labor in times of need, but to restrict migration or cheap labor when that labor is a threat to White jobs and employment.
   a) Discuss the repatriation of Mexican and Mexican American people during the Depression years.

   b) During World War II and after the war, the United States negotiated with the government of Mexico to allow seasonal workers into the country. Discuss the Bracero Program that began in 1942 and concluded in 1964.

   c) What was "Operation Wetback"?

Name _____ *Date* _____

Questions, Exercises, and Topics for Discussion and Debate (continued)

7) The period following the Mexican Revolution brought many immigrants to the United States who struggled to make a living and raise their families. But in their hearts, these migrants still longed for Mexico and looked fondly upon their roots and culture. Following the Mexico Lindo Generation of the 1920s, many Mexican Americans sought respectability and acceptance into the dominant society.

a) What was the Mexican American Generation?

b) What is LULAC and what were its organizational goals?

c) Young Mexican Americans during World War II struggled between their identities as Mexicans and their place in U.S. society. Who were the Pachucos?

d) Discuss the Sleepy Lagoon Case and the Zoot-Suit Riots.

8) Prior to the *Brown v. Board of Education* decision of 1954, there was an important precedent set that involved Mexican Americans. Research and discuss the **Westminster v. Mendez** case and its significance for Chicano education.

9) By the late 1950s throughout the Southwest, as a result of Mexican American involvement in World War II and the Korean War and the rising up of raza, a new working-class insurgency and an activist consciousness began to percolate through the colonias and barrios of Aztlán.

a) What is meant by the Chicano Generation?

b) What does the term *Chicano* imply?

c) What is Chicanismo?

d) Discuss the Chicano movement in terms of listing key leaders, organizations, and significant events.

10) In what ways do you think that the East L.A. school blow-outs were important in generating Chicano consciousness and community activism? Explain.

11) Chicanos and Mexican Americans have played a significant role in agricultural labor—particularly in California, Texas, and the states of the Pacific Northwest and the Midwest. Yet, they were degraded, stereotyped, and exploited.
   a) Discuss the life and activism of César Chavez as a labor organizer and as an icon of the Chicano movement.

   b) What was the significance of the Delano-to-Sacramento March?

   c) Who is Dolores Huerta, and what was her contribution to the UFW union and the labor movement and other progressive causes?

12) Research Reies Lopez Tijerina and his contributions to the Chicano movement—particularly in Arizona and New Mexico in relation to the Spanish land grants and the Treaty of Guadalupe Hidalgo.

13) Education, community, and organizing are important components of the Chicano struggle for political empowerment and the creation of Chicano studies.
   a) Discuss the role of the blow-outs for Mexican American high school students.

   b) What was the significance of the 1968 Santa Barbara Conference, and how did **El Plan de Santa Barbara** contribute to the establishment of MEChA and Chicano studies?

   c) Who was Rodolfo "Corky" Gonzales and why was he such a significant force in the Chicano movement?

   d) Discuss the evolution of Corky Gonzales from Golden Gloves boxer to city politics and Chicano activist and revolutionary. What was the Chicano Youth Conference and the Crusade for Justice?

   e) Why is the poem "I Am Joaquín" relevant to Chicanos?

Questions, Exercises, and Topics for Discussion and Debate (continued)

14) Discuss the rise and contributions of José Angel Gutiérrez in Cristal City, Texas, and as the founder of the organization MAYO and the Raza Unida Party.

15) What is the significance of August 29, 1970, for the Chicano movement? Who was Ruben Salázar and how and why did he die?

16) The Chicano movement challenged both the racist institutions and practices of Anglos as well as the complacency of Mexican American accommodationists. But in time the movement was weakened from within and there was reactionary resistance from the mid-1970s to the present. Discuss the following topics:
   a) David Sanchez and the Brown Berets
   b) Religion, the Virgen de Guadalupe, and Católicos Por La Raza
   c) Chicano machismo and the rise of Chicana feminism
   d) The sanctuary movement of the 1980s
   e) The role of maquiladoras and the Border Industrial Program inside Mexico
   f) The Simpson–Mazzoli Bill, racism against Mexican immigrants, Proposition 187, and the Minute Man Project and militarization of the U.S. Mexican Border
   g) English-only education and Proposition 227
   h) Anti–affirmative action and Proposition 209

17) What is the **Hispanic Generation?** Has the Chicano Generation ended? Explain.

Asian Americans

Chapter Ten

Key Terms

Alien Land Bill

Asians as middle man minorities

Asians as perpetual foreigners

boat people

Chinese Americans

Chinese Exclusion Act

East Indian Americans

Executive Order 9066

Filipino Americans

Gentleman's Agreement

Immigration Act of 1924

Immigration Reform Act

Japanese Americans

Japanese internment

"Killing Fields" of Cambodia

Korean Americans

Korean–Black conflict

model minority

outsourcing of labor

Pearl Harbor attack

picture brides

South Asian brain drain

stereotypes of Asians

sweat shop workers

Tydings–McDuffie Act

Vietnamese Americans

Vietnam War

Vincent Chin case

yellow peril

Key Lesson

The history of Asia extends back thousand of years and encompasses the languages, cultures, religions, and civilizational contributions of many peoples from diverse societies and nations.

Contact between the peoples of Europe, the Mediterranean world, and the Far East developed as a result of exploration and travel, long-distance trade, colonization, strategic military considerations, the search for inexpensive and contract labor, and the globalization and expansion of Western markets to distant shores.

European expansion into the New World and the subsequent history of the United States drew Asians into the Americas, particularly after the 1840s when Chinese laborers began migrating to California in search of better fortune in the goldfields than they were experiencing under the rulers of the Qing Dynasty or local warlords.

The history of Asians in America can best be analyzed by examining the voluntary migrations of Chinese, Japanese, and Filipino laborers or the recruitment of contract laborers in Hawaii and other parts of the world from the late 1840s through the first third of the twentieth century. **Chinese Americans** were exploited as a source of cheap labor in menial work, on the transcontinental railroad, and in the emerging Chinatowns of the West Coast, as well as strikebreakers on the East Coast and farmworkers in the deep South following the Civil War. Wherever they were, Chinese Americans were viewed as a danger to White free labor and as a cultural threat to the White civilization of the United States. Thus, they were exploited, segregated, scapegoated, and finally excluded from immigration. A disproportionately male bachelor society precluded a dynamic of holistic growth and development for many decades.

Every time one Asian group was successfully excluded through the efforts of nativist interest groups, racist politicians, biased newspapers, discriminatory legislation, and horrific court decisions and precedents, a new wave of immigrants would find their way to American and Hawaiian shores to fulfill their role as plantation laborers, menial workers, or scapegoats. **Japanese Americans** were also subjected to racism, restriction due to their success in truck farming and agriculture, and legislative exclusion in 1924 following legislation such as the 1913 **Alien Land Bill.** But the strength of Japan as an emerging twentieth century power led to the **Gentleman's Agreement of 1907–1908,** and the legal importation of **picture brides** until that practice was banned in 1920 at least allowed a more balanced sex ratio and the development of Japanese families and communities.

The arrival of Filipinos, initially as students, but then as a third wave of contract laborers and workers for Hawaiian plantations and West Coast farmworkers, also resulted in their subordination. The racist war against the Philippines, with its genocidal and exterminationist tactics, resembled American frontier warfare against her own native populations far more than a battle to extend freedom and democracy to "the little Brown brothers" of the Philippines. Only a loophole in the 1934 **Tydings–McDuffie Act,** which allowed fifty Filipinos a year to enter the United States because the Philippines were a territorial possession, placed a thin veneer over America's efforts to completely prevent Asian immigration or rights of citizenship in Hawaii or on U.S. soil.

The major presence of other Asian ethnic nationals in the United States in a few instances reaches back to the early twentieth century, but for the most part occurred in the post–World War II era and specifically in the post-1965 period following the **Immigration Reform Act,** which brought greater equity between immigration quotas for western and eastern hemispheric countries. Also, the dividing of North and South Korea, North and South Vietnam, and the post-1947 partitioning of Muslims and Hindus in India and East and West Pakistan all impacted the politics of Southeast and Southern Asia during the era of the cold war.

From World War II to the present, the dynamic between the United States and Asia reflects changes in international racial and political economic realities in the reorganized global system of capitalism. The Japanese were imperialist aggressors in Asia and the Pacific, especially following the December 7, 1941, attack on Pearl Harbor. The 110,000 mainland Japanese Americans were relocated and interned in concentration camps, and at war's end, America dropped atomic bombs over Hiroshima and Nagasaki, which ended World War II but also ushered in the cold war, the nuclear age, and the longstanding fear of World War III and the superpower madness and competition between the United States, the Soviet Union, and communist China.

Because of shifting alliances during and after World War II, Chinese exclusion ended in 1943 and the Japanese internment camps were closed by 1946. Japan was able to develop her economy and technology because the United States had occupied Okinawa and the Japanese were not responsible for their own military defense. New organizations such as the United Nations, the World Bank, and the International Monetary Fund were created to help the European nations to be reconstructed as well as to regulate and oversee emerging relations between former colonial powers and the newly independent countries that represented the nonaligned nations or the developing nations of the third world.

New political alignments and conflicts occurred in conjunction with moral, political, and economic migrations and population movements. The United States fought the Viet Cong and North Vietnam for eight long years but could not prevail in Vietnam—thus, the hasty and highly visible helicopter evacuations of American and South Vietnamese officials and people who desperately sought escape after the April 30, 1975, fall of Saigon. Later came the first and second waves of Vietnamese and Indochina people to refugee camps, resettlement stations, and absorption into the languages, cultures, and lifestyles of new host countries—whether in the United States, Australia, Canada, or other places in the world.

There were the **"Killing Fields" of Cambodia,** the **"boat people,"** the politics of the CIA and local tribal people in Laos or Thailand, which had such a devastating impact on the international drug trade and the secret wars of the United States to prop up dictators or clandestinely overthrow foes.

By the 1970s and beyond, South Koreans, Filipinos, and Asian Indians migrated in unprecedented numbers to various areas of the United States. The rising competition between Japan's economy and the United States—especially when Detroit's automobile industry could no longer monopolize the sale of large gas-guzzling cars following the oil crisis in the 1970s—led to strong anti-Japanese sentiment in the 1980s as Americans reacted to Japan's capitalist success, new management styles, and international investment and acquisitions outside of Japan.

The resulting racism was felt in the United States in 1982 with the killing of **Vincent Chin,** who was beaten to death by Whites who argued with him because they had mistakenly believed he was Japanese. Only strong and vigorous protest by Asian activists kept the offensiveness of the killing from being swept under the carpet of American racism as usual. Clearly, despite Asian American struggles in the 1960s and beyond for recognition, Asian American studies in universities, for compensation and reparations for the wrongs of the World War II internment, and the loss of dignity and millions of dollars in property and possessions, the United States could not, or would not, take Asian American assertiveness seriously.

The United States supported the dictatorship and martial law in the Philippines of Ferdinand Marcos because the islands had strategic military bases. The United States nurtured the notion of Asian Americans as a **model minority** representing the best of racial minorities who, despite obvious histories of oppression, exploitation, and racism from government and U.S. citizens, had quietly assimilated, found their place (often as entrepreneurs and **middle man minorities**), and were well on their way to fulfilling the American Dream.

Compared to the highly visible Black, Indian, and Chicano activist and nationalist movements, the ghetto rebellions, barrio protests, and Indian activism from Alcatraz to Minneapolis, and the Trail of Broken Treaties and BIA building takeover, to the occupation of Pine Ridge, and other American Indian movement campaigns—the Japanese, Chinese, Filipino, Korean, East Indian, Indochinese, and Vietnamese seemed to be ideal exemplars of what many paternalistic Anglo Americans felt was the appropriate response that "grateful" minorities should display for America's long-term historical welcome and generosity toward her Asian immigrants.

The model minority myth was a useful political weapon through which conservative politicians could shield themselves against charges of racism, while they chastised militant Blacks, Chicanos, Puerto Ricans, and Indians for not emulating the "overachieving" and "whiz kid" Asians who succeeded educationally and overcame language barriers in order to suffer their own discrimination. Underachieving African Americans, Latino, and Indian students were able to enter college through affirmative action programs, while Asian Americans were held down in spite of their grades and SAT scores, so that Whites would not become statistical minorities on some prestigious multiracial campuses.

Asian Americans were also stereotyped as **perpetual foreigners** regardless of the number of generations they and their families had lived in America and even if they had no knowledge of their ancestral culture, language, or religion. Other stereotypes persisted in the movies and new images came out of the martial arts films that were cheaply produced in Asian markets such as Hong Kong and poorly dubbed into English. Controversy even followed the rise of Bruce Lee's action films such as *Enter the Dragon* and the highly successful television series "Kung Fu," which starred David Carradine.

In the late 1980s and early 1990s, conflict between **Korean-American** grocers and small business owners of liquor stores in predominantly Black communities led to boycotts, marches, violence, and retribution as Koreans failed to trust or understand Black patrons who entered their stores, while angry African Americans accused Asians of racism for following them around in their stores, not looking them in the eye, or putting change on the counter instead of in their hands. These behaviors, which Korean store owners did not intend as racist from their cultural norms, coupled with actual hostility and unfortunate shootings—particularly the Latasha Harlins case in Los Angeles—led to serious **Korean–Black conflict** following the April 30, 1992, L.A. uprising in response to the acquittal of the four Los Angeles police officers in the Rodney King beating trial.

The other major issues that affect Asians in America and throughout the world have to do with the oppression of garment laborers and **sweat shop workers** in the United States and many Asian nations such as India, Bangladesh, the Philippines, and Indonesia. Many South Asian Indian middle-class and professional workers and technicians came to the United States in the 1950s and 1960s in what was termed the **"South Asian brain drain,"** and in the increasingly global economy of the new century, the **outsourcing of labor** and jobs—that are costly in America due to union wages—has been shifted to India, China, the Philippines, and other areas where there is a tremendous competition to qualify for positions by middle-class and educated individuals, or among the poor for unskilled labor similar to the kind many young girls and even children perform in maquiladoras in Latin America to produce materials for corporations who will do almost anything to keep tight or unconscionable profit margins from slipping at home or around the world.

Notable Quotes

The presence of Asians on America soil highlighted some fundamental cleavages in American society. This fact makes Asian immigration history more important than the small numbers of Asians in the United States might otherwise warrant. During the first period of their migration, vested interests that stood to gain by their labor promoted their influx, while other groups threatened by their coming strove to exclude them. But both those who wanted them and those who did not agreed on one point: like the indigenous population of Hawaii, Alaska, and the continental United States pushed aside by Euro-Americans who desired their land, like Africans enslaved and condemned to hard labor in the New World, like Mexicans conquered and subjugated, Asians were deemed members of "inferior races." Negative perceptions of nonwhite peoples have a long history in the Western World. Color prejudice has become such a habit of heart and mind among Euro-Americans by the time Asians started coming that the former had no difficulty justifying hostile actions that culminated in efforts to expel Asians from some parts of the United States as well as to prevent them from entering the country altogether.

(Chan, 1991, p. 45)

In the late 1870s, the anti-Chinese "Yellow Peril" movement gripped the West. Cities erupted in riots against the Chinese—homes, laundries, and shops were burned to the ground. Murders and lynchings of Chinese were commonplace. Chinese women—the very small numbers who were admitted to the United States—were molested by angry gangs of whites. In rural areas, white farm workers set fire to the barns and fields where Chinese lived and worked. These egregious acts established a particular brand of American racism that would be directed against Asian Americans into the next century.

(Zia, 2000, p. 27)

Hostility against Asian immigrants may be divided into seven categories; prejudice, economic discrimination, political disenfranchisement, physical violence, immigration exclusion, social segregation, and incarceration.

(Chan, 1991, p. 45)

By the turn of the century, Asian immigrants were represented as the yellow peril, a threat to nation, race, and family. The acquisition of territories and colonies brought with it a renewed threat of "Asiatic" immigration, an invasion of "yellow men" and "little brown brothers." At the moment when the United States prepared to pick up "the white man's burden" in the Caribbean and the Pacific, "Asian immigration" was said to pose "the greatest threat to Western Civilization and the White Race." . . . Through its supposed subversion of the family, the yellow peril threatened to undermine what Lothrop Stoddard, a popular advocate of eugenics and racial geopolitics, called the "inner dikes" of the white race.

(Lee, 1999, p. 10)

Stereotypes of Asian immigrants as plodding, degraded, and servile people—indeed, virtual slaves—notwithstanding, members of every Asian immigrant group did stand up for their rights and fought oppression in myriad ways. . . . Looking at the principal ways they have used to fight against their lowly status—strikes, litigation, and involvement in efforts to liberate their homelands—it is clear that the immigrants themselves realized their suffering had multiple causes. As workers they struck for higher wages and better working conditions; as nonwhite minorities "ineligible to citizenship" they challenged laws that denied them civil rights on account of their race; and as proud sons and daughters of their countries of origin, they supported political movements to free those lands from foreign encroachment.

(Chan, 1991, p. 81)

Our concentration camps were places where men, women, and children, citizen and alien, were detained. On the basis of one executive order a whole community, the West Coast Japanese, was ordered from its homes and confined without a trace of due process or even an allegation of personal guilt. Japanese Americans were all judged guilty, deprived of much of their real property, and incarcerated, some of them for more than three years, merely by reason of their ancestry.

(Daniels, 1988, p. 228)

On February 19, 1942, President Roosevelt issued Executive Order 9066, which authorized the evacuation and internment of Japanese Americans. Soon after, all Americans of Japanese descent were prohibited from living, working, or traveling on the West Coast. Families were given no more than a week to somehow dispose of all their household goods and property before moving to points unknown with only what they could carry in clothing, bedding and linen, kitchen and toilet articles, and "personal effects."

With numbered tags tied around their necks, the Japanese Americans were [packed onto buses and trains with blinds drawn down. They were sent first to racetracks and fairgrounds, which became makeshift assembly centers; they were forced to live in filthy animal stalls. There they awaited a more permanent incarceration at one of ten internment camps in the barren hinterlands of California, Idaho, Wyoming, Utah, Arizona, Colorado, and Arkansas. About half of the incarcerated were children. At the internment camps, the families were told they needed barbed wire and armed guard towers for their own protection—but the guns pointed inward. Families lived in prison-style blocks with communal latrines and showers.

(Zia, 2000, p. 42)

The representation of Asian Americans as a model minority, although popularly identified with the late 1960s and 1970s, originated in the racial logic of Cold War liberalism of the 1950s. The image of Asian Americans as a successful case of "ethnic" assimilation helped to contain three spectres that haunted Cold War America: the red menace of communism, the black menace of racial integration, and the white menace of homosexuality. In place of a radical critique calling for structural changes in American political economy, the model minority mythology substituted a narrative of national modernization and ethnic assimilation through heterosexuality, familism, and consumption. By the late 1960s, an image of "successful" Asian American assimilation could be held up to African Americans and Latinos as a model for nonmilitant, nonpolitical upward mobility.

(Lee, 1999, p. 10)

Introduction

The study of patterns of race and ethnicity in New World North American colonial and U.S. history provides the scholar with the opportunity to explore the unique experiences of peoples who are culturally diverse but have been defined as racially alike by the dominant society and its power elites.

Dominant European nation-states and their Protestant and Catholic rulers formed a unique panethnic spiritual unity in the 1400s to 1600s relative to non-Europeans based upon the community of a shared faith known as Christendom; but national, cultural, linguistic, and economic interests also divided the peoples of Europe as they fought one another over the control of territories, strategic locations, raw materials, access to the labor of others, and markets and trade. At times Europeans were unified in linking their racial heritage with their sense of cultural superiority over non-Europeans, while at other times the descendants of Western and Northern Europeans defined other European immigrants to North America as racially distinct and as culturally inferior.

The confusion over the social meanings of race, ethnicity, nationality, and culture are important for interpreting the relationships between the religious, national, and racial cultures of Europeans and their descendants and the peoples they defined as racially inferior to themselves.

Indians were and are culturally distinct, but there is a tendency to assume that they were generically alike in terms of their oppression by Whites. Africans represented diverse social, linguistic, ethnic, and regional cultures but in relation to their experiences of enslavement, the Middle Passage, and forced entry into colonial societies, are viewed as racially alike despite cultural differences of European New World colonies and societies.

Latinos can be defined as racially and ethnically diverse and yet they share exposure to Catholicism, Spanish and Portuguese languages, indigenous origins, and Caribbean and Latin American slave traditions. In the U.S. context, one can study each Latino culture as unique based upon America's diverse history with each Latino country. In this case, I chose to concentrate on the Mexican and U.S. Chicano experience because of the preeminent impact of Mexico in the Southwest and in the development of Chicano studies.

In this final chapter dealing with Asian Americans, I cannot lump the diverse groups of Asian national origins into a pan-ethnic experience that reflects similarities in the treatment of Asian Americans by Whites. The reason for this is that Asians have entered the United States at different times and have been exposed to prejudice, discrimination, and racism that varied in relation to the stage of political and economic development, as well as the relations between the United States and particular Asian nations.

Asian Americans who have assimilated into the dominant society over three or more generations and those who are the most recent immigrants must contend with prejudice, stereotypes, and the racist assumption that they are "perpetual foreigners" no matter how culturally well adjusted they may be, or because they are racially "other" and can never be truly loyal to the United States.

Finally, Asians in the United States have had to contend with the post–World War II stereotype of the "model minority." This seemingly positive notion has been used by well-meaning non-Asians to treat Asian Americans as an exceptional racial minority who do not fit the pattern of militance, protest against the racist system, or negative and dysfunctional behaviors that are commonly associated with Blacks, Latinos, and Indians during the radical era of the 1960s and 1970s.

Asian Americans have been subjected to extreme prejudice, stereotyping, discrimination, and labor exploitation as well as racist exclusion from immigration and citizenship. Then the nation's politicians, elites, and culture-makers played them off as groups to be emulated and imitated by more problematic racial populations.

In this chapter I will provide an overview of Asian American experience by discussing the nineteenth- and early-twentieth-century waves of immigration to California, the West Coast, and Hawaii; the forms of nativism and racism that Asians faced; and the difference between pre- and post-1965 Asian immigration to the United States.

I will provide a framework for understanding the generic experience of the Chinese, Japanese, Koreans, Filipinos, Vietnamese, Southeast Asians, and Asian Indians in the United States and will emphasize their experiences with discrimination and racism historically and in the present.

Sources

The field of Asian American studies has been an important outgrowth of the diverse movements of the 1960s. At colleges and universities such as San Francisco State, Cal State Los Angeles, UC Berkley, UCLA, and elite East Coast universities, Asian American studies has developed and flourished. Also, Hawaii is a location characterized by great Asian and ethnic diversity. In some academic settings, Asian American and Pacific Islanders are a combined field of study and research.

The available literature on Asians, Asian Americans, and Pacific Islanders is huge due to the number of Asian countries that have been colonized by non-Asians or from which immigrants, sojourners, contract laborers, and secondary migrants left to settle elsewhere.

The books that I have selected about Asians and Asian Americans include the following topics:

- Asian American movement
- Asian ethnic experience
- Asian Indian Americans
- Asian panethnicity
- Bangladesh politics

- ▦ "Boat people"
- ▦ Chinese Americans
- ▦ Chinese and Japanese literature
- ▦ Chinese women in San Francisco
- ▦ Contemporary Asian American politics
- ▦ Filipinos
- ▦ Hawaiian sovereignty
- ▦ Hmong in Laos and America
- ▦ Japanese internment during World War II
- ▦ Koreans in America
- ▦ Model minority
- ▦ Pacific Islands history
- ▦ Stereotypes of Asian Americans
- ▦ Vietnamese Americans
- ▦ Yellow peril

The books I have chosen on Asian Americans are listed in alphabetical order by author.

1) Alexandra Bandon

   Asian Indian Americans

2) Carlos Bulosan

   America Is in the Heart

3) Lan Cao and Himilce Novas

   Everything You Need to Know About Asian-American History

4) Nathan Caplan, John F. Whitemore, and Marcella H. Choy

   The Boat People and Achievement in America

5) Jeffrey Paul Chan, Frank Chin, Lawson Fusao Inada, and Shawn Wong (Editors)

   The Big Aiiieeeee!: An Anthology of Chinese American and Japanese American Literature

6) Sucheng Chan

   Asian Americans: An Interpretive History

7) Sucheng Chan

   Hmong Means Free: Life in Laos and America

8) Iris Chang

   The Chinese in America: A Narrative History

9) Philip P. Choy (Editor)

   The Coming Man: 19th Century American Perceptions of the Chinese

10) Roger Daniels

   Asian America: Chinese and Japanese in the United States Since 1850

11) Roger Daniels

   Prisoners Without Trial: Japanese Americans in World War II

12) Yen Le Espiritu

   Asian Panethnicity: Bridging Institutions and Identities

13) Yen Le Espiritu

   Filipino American Lives

14) Steven Roger Fischer

   A History of the Pacific Islands

15) Timothy P. Fong

   The Contemporary Asian American Experience: Beyond the Model Minority

16) James M. Freeman

   Changing Identities: Vietnamese Americans, 1975–1995

17) Jessica Tarahata Hagedorn (Editor)

   Charlie Chan Is Dead: An Anthology of Contemporary Asian American Fiction

18) Jean Wakatsuki Houston and James D. Houston

   Farewell to Manzanar

19) Nazli Kibria

   Family Tightrope: The Changing Lives of Vietnamese Americans

20) Peter Kwong

   The New Chinatown

21) Joann Faung Jean Lee

   Asian American Experiences in the United States: Oral Histories of First to Fourth Generation Americans from China, the Philippines, Japan, India, the Pacific Islands, Vietnam, and Cambodia

22) Robert G. Lee

   Orientals: Asian Americans in Popular Culture

23) Karen Isaksen Leonard

   The South Asian Immigrants

24) Lawrence Lifschultz

   Bangladesh: The Unfinished Revolution

25) Lisa Lowe

   Immigrant Acts: On Asian American Cultural Politics

26) Stanford M. Lyman

   Chinese and Japanese Americans

27) H. Brett Melendy

   Asians in America: Filipinos, Koreans, and East Indians

28) H. Brett Melendy

   Chinese and Japanese Americans

29) Victor G. Nee and Brett de Bary Nee

   Longtime Californ': A Documentary Study of an American Chinatown

30) Gary Y. Okihiro

   Margins and Mainstreams: Asians in American History and Culture

31) Vijay Prashad

   The Karma of Brown Folk

32) Sheridan Prasso

   The Asian Mystique: Dragon Ladies, Geisha Girls and Our Fantasies of the Exotic Orient

33) Paul James Rutledge

   The Vietnamese Experience in America

34) Epifanio San Juan et al.

   From Exile to Diaspora: Versions of the Filipino Experience in the United States

35) Alexander Saxton

   The Indispensable Enemy: Labor and the Anti-Chinese Movement in California

36) Stan Steiner

   Fusang: The Chinese Who Built America

37) Ronald T. Takaki

   Strangers from a Different Shore

38) Ronald Takaki

   From the Land of Morning Calm: The Koreans in America

39) Richard Austin Thompson

   The Yellow Peril, 1890–1914

40) Benson Tong

   The Chinese Americans

41) Haunani-Kay Trask

   From a Native Daughter: Colonialism and Sovereignty in Hawai'i

42) Mia Tuan

   Forever Foreigners, or Honorary Whites: The Asian Ethnic Experience Today

43) Yoshiko Uchida

Desert Exile: The Uprooting of a Japanese-American Family

44) Michi Weglyn

Years of Infamy: The Untold Story of America's Concentration Camps

45) William Wei

The Asian American Movement

46) Stanley Wolpert

A New History of India

47) Frank H. Wu

Yellow: Race in America Beyond Black and White

48) Marilyn B. Young

The Vietnam Wars 1945–1990

49) Judy Yung

Unbound Feet: A Social History of Chinese Women in San Francisco

50) Min Zhou and James V. Gatewood (Editors)

Contemporary Asian America: A Multidisciplinary Reader

51) Helen Zia

Asian American Dreams: The Emergence of an American People

Asian American Origins and Diversity

Although some Chinese and Filipinos reached Mexico on the ships of the Manilla galleon in the 1600s and by the 1830s Chinese "sugar masters" were working in Hawaii and Chinese sailors and peddlers had come to New York, the beginning of Asian immigration to the United States properly begins in the late 1840s and the 1850s (Sucheng Chan; 1991, p. 192).

The immigration of Asians to the United States can be roughly divided into two periods:

■ Early Asian immigration from largely feudal or traditional societies of the nineteenth and early twentieth centuries.

The immigration of Chinese, Japanese, Filipino, and some Koreans and Asian Indians and the U.S. policies, laws, and court decisions that systematically exclude Asians from immigration and/or citizenship highlighted by the Chinese Exclusion Act of 1882, the Immigration Act of 1924, and the Tydings–McDuffie Act of 1934.

■ Post-1965 to the present.

The passage of the 1965 Immigration Reform Act finally abolished "national origins" as the basis for allocating immigration quotas to various countries—thus placing Asian countries on an equal footing with western hemispheric countries.

The post-1965 immigrants from Asian nations differed significantly from the older waves of Chinese, Japanese, and Filipino migrants. According to Martin N. Marger:

. . . most of the new immigrants have been noticeably higher in class origin, and many have been well educated and occupationally skilled. Moreover, the new Asian immigration has been considerably more diverse in national origin, made up of people from almost every contemporary Asian society. Today, except for the Japanese, Asians in the United States are predominantly foreign-born. Over 60 percent of the Chinese and Filipino population, 80 percent of the Koreans, 70 percent of the Asian Indians, and 90 percent of the Vietnamese are first-generation immigrants.

(Marger, 2000, p. 323)

While the Asian American population is quite diverse, it represents only about 3.6 percent of the total U.S. population. But Asian Americans as a population are increasing both in terms of size and economic and cultural significance. Marger points out some interesting facts and significant trends with respect to Asians:

- The Asian American population is today the fastest-growing ethnic minority in the United States.

- Between 1970 and 1980, it grew by 128 percent, and between 1980 and 1990, by 128 percent.

- By 2020 the current Asian population of 10 million will double.

- By 2054 the Asian American population will reach 34 million.

- The rapid and sizable population growth is due to the fact that Asians now account for almost half of all immigrants to the United States.

- In 1970 most Asian Americans were either Chinese or Japanese, but these groups were projected to only constitute 25 percent of Asian Americans after the year 2000.

- In the 1980s, the Hmong population in the United States increased from 5,200 to 90,000, and the Cambodian population increased from 16,000 to 147,000. Of all Filipinos in the United States, 32 percent arrived in the period between 1980 and 1990. During the same decade, the rates for other Asian groups were equally amazing: 49 percent for Chinese; 41 percent for Koreans; 44 percent for East Indians; and 62 percent for Vietnamese.

(Marger, 2000, pp. 331–332)

These facts and figures help to define the periods of Asian immigration, the diversity of Asian Americans, and the expected growth of the Asian American population.

In the following section I will provide brief overviews of the major Asian populations that began to immigrate to the United States, beginning with the Chinese and concluding with Asian Indians.

Overview of Asian Immigrant Groups

Chinese Americans

Toward the middle of the nineteenth century, young Chinese males began to migrate from China's southeastern coastal provinces in search of labor opportunities in Spanish, Portuguese, Dutch, and British colonies as well as to California following news of the discovery of gold. The Chinese laborers were also responding to unfavorable political and economic condition inside China, such as upheaval and political unrest, famine and local warfare, and excessive taxation within a depressed economy.

The Chinese who came to the United States were overwhelmingly young men who intended to sojourn long enough to make enough money and then return to their villages to support their families or relatives. Those who came to the goldfields of California referred to the state as "Gold Mountain."

The Chinese also entered the United States as contract laborers who were recruited through agreements negotiated between the U.S. and Chinese governments. In the 1860s, large numbers of Chinese laborers worked on the construction of the Transcontinental Railroad.

It was not easy for the Chinese to live or work in the United States. They were forced to pay the foreign miners tax to mine for gold in California, they were often subjected to racial prejudice and physical violence because of their race and distinct culture, and they were perceived to be an economic threat to White workers—in part because capitalists were willing to employ the Chinese as strikebreakers when White laborers tried to organize unions or demand higher wages or better working conditions.

The Chinese usually were severely limited both in terms of what occupations they could enter as well as where they could live. Because of racist **stereotypes of Asians** and organized anti-Chinese interest groups, as well as vicious media campaigns and the response of politicians at the state and national levels, the Chinese were targeted for exclusion and immigration restrictions that led to the passage of the **Chinese Exclusion Act** in 1882 and a series of additional laws and court decisions that prevented virtually all Chinese immigration to the United States until 1943, when the Chinese became an ally of the United States in the war against imperial Japan following her attack on Pearl Harbor in Hawaii and her aggression throughout Asia and the Pacific.

The Chinese Exclusion Act marked the first time in U.S. history that a specific group was formally barred from entrance into the country, and it became a precedent for the barring of other immigrant groups during the first third of the twentieth century.

The Chinese population in the United States prior to 1965 was never very large. According to Marger (p. 324), there were about 125,000 Chinese in America in 1882. Before 1882, more than 100,000 men but only 9,000 women had immigrated. The disproportionate ration of males to females led to the creation of Chinatowns in which population growth was impossible. After 1882 and for the next 60 years, the Chinese population failed to grow. By 1910 there were only 70,000 Chinese in the United States.

Thus, the first wave of Asian immigrants to America resulted in the restriction of the Chinese to menial, labor-intensive occupations and traditionally Chinese jobs. The Chinese were miners, farmers, railroad workers, and, with the growth of Chinatowns, they operated laundries, restaurants, and other forms of labor that non-Chinese did not do. The Chinese were excluded from immigration and those who remained in the United States did not become dispersed from the urban Chinatowns until the post–World War II period.

Some growth in the Chinese population began to occur by the 1960s due to the repeal of the Exclusion Act in 1943, the entry of war brides, refugees, and scientific personnel following the communist Chinese victory and assumption of power in 1949. With the Immigration Reform Act of 1965 the number of Chinese entering the United States and the number of women skyrocketed. Many of the new immigrants came from Taiwan, Hong Kong, and even Vietnam, where ethnic Chinese were a population segment.

Japanese Americans

After the exclusion of the Chinese, a second wave of Japanese immigrants began arriving toward the end of the nineteenth century. The first Japanese to enter the United States were mostly males and were confined to menial jobs. The Japanese who had largely settled in California were also viewed as a threat, and anti-Japanese antagonism resulted in formal legislation to prohibit further migration.

In 1907–1908, the United States and Japan negotiated what became known as the Gentlemen's Agreement, which restricted further Japanese immigration to the United States. Based on this agreement, "only non-laborers and relatives of resident Japanese would be permitted to enter. The Oriental Exclusion Act of 1924 carried the restriction a step further, barring all subsequent Japanese immigration" (Marger, 2000, p. 325).

But the Japanese experience only partially resembled that of the Chinese. Even though Japanese workers were also occupationally limited, in time most would turn to farming, where they were able to carve out a competitive niche in California's growing agricultural sector in the early twentieth century.

Also the Japanese male-to-female ratio of migrants, which began with mostly males coming to the United States, over time became more evenly balanced as more women were legally permitted to migrate with their children to join Japanese men already living in the United States, based on the terms of the Gentlemen's Agreement.

Because the Japanese were able to establish unified families, their ethnic communities did not suffer the fate of the so-called Chinese bachelor societies.

> With families intact, the base for a second generation was provided and thus a natural increase in the Japanese American population. By 1940, nearly two-thirds of the Japanese in the United States were native-born. Today unlike other Asian-American groups, the Japanese have not increased their numbers through large-scale immigration. As a result, the Japanese-American population stabilized and is rapidly being surpassed by other, more recent Asian groups.
>
> (Marger, 2000, p. 325)

I will discuss the anti-Japanese movement and the internment of the Japanese during World War II later in this chapter. What is significant about Japanese Americans is that over two-thirds are native born, giving them a longer history in the United States and greater generational divergence than other Asians who have migrated in the post-1965 period.

Japanese Americans as a group are more completely assimilated into American society and culture than other Asian groups. Many of the more recent Asian immigrants to America harbor resentment or anti-Japanese sentiments due to the harsh experience that their countries of origin endured during World War II as a result of Japanese colonialism.

Korean Americans

In the early twentieth century a few thousand Koreans were brought to Hawaii to work on the sugar plantations following labor shortages that resulted from the exclusion of the Chinese. Prior to the 1950s, there were a limited number of Korean Americans on the mainland, but it was in the aftermath of the Korean War that significantly larger numbers of Koreans entered the United States as either refugees or war brides.

After 1965, the growth of the Korean ethnic community became a virtual flood. In the decade of the 1970s, the Korean American population grew from 70,000 to 355,000. By 1990 the Korean American population stood at about 800,000.

Most Koreans who migrated after 1965 came from the urban middle class, and many were professionals with college training. Most Koreans came to the United States as family units, and a very high proportion are Christians. About one-third of all Korean Americans live in California and 17 percent of California's Koreans reside in Los Angeles.

Many Korean American families have become operators of small businesses such as grocery stores or liquor stores located in inner cities or urban ghettos. During the late 1980s and into the 1990s, conflict between Korean grocers on the East Coast and in Los Angeles was well publicized. Cultural differences between Koreans and African Americans led to boycotts of Korean stores, a well-publicized shooting of an African American fifteen-year-old girl named Latasha Harlins by Soon Ja Du of the Empire Liquor Market in South Central L.A. on March 16, 1991, and violence against Korean-owned businesses during the April 30, 1992, Los Angeles uprising that occurred after the acquittal of four Los Angeles police officers in the trial that followed the March 3, 1991, beating of Rodney King. For a detailed account of racial conflict between Korean and African American communities in the New York and Los Angeles, see Helen Zia's "To Market to Market, New York Style" (pp. 82–108) and "Lost and Found in L.A." (pp. 165–194) in *Asian American Dreams* (2001).

During the 1990s, many Koreans decided to return to Korea due to a stronger economy and greater political stability than had existed in the previous two decades. In the case of Koreans who ran successful businesses in the United States or who obtained university degrees, returning to Korea represented an opportunity to be more successful in a more familiar cultural environment.

> Return is also appealing for those who have experienced increasing difficulties in adapting to American culture or who find that operating a small business, so common among Korean Americans, is simply too risky in terms of physical safety as well as economic security. The image of Korean shops being burned and looted during the Los Angeles riots of 1992 and the frequent harassment of Korean shop owners in other cities have made Korean Americans more conscious of ethnic conflict, a condition not encountered in a homogeneous Korea.
>
> (Marger, 2000, p. 327)

The plight of Korean small business owners illustrates a structural condition that has affected diasporic Asians and other entrepreneurial populations operating in heterogeneous or multiracial societies around the world. The small business owner represents a middleman minority who is forced to service other subordinate or racially marginalized populations because of his or her own precarious position relative to the dominant racial and capitalist social order.

Asians have thus served as a buffer between Anglos who do not want to welcome them but who would rather allow them to face the risks associated with running businesses in inner-city locations. Interethnic conflict and competition have often led racial minorities to accuse each other of racism or to have to seek reconciliation and possible political and economic realignments or coalitions. This dynamic has also been problematic because of the use of the label "model minority" to stigmatize non-Asian groups as less intelligent or as coming from dysfunctional families and violent neighborhoods and communities. Debates on the subject of affirmative action have also pitted Asians against Blacks, Latinos, and Indians for admissions to colleges and universities based upon meritocratic principles.

Filipino Americans

A third wave of Asian immigration to the United States and Hawaii involved Filipinos who began emigrating around 1907 to work on Hawaiian sugar plantations. Planters had turned to Filipino and Korean workers following labor strikes by the Japanese. In 1915, the Hawaiian labor force was 54 percent Japanese and 19 percent Filipino, but by 1932 the Filipinos represented 70 percent of the workers while the Japanese were reduced to 19 percent (Hraba, 1994, p. 507).

Historically, Spain had colonized the Philippines for over 300 years. Most Filipinos therefore have Spanish surnames and are predominantly Roman Catholic. Following the Spanish–American War of 1898, the United States took possession of the Philippines in a violent and racist war.

Hraba (p. 507) describes the condition of Filipino workers in Hawaii:

> Early Filipino migration to Hawaii consisted mainly of single men, who were joined after 1920 by women. Nevertheless, the migration to Hawaii was predominantly male; there was fewer than one woman for each ten Filipino males. . . . Filipinos were a bachelor society on the bottom of the plantation's labor hierarchy, facing a segmented and split labor market, and living in segregated housing. . . . In 1950 Hawaiian plantation workers were the best-paid agricultural labor in the world.
>
> (Hraba, 1994, p. 507)

Filipino American workers were eventually pushed off the land due to mechanization of agriculture, and second-generation workers found employment in the canneries and in the tourist industry in the cities of Hawaii (Hraba, p. 507).

In the United States, Filipino migration followed the flow of workers to Hawaii. Some Filipino students came to the United States in 1903 (Sucheng Chan, p. 195) but there were only 405

Filipinos in the United States as of 1910. By 1930, the number of Filipinos had climbed to more than 45,000 (Hraba, p. 508).

The students that Sucheng Chan referred to were called *pensionados*. They came to the United States and then returned to the Philippines. The Filipino laborers who entered the United States in the 1920s settled on the West Coast to replace the Japanese as agricultural laborers. By the 1930s, Filipino migration dropped off due to the impact of the Great Depression and because of the Tydings–McDuffie Act, which only allowed 50 Filipinos per year to enter the United States.

From 1946 to 1964, the third wave of Filipino migrants was about 71 percent women, "many of them spouses, children, or other family members of U.S. servicemen stationed in the Philippines after the Second World War" (Hraba, p. 508).

Before World War II, Filipinos faced Anglo prejudice, hostility, racism, and violence, but during World War II the Philippines was a key American ally, and attitudes toward Filipinos improved considerably.

Whereas the early Filipino laborers had very little education and were forced to engage in seasonal agricultural labor or to take low-status service positions as restaurant workers, hospital attendants, and hotel workers, those Filipinos who arrived during the decade of the 1960s were better able to adjust to life in America and were culturally and politically ready to do so.

The Philippine Islands became independent on July 4, 1946. Filipinos were attracted to the United States and there was a strong U.S. military presence in the Philippines for forty years. Many of the Filipinos who came to the United States after the 1970s were women married to American servicemen.

The most recent Filipinos in America represented families with children who were seeking the promise of better economic opportunities. They have been better educated than pre–World War II migrants and many come with professional credentials that allow them to gain highly skilled jobs in fields such as medicine and education.

Filipinos now constitute the second largest Asian American group, behind the Chinese. Most Filipinos in the United States have come within the past forty years or so. Between 1961 and 1970, 101,500 Filipinos came. From 1971 to 1980, the number was 360,200, and between 1981 and 1990, an additional 431,000 Filipinos arrived. Two other facts are worth noting. In 1980 there were 774,640 Filipinos in the United States, of whom 501,440 were born in the Philippines. In 1980, four-fifths of the Filipino population had lived in the United States less than fifteen years (Hraba, p. 512).

Vietnamese and Indochinese Americans

Prior to American involvement in Vietnam and the neighboring Indochinese countries of Laos, Thailand, and Cambodia, most Americans knew virtually nothing about the people or history of Indochina.

In 1964 there were only 603 **Vietnamese Americans** living in the United States. Between 1966 and 1975, only 20,000 Vietnamese came to the United States. The Vietnamese in America are almost all political refugees who came here following the fall of Saigon on April 30, 1975.

In the period between 1975 and 1984, more than 700,000 Southeast Asians entered the United States. Most were Vietnamese. They migrated in two waves.

The first wave of 130,000 people came at the time of the American evacuation of Vietnam because they has been connected with the American government in Vietnam during the war and thus at risk after the fall of Saigon in 1975. They were educated and two thirds could speak English. Most came from urban South Vietnam, especially Saigon, and one-half were Christians, although only 10 percent of the Vietnam population was Christian.

(Hraba, 1994, p. 513)

The first-wave refugees left Vietnam because their lives were at risk, but they were also able to anticipate what the fall of Saigon might mean. According to James A. Banks (1987, p. 465), most of the refugees came as part of a family unit. Sixty-two percent of the refugees belonged to households with more than five persons, and "sixty-two families had seventeen or more members of their families with them." Over 45 percent of the refugees were under the age of 18 when they came to America, and over 700 children were not accompanied by relatives or adults (Banks, p. 469).

In short, the first-wave refugees included the rich and poor, skilled and unskilled workers, and well-educated and illiterate individuals. The refugees came to the United States in stages. Refugees initially went to refugee camps in Thailand or the Philippines, which were operated by the governments of those countries with the support of the Red Cross or other relief agencies.

From these camps refugees were sent to receiving stations on Wake Island or Guam,

> When additional bases were needed to process the refugees, four relocation stations were opened on the mainland at Camp Pendleton outside San Diego, Fort Chaffee in Arkansas, Elgin Air Force Base in Florida, and Fort Indian Town Gap near Harrisburg, Pennsylvania.
> (Banks, 1987, p. 469)

The refugee camps in the United States were administrated by an Inter-Agency Task Force. The camps were deliberately set up in different areas of the country so that the Vietnamese population could be settled in various communities and sections of the country. The goal in the refugee camps was to process the refugees in an orderly manner and to encourage the rapid assimilation of individuals and families into American society. The Vietnamese did not always agree with the forced assimilation and English as a second language because they felt they were being denied their own cultural traditions (Banks, p. 470).

According to Hraba (p. 517), the average stay at the refugee centers was seven months.

> There were four ways in which refugees could leave these centers. A refugee could go to another country for resettlement, repatriate to Vietnam, prove financial self-support and be released in the United States, or have an American sponsor. The sponsors were expected to provide ". . . food, clothing, and shelter; assistance in finding employment; help with school enrollment; and coverage of ordinary medical costs until the refugees became self-sufficient."
> (Hraba, 1994, p. 517)

The second wave of refugees began arriving in the United Sates in late 1978 after the American evacuation in Saigon. Between 1975 and 1978, circumstances in Indochina caused a large number of ethnic Chinese, Vietnamese, Laotian, Hmong, and Kampucheans to leave their countries. These were the second wave of Indochinese refugees who became known as "boat people" because of the chaos and desperation that motivated them to escape the region.

> These ethnic Chinese, Laotian, Hmong, Kampucheans, and Vietnamese used their own resources to leave Indochina. Some paid large sums of money to escape in fishing boats. The boats were small, poorly constructed, and unsuitable for travel on the high seas. The refugees sailed to places as near as Thailand and as far away as Australia. The journeys were long, tiring, and dangerous with the threat of unpredictable weather, pirates, and mechanical breakdowns. If the refugees survived the sea journey, they often faced hardships in refugee camps in the Far East. Many of these refugees were called "Boat People" by the press. Their journey to the United States and their experience in the United States has been difficult.
> (Banks, 1987, p. 473)

The boat people were more homogeneous than the 1975 refugees. They were less educated, most did not speak English, and they had few marketable skills. They were not urbanized or Westernized and most had a large number of severe health problems (Banks, p. 473).

Whether the Vietnamese and Indochinese were in the first wave or the second wave, adjustment to a new life in the United States has not been easy. James Banks explains the nature of the adjustment that the refugees from Vietnam and Indochina had to make:

> Many Indochinese refugees have had to make a number of psychological, social, and economic adjustments. Their arrival in the United States was filled with traumatic and emotional circumstances associated with the war and evacuation. The uncertainty of refugee status itself can cause psychological stress. Many refugees had to leave family members in Indochina; in some cases, this has resulted in long-term depression. Some refugees have not made the adjustment to life in the United States. A few have taken their own lives, some have been divorced.

> The cultural shock of being thrust almost overnight into a new and different environment has jolted many refugees. This relocation has meant exposure to a new language, values, lifestyles, and statuses. Most of the Indochinese left nations where they were part of the ethnic majority. They now have to adjust to being ethnic and racial minorities.
>
> (Banks, 1987, p. 475)

The Vietnamese in the United States are concentrated in urban areas in California, Texas, Louisiana, and Washington, D.C.

The tragedy of the **Vietnam War** represents not only the U.S. military and diplomatic efforts in Indochina, but the previous colonization of the region by the French and the decades of struggle by the Vietnamese against French colonialism and American imperialism that was carried out during the height of the cold war and the fight to contain communism.

The United States is well over thirty years removed from the height of the Vietnam conflict, and still the wounds from that era are not entirely healed. But relations between the United States have been normalized with Vietnam, and the Vietnamese people in Vietnam and the United States are resilient and courageous.

Time and circumstances will determine how the present generation resolves its War on Terrorism, which has so far impacted Afghanistan and Iraq—and, given the international situational globally, there is no end in sight.

Asian Indians

The subcontinent of India in South Asia has a lengthy history, rich cultural heritage, and great ethnic, linguistic, and religious diversity. The British colonized India and in the twentieth century had to contend with Indian nationalism and independence in 1947. Because of the religious conflict between Muslims and Hindus, the nation was partitioned into India and West and East Pakistan. By the early 1970s, the Bengali-speaking Muslims of East Pakistan fought West Pakistan and established the nation of Bangladesh.

Throughout India, there have been many religious and political conflicts. There has also been a long history of Indian immigration to societies all over the world. In South Africa, Uganda, and other countries in Africa and the Caribbean, Indians served as laborers, shopkeepers, and middleman entrepreneurs.

Indians only moved into the United States as agricultural laborers early in the twentieth century. But because Indians recruited to work in California and Washington faced immigration restrictions, their population numbers did not expand.

Indians faced racism and extremely harsh forms of discrimination. Most Indian agricultural workers were isolated in the state of California. It was only after the liberalization of U.S. immigration policy after 1965 that large numbers of Indians began to enter the United States.

The post-1965 Indian immigrants tend to be highly educated and a highly skilled population. According to Marger (2000), almost 60 percent of adult Asian Indians are college graduates and about one-third have earned graduate or professional degrees (p. 330). Indians are one of the most educated segments of the U.S. population and their income is far above average (p. 330).

Clearly, the Indian immigrant population coming to America is not typical of the Indian population on the subcontinent. They are more educated, skilled, and privileged. In the world economy, those people with education and occupational skills usually seek to move into the most industrialized societies of the West.

But many **East Indian Americans** have also been students who have attended American universities and then found employment after completing their degrees. The educational and professional standing of the Indians in the United States has allowed them to adjust both economically and socially to life in America.

Most Indian immigrants are already fluent in English and are strongly committed to Western values. In recent years the professional Indian class has been complemented by a growing commercial class. Asian leaders run small businesses and are particularly influential in the ownership of motels throughout the country.

The Asian Indian population is extremely diverse and it is not the only country in South Asia to be present in the United States. Many migrants to the United States also come from the nations of Pakistan, Bangladesh, and Sri Lanka.

The migration of highly educated and professional Indians to the United States and other industrialized countries during the 1960s and beyond has been referred to as a "brain drain" because the best and the brightest individuals who could be helping a developing nation instead add their talents to an already modern economy somewhere else.

Because of the ramifications of globalization in recent decades, there has been an interesting development with regard to nations such as India. Many well-educated Indians or professional nationals in various countries perform services in their own countries that would cost much more if done by American workers. Whether it is work pertaining to computer programming, preparing income tax returns, marketing, billing, or any number of services, the process of outsourcing has become an important issue.

Many Americans view the outsourcing of jobs as a threat to American workers who cannot compete with their counterparts around the world. But the dynamics of corporate capitalism allow companies to make huge profits if they can cut the cost of labor and still compete with other firms.

The immigration of Asian laborers to various parts of the world was intimately connected to the expansion of capitalist markets. In the beginning, conquest and colonization created racial and ethnic inequality. Labor and capital interacted dialectically. Whether as slave labor, free labor, contract labor, or outsourced labor, there has always been an association between capitalist production, class inequality, racial and ethnic exploitation, and economic markets and consumption. The Asian American experience is in part a reflection of political economic reality as well as the reality of prejudice, discrimination, and racism in society.

Prejudice and Racism against the Chinese

Even though Asians immigrated voluntarily to the United States, they suffered worse forms of prejudice and discrimination than any other voluntary immigrant group.

> Indeed, if there is a common thread running through the early history of Asian-American groups, it is the experience of rampant prejudice and discrimination of the most vehement and often violent nature.
>
> (Marger, 2000, p. 342)

Anti-Asian sentiment first manifested itself against the Chinese who came to California to work in the goldfields. But wherever the Chinese settled in the West Coast or around the country, they "met with derision and hostility" and were common targets of assault and even murder (Marger, 2000, p. 342). The primary reason the Chinese were scapegoated is that they were different. They did not speak English, they dressed in non-Western attire, they were culturally distinct, and most Whites viewed the Chinese workers as a threat to the economy—especially during the post–Civil War period when there were economic panics, labor strikes, capitalist lockouts, the use of workers of color as scabs or strike-breakers, union organizing, and a genuine fear of class warfare between capital and labor.

The Chinese were in a constantly precarious position and were subjected to "every variety of fraud and chicanery" because favorable public opinion was not with the Chinese, the police and courts were seldom told of abuses against the Chinese, and the law itself did not permit the Chinese to testify against Whites (Marger, 2000, p. 43).

Prejudice against Asians was supported by degrading stereotypes that were first leveled against the Chinese in the nineteenth century. First the Chinese immigrants were labeled as "dirty," "immoral," and "unassimilable." The list of negative traits was expanded to include "sly, untrustworthy, and inscrutable" (Marger, 2000, p. 343). Other stereotypes such as "coolie labor" were meant to define the Chinese as an economic threat to Whites and to paint them as willing to perform "undignified work."

Whites accepted without question that they were superior to Asians. In a stereotype that can be viewed as the beginning of all subsequent forms of "immigrant bashing," the Chinese were labeled as the "**yellow peril,**" meaning that their limited or minimal presence in the American West was defined as "an invasion of people who were loyal only to their country of origin and who, if not stopped, would eventually take over the United States" (Marger, 2000, p. 343).

The anti-Chinese prejudice, discrimination, and racism was fueled by newspapers that promoted racist stereotypes, nativist politicians who argued that the Chinese could never be assimilated, and by anti-Asian interest groups—such as labor—that were concerned about class warfare that could only become worse if the Chinese were able to be in the labor force.

In addition to the racism that negatively affected the Chinese, there were volatile and highly inflammatory stereotypes about the Chinatowns that grew up in the cities with large settlements of Chinese immigrants. For many Americans, Chinatowns were dangerous environments where men congregated in opium dens, engaged in peddling illicit drugs, belonged to violent secret societies such as the Tongs, and perhaps the strongest accusation was that the Chinese promoted prostitution through importing women from China into corrupt and debased activities.

The process that led to the passage of the Chinese Exclusion Act in 1882 and all legislation that targeted the Chinese demonstrates the relationship between group prejudice, stereotyping, scapegoating of the Chinese, and ultimately of institutional racism that reinforced White supremacy in America.

The anti-Chinese sentiment that manifested itself in California, the West Coast, and other areas of the country resulted in violence, legal restrictions against the Chinese, anti-miscegenation laws, exclusion from immigration, the denial of the right to become naturalized citizens, and countless other abuses. Joseph Hraba summarizes the treatment of the Chinese as follows:

The Chinese were historically excluded from American society. They were forced to assume a subordinate position in the nation's system of ethnic stratification, on the one hand, and their entry into the country was restricted on the other. Their rights to naturalization and in the courts were also curtailed. Competition between the Chinese and white workers, demands of the Chinese on white growers in California, the superior political power of their Sinophobic foes, especially on the West Coast—all these set into motion the forces for Chinese exclusion.

Furthermore, politicians from California allied in congress with those from the South to legalize the racial stratification of all non-whites, Asian or African. . . . The foes of the Chinese controlled the political process, and through it they got the upper hand in their conflict with the Chinese. The Chinese were virtually powerless in politics. Chinese aliens in the United States could not vote, and China, because of its weakness in world politics, was unable to protect its nationals in this country.

(Hraba, 1994, p. 434)

The following chronological summary of anti-Chinese acts, legislation, and court cases is taken from Sucheng Chan's "Chronology" in *Asian Americans: An Interpretive History* (1991):

- 1869, 1871, 1880, and 1882—Anti-Chinese riots in San Francisco, Los Angeles, Denver, and Rock Springs.

- 1870—California passes a law against the importation of Chinese, Japanese, and "Mongolian" women for prostitution.

- 1875—Page Law bars entry of Chinese, Japanese, and "Mongolian" prostitutes, felons, and contract laborers.

- 1877—Anti-Chinese violence in Chico, California.

- 1878—*In re Ah Yup* rules Chinese ineligible for naturalized citizenship.

- 1882—Chinese Exclusion Act suspends immigration of Chinese laborers for ten years.

- 1886—Residents of Tacoma, Washington, Seattle, and many places in the American West forcibly expel the Chinese. End of Chinese immigration to Hawaii.

- 1888—Scott Act renders 20,000 Chinese reentry certificates null and void.

- 1889—*Chae Chan Ping v. U.S.* upholds the constitutionality of Chinese exclusion laws.

- 1892—Geary Law renews the exclusion of Chinese laborers for another ten years and requires all Chinese to register. *Fong Yue Ting v. U.S.* upholds the constitutionality of the Geary Law.

- 1900—Organic Act makes all U.S. laws applicable to Hawaii, thus ending labor in the islands.

- 1902—Chinese exclusion extended for another ten years.

- 1904—Chinese exclusion made indefinite and applicable to U.S. insular possessions.

- 1943—Congress repeals all Chinese exclusion laws, grants the right of naturalization and a small immigrant quota to Chinese.

- 1947—Amendment to 1945 War Brides Act allows Chinese American veterans to bring brides into the United States.

- 1965—Immigration Law abolishes "national origins" as basis for allocating immigration quotas to various countries; Asian countries are finally placed on an equal footing.

- 1982—Vincent Chin, a Chinese American draftsman, is clubbed to death with a baseball bat by two Euro-American men.

The treatment of the Chinese established the pattern for anti-Asian racism in the twentieth century.

Prejudice and Racism against the Japanese

In 1900, 41.7 percent of the Japanese in the United States lived in California, where they worked in agriculture and competed with Chinese workers for jobs. By 1930, their percentage had risen to over 70 percent. The Japanese were welcomed in the beginning by growers because they were willing to work for significantly lower wages than the Chinese, and that lowered labor costs considerably.

Even though the Japanese were willing to take jobs in diverse occupations such as "urban trades, mining, on railroads, in general construction, logging and fishing, and domestic service," about 40 percent were concentrated in agriculture by 1911 (Hraba, pp. 456–457).

In the early years of Japanese immigration, California growers needed gangs of laborers. The first-generation Issei ran clusters of boardinghouses and became small-scale labor contractors.

> The boardinghouse keepers had connections with the Japanese labor bosses who placed Japanese crews into the fields of California. Other immigrants were placed in the United States by emigration companies and labor contractors in Japan. . . . These funnels moved immigrant laborers fresh off the boat directly into the fields.
>
> (Hraba, 1994, p. 457)

Within a few years, many of the Japanese immigrants were able to become independent farmers by "leasing land, sharecropping, or buying land of their own" (p. 457). Through the kinship networks that tied the Japanese to a labor supply and to Japanese labor contractors who represented the collective interests of their laborers to White growers, the Japanese were able to move from agricultural wage laborers into the positions as landowners.

It is this process of upward mobility and their skills in agriculture that brought the Japanese into direct competition with the White farmers and landowners in California and created a climate where anti-Japanese feelings could fester and grow in California. Hraba summarizes the process that led to Japanese success and that angered their White competition in the early years of agribusiness in the state.

> The Japanese value commitment to farming and landownership and their skills at labor-intensive agriculture must also be counted among the reasons for their rapid rise out of field labor. The Japanese typically bought marginal land, often swamps and marshes which they drained, and cultivated crops from their homeland. This required hard continuous, intelligent effort. Japanese farmers in California concentrated in the areas around Vacaville, Florin, the San Joaquin Valley, Fresno, the Parajo Valley, and later in Imperial and Orange Counties in Southern California . . . When the Japanese immigrants became independent farmers, they continued to use their network of ken ties for their mutual advantage and economic growth. In the process, the Japanese became increasingly competitive with white growers in California, which ushered in the era of intergroup competition, ethnic stratification, and the exclusion of the Japanese.
>
> (Hraba, 1994, pp. 457–458)

The fact that Whites perceived the Japanese as an economic threat to their own dominance testifies either to the phenomenal skill and work ethic of the Japanese, or to the intensity of their own racism. While the Japanese worked in subordinate positions, farm owners and manufacturers welcomed them as a cheap replacement for the excluded Chinese.

But in the years following the Gentlemen's Agreement of 1907–1908 up until their exclusion in 1924, anti-Asian stereotypes such as the "yellow peril" were applied to the Japanese. The Japanese population of California was only 70,000 in 1919, which was 2 percent of the total, and despite their success in farming, they only controlled about 1 percent of the farmland. But because the Japanese produced 10 percent of the value of California's crops, the Whites:

> . . . began to agitate for restriction not only on further immigration but on the right of the Japanese to own land in the state. California newspaper publishers William Randolph Hearst and U.S. McClatchy emerged as two of the leading figures in the anti-Japanese movement. . . . Their propagandistic attacks claimed that the Japanese refused to assimilate, that their birthrate was so great they would eventually outnumber whites, and that "their low standard of living" presented an unfair advantage in economic competition with whites.
>
> (Marger, 2000, p. 344)

The Japanese exclusion movement gained strength in California after World War I, and at least one California politician proposed that legislation supporting exclusion be passed even if it required an amendment to the Constitution to "protect the white race against the economic menace of the unassimilable Japanese" (Marger, 2000, p. 344).

The reasons that the Japanese were so vehemently attacked during the years of the social Darwinist and anti-immigrant era were:

- The Japanese were racially distinctive compared to Southern and Eastern European groups.

- The Japanese were economically successful in both agriculture and business, which allowed them to be resented and targeted as a competitive threat to Whites.

- The Japanese in America were also feared because of the reputation that Japan gained in the early decades of the twentieth century as "an aggressive, militaristic international power" (Marger, 2000, p. 344). The press covered Japan's actions and argued that their readers should be equally suspicions of the motives and intentions of the Japanese in America.

- Because "California, by virtue of its anti-Chinese tradition and frontier psychology, was already conditioned to anti-Orientalism before the Japanese arrived," according to a historian quoted by Roger Daniels, the state represented an ideal setting for an anti-Asian movement since so many Japanese were concentrated there (Marger, 2000, p. 344).

Racism and prejudice against the Japanese in California stiffened as the former employers of laborers who had worked for them became aware of the direct competitive threat that independent Japanese farmers represented to White economic success.

- The Japanese immigrants were very successful.

- They competed directly against Whites in some of California's produce markets.

- The Japanese often had a competitive edge because of their ethnic marketing associations.

- The movement of the Japanese into a class of independent farmers meant a decline in the supply of cheap Japanese field labor for White growers in the years before large numbers of Mexican farmworkers entered California.

- Japanese farmers also hired dependable Japanese laborers to work on their own farms, and "it was the loss of their labor supply that most antagonized white ranchers against the Japanese" (Hraba, 1994, p. 459).

Prior to the passage of the Alien Land Bill in 1913, racism and prejudice against the Japanese "took the form of barn burning, verbal assaults on individual Japanese, and other expressions of hostility" (Hraba, 1994, pp. 459–460).

The purpose of legislation was to drive the Japanese out of agriculture, and perhaps out of California, according to Kitano (in Hraba, 1994, p. 459). The Alien Land Bill was supposed to ban alien Issei from owning land in California, but the Japanese and lawyers defending their interests circumvented the intent of the law through a number of technicalities and legal loopholes. According to Roger Daniels (in Hraba, p. 460), the Japanese formed corporations so that their land was "ostensibly held by whites," and for the Issei who had children who were born in the United States, and therefore were American citizens, "they simply transferred the stock or title to their citizen children whose legal guardianship they naturally assumed" (Hraba, p. 460).

There was an increased demand for farm produce during World War I, so the Japanese actually prospered in spite of the intent of the Alien Land Law. But in 1920, the Alien Land Bill was amended in an act designed to prevent the Issei from acting as guardians for the property of a native-born minor if the property could not be held legally by the alien himself (Hraba, 1994, p. 460).

The loophole that was used to undermine the first-generation Issei from owning land was that they were illegible for citizenship in 1922 and according to the 1913 law, only American citizens had the right to own property.

Many anti-immigrant groups supported the proposed legislation, including: The Exclusion League, the American Legion, the Native Sons and Daughters of the Golden West, and the Hearst Press. The Japanese did lose farmland due to the Alien Land Bill of 1920, but the value of their land increased in the 1920s due to improvements and, even by 1940, 40 percent of the Japanese in California were still in agriculture (Hraba, 1994, p. 461).

The final victory for anti-Asian restrictionists came in 1924 when the **Immigration Act of 1924** was passed. For the groups opposed to the Japanese presence in California, the Alien Land Law of 1920 did not go far enough. They wanted a complete halt to immigration and the removal of the Japanese from California.

The Gentlemen's Agreement of 1907–1908 was a compromise negotiated by Theodore Roosevelt because of the complaint of Japan against a San Francisco School Board decision in 1906 that directed the segregation of Japanese children in the city's schools. Roosevelt denounced the school board decision and reassured Japan that it would be changed, but he also had to deal with the anti-Asian sentiments of the West Coast, therefore, he got the Japanese government to restrict the number of immigrants coming to the United States.

The restrictionists objected to the number of so-called "picture brides" entering the United States since their presence in California ensured that the Japanese population would grow even if immigration was restricted. The practice of importing picture brides was made illegal in 1920 (Hraba, p. 463).

The Immigration Act of 1924 "granted absolutely no quota for Japanese" (Hraba, p. 463):

> The Japanese were excluded in two senses. They were forced to assume a subordinate position in the nation's system of ethnic stratification, on one hand, and the immigration into the country was restricted, on the other. The foes of the Japanese had gotten the upper hand through politics, as they had with the Chinese, for, like the Chinese Alien, the Japanese immigrant did not have the franchise.
>
> (Hraba, 1994, p. 463)

The successful exclusion of the Japanese is proof of the strength of American racism in the first quarter of the twentieth century.

> The proportion of Japanese immigrants in the United States has always been small. During the period 1915–1924, when the movement to exclude Japanese immigrants was intense, 85,197 Japanese immigrants entered the United States which comprised only 2.6% of all immigrants who came to the United States during this period. A total of 45,531,116 immigrants came to the United States between 1820 and 1971; only 370,033 of these were Japanese immigrants in the United States. . . . Politics, economic competition, and racism rather than the large numbers of Japanese immigrants . . . caused alarm about the "swelling" Japanese population in the United States.
>
> (Banks, 1987, p. 430)

Summary of Anti-Japanese Sentiment

I have described the basis for the exclusion of the Japanese. The following summary is based upon Sucheng Chan's "Chronology" quoted earlier:

- 1906—San Francisco School Board attempts to segregate Japanese school children.

- 1906—Asiatic Exclusion League formed in San Francisco.

- 1906—Japanese scientists studying the aftermath of the San Francisco earthquake are stoned.

- 1907—Japan and the United States reach Gentlemen's Agreement, whereby Japan stops issuing passports to laborers desiring to emigrate to the United States.

- 1913—California passes Alien Land Law prohibiting "aliens ineligible to citizenship from buying land or leasing it for longer than three years."

- 1920—Japan stops issuing passports to picture brides due to anti-Japanese sentiments.

- 1920—Initiative in California ballot plugs up loopholes in the 1913 Alien Land Law.

- 1921—Japanese farmworkers driven out of Turlock, California.

- 1922—*Yakao Ozawa v. U.S.* declares Japanese ineligible for naturalized citizenship.

- 1922—Cable Act stipulates that any American female citizen who marries an alien ineligible for citizenship would lose her citizenship.

- 1923—*Porterfield v. Webb* upholds the constitutionality of California's Alien Land Law.

- 1923—*Frick v. Webb* forbids aliens "ineligible to citizenship from owning stocks in corporations formed for farming."

- 1924—Immigration Act denies entry to virtually all Asians.

Summary of the Japanese Internment

- 1941—United States declares war on Japan following **attack on Pearl Harbor.** Japanese **internment** follows, and 2,000 Japanese community leaders along Pacific Coast states and Hawaii are rounded up and interned in Department of Justice camps.

- 1942—President Franklin D. Roosevelt signs **Executive Order 9066** authorizing the secretary of war to delegate a military commander to designate military areas "from which any and all persons may be excluded."

- 1942—Congress passes Public Law 503 to impose penal sanctions on anyone disobeying orders to carry out Executive Order 9066.

- 1942—Incidents at Poston and Manzanar relocation centers.

- 1943—Incident at Topaz relocation center; registration crisis; Tule Lake relocation center made a segregation center.

- 1944—Tule Lake is placed under martial law; draft reinstated for Nisei draft resistance at Heart Mountain relocation center; 442nd Regiment Combat Team gains fame.

- 1945—World War II ends.

- 1952—One clause in the McCarran–Walter Act grants the right of naturalization and a small immigration quota to Japanese.

- 1976—President Gerald Ford rescinds Executive Order 9066.

- 1978—National Convention of the Japanese American Citizenship League adopts resolution calling for redress and reparations for the interment of Japanese Americans.

- 1981—Commission on Wartime Relocation and Internment of Civilians (set up by Congress) holds hearings across the country and concludes the internment was a "grave injustice" and that Executive Order 9066 resulted from "race prejudice, war hysteria and a failure of political leadership."

- 1983—Fred Korematsu, Min Yasui, and Gordon Hirabayashi file petitions to overturn their World War II convictions for violating the curfew and evacuation orders.

- 1987—The U.S. House of Representatives votes 243 to 141 to make an official apology to Japanese Americans and to pay each surviving internee $20,000 in reparations.

- 1988—The U.S. Senate votes 69 to 27 to support redress for Japanese Americans.

- 1989—President George Bush signs into law an entitlement program to pay each surviving Japanese American internee $20,000.

American Concentration Camps during World War II

The Japanese bombing of Pearl Harbor on December 7, 1941, was that generation's equivalent to the September 11, 2001, attack on the World Trade Center in New York City. With Roosevelt's declaration of war the following day, the United States entered the war on the side of the European Allies and against the Axis powers of Nazi Germany, imperial Japan, and fascist Italy.

There has been more than enough written about World War II, the attack on the American fleet, and the interment of 110,000 West Coast Japanese. In the post–September 11 climate many comparisons have been made regarding the two events, which catapulted America into World War II and into what George W. Bush called the "War on Terrorism." There are controversies that center around America's entry into World War II. The U.S. public was quite isolationist in the late 1930s as war loomed over Europe because of the impact of the Great Depression and FDR's New Deal. Jim Marrs (2003), in analyzing the events surrounding September 11, 2001, has argued that FDR could not have declared war without some major provocation.

In *The War on Freedom: The 911 Conspiracies* (2003), Marrs writes about the emerging "national security apparatus that grew out of FDR's policies during the Depression and about Roosevelt's foreknowledge of the attack on Pearl Harbor":

> Petroleum has been behind all recent wars, beginning in the early 1940s, when a mostly rural and isolationist America was suddenly thrown into a World War as a reaction to the Japanese attack on Pearl Harbor. Americans mourned the loss of some three thousand soldiers and civilians in Hawaii and, in righteous indignation, allowed their country to be turned into a giant military camp. The federal government, which had consolidated so much power unto itself under President Franklin Delano Roosevelt, grew even stronger and more centralized under the aegis of "national security."
>
> (Marrs, 2003, p. 76)

> It has now been well established that Roosevelt and a few close advisers knew full well that Pearl Harbor would be attacked on December 7, 1941, but chose to allow it to happen to further their agenda for dragging the isolationist population into war.
>
> (Marrs, 2003, p. 77)

Controversial as the preceding two quotes may be, it is clear that a consequence of Japan's attack on Pearl Harbor and America's declaration of war was that the same racism that led to the exclusion of the Chinese and the Japanese would have an even more devastating impact on the West Coast Japanese during World War II.

> Fueled by the shock of Pearl Harbor and reinforced by the stereotype of Japanese treacherousness, the anti-Japanese movement culminated after the start of World War II with the interment of the Japanese population living on the West Coast. No other series of events in American ethnic history, other than the enslavement of African Americans and the genocidal measures employed against Native Americans, were comparable to this action.
>
> (Marger, 2000, pp. 344–345)

According to James A. Banks, following the attack on Pearl Harbor, hysteria emerged on the West Coast—fueled by anti-Japanese groups:

- They spread rumors about so-called fifth-column espionage activities among the Japanese.

- Whites claimed that the Japanese were still loyal to their mother country.

- People said that you could not tell a "good Jap" from a "bad Jap."

- Rumors suggested that the United States was in danger of being attacked by a fleet of Japanese soldiers who were being helped in their planning by Japanese Americans.

- The term "yellow peril" resurfaced and the media exacerbated American fears by printing highly fictionalized and sensationalized news stories about the "threat."

(Banks, 1987, p. 430)

FDR's Executive Order 9066, which was based on recommendations of Secretary of War Stimson, authorized the U.S. Army to remove "any group viewed as a security risk" (Marger, 2000, p. 345). Between 110,000 and 120,000 people of Japanese ancestry living in California, Oregon, Washington, and Arizona were rounded up and sent to ten "relocation centers" or internment camps.

The tragedy for the Japanese who were rounded up is difficult to imagine even in the context of today's War on Terrorism, and given the draconian possibilities for civil and human rights abuses under the Patriot Acts, the Department of Homeland Security, and the measures in operation at Guantánamo Bay, Cuba.

Having no time to prepare, most [of the Japanese] were forced to quickly liquidate their businesses, and many abandoned their homes and possessions, losing their life savings. They were permitted to carry with them only a single suitcase of personal belongings.

(Marger, 2000, p. 345)

More than 110,000 of the 126,000 Japanese in the United States were affected by the order to evacuate the military areas in the western states, and two-thirds of the evacuees were American citizens (Hraba, p. 471). The removal of the Japanese involved two phases: (1) the Japanese were sent to Assembly Centers temporarily; and (2) they were placed in ten concentration camps located as follows:

- Tule Lake and Manzanar in interior California

- Minidoka in Idaho

- Topaz in Utah

- Poston and Gila River in Arizona

- Heart Mountain in Wyoming

- Granada in Colorado

- Rohwer and Jerome in Arkansas

(Banks, 1987, p. 431)

The camps were located in "desolate and barren areas that had hot weather in the summer and cold weather in the winter" (Banks, p. 431), and they were fenced with barbed wire and guarded by soldiers.

Space does not permit a complete and detailed analysis of the experience of the Japanese during World War II and their subsequent reintegration into American society after the war, but I have provided a number of excellent books on the topic under the sources for this chapter.

The conclusions that one can draw from the Japanese internment experience are the following:

- Anti-Japanese sentiment was constant in West Coast America for much of the twentieth century.

- Most of the internees had been born in the United States and were American citizens.

- The Japanese were denied their fundamental rights on the basis of their ethnicity.

- The removal of the Japanese was racially motivated. This fact is based on the reality that neither Americans of German nor Italian ancestry were treated in a similar fashion despite the fact that the United States was at war with both Germany and Italy.

- After the war, it was acknowledged that the Japanese on the West Coast "had never presented a military threat, and in fact, their incarceration may have actually retarded the war effort" (Marger, p. 345).

- If national security was so critical an issue after the attack on Pearl Harbor, one must question why the larger Japanese population on Hawaii was never removed despite its more strategic location.

Marger provides a fitting summary for this section and the issue of prejudice and racism against the Japanese in the United States:

> In the end, the exclusionist movement that had begun in California in the early years of the century had accomplished its objective—removal of the Japanese. The fear, suspicion, misperception, and envy, bred by the decades of negative stereotypes, were released in a grievous deed, responsibility for which was shared by nativist groups, farmers, entrepreneurs, the military, and state and federal politicians.
>
> (Marger, 2000, p. 345)

Conclusion for Asian Americans

Rather than attempt to describe the forms of racism that have affected Koreans, Filipinos, Vietnamese, Southeast Asians, or Asian Indians, I will refer the reader to the list of sources. Each Asian group in the United States faces the forms of racism that shape the particular political-economic formation under which they have found themselves along with the ideological forms of consciousness that shape inter- and intraracial relationships. I have provided historical overviews of the Asian populations that are most important for the field of Asian American studies. I would recommend the books by Helen Zia and Frank H. Wu for discussions of contemporary Asian American political issues. Ronald Takaki's *Strangers from a Different Shore* is an excellent overview of Asian American history. The work of Gary Y. Okihiro and Yen Le Espiritu's *Asian Panethnicity* are both theoretically important in Asian American studies.

Finally, the edited reader by Min Zhou and James V. Gatewood, *Contemporary Asian America: A Multidisciplinary Reader,* is a rich source of insightful articles covering a full range of important Asian American issues.

The diversity of Asian Americans and their generations of experience in the United States make them a fascinating group for exploring racial and ethnic reality. But the experiences that all Asians share in terms of facing and overcoming prejudice, stereotyping, discrimination, and racism stand as stern warnings to all of us to remain vigilant and to remember that the unthinkable can occur, and that if we do not learn from the past, we may in fact be doomed to repeat it.

Questions, Exercises, and Topics for Discussion and Debate

1) Discuss the history of the Chinese in America and the types of anti-Chinese sentiment, laws, and court decisions that developed during the years of the exclusion movement through World War II.

2) Explain the basis of Japanese migration to Hawaii and the U.S. mainland.
   a) What key factor differentiated the social and community structure of the Japanese immigrants, but was lacking for nineteenth and early twentieth century Chinese and Filipino laborers?

   b) What was the Gentleman's Agreement?

   c) Discuss the forms of prejudice, stereotyping, and racism that the Japanese had to confront from 1906 through 1924.

3) In what ways do the experiences of Filipinos in the United States resemble those of the Chinese and Japanese? Discuss the Spanish–American War of 1898 and the role the U.S. military played in the war against Aguinaldo in the Philippines.

4) Why did Filipinos not face exclusion as a result of the 1924 Immigration Act? Explain the effect of the Tydings–McDuffie Act on Filipino immigration.

5) Discuss the history of Korean immigration to the United States, particularly during the post–World War II period.

6) When and how did East Indians, Pakistanis, and Bangladeshis come to the United States, and how did immigration of South Asians during the 1950s and 1960s differ from that of earlier Asian labor?

7) What stereotypes were developed against various Asian immigrants during the nineteenth and twentieth centuries? What roles have nativists, politicians, newspapers, literature, and television played in creating, recycling, or transmitting stereotypes of Asians in America and around the world?

8) Explain the experience of the Japanese living in Hawaii and those on the West Coast mainland because of the December 7, 1941, bombing of Pearl Harbor by the Japanese Imperial Navy and air force. Your discussion should include:

   a) FDR and Executive Order 9066

   b) The round-up of West Coast Japanese

   c) What did people on the mainland claim as a justification for the Japanese internment?

   d) In your opinion, should the Japanese in America have been rounded up, sent to staging areas, and interned in ten concentration camps around the country? Explain your answer.

   e) Does the treatment of Japanese Americans during World War II resemble or differ from the treatment of detainees of Guantánamo Bay, Cuba, or those suspected of terrorism in the aftermath of September 11, 2001, and the policies of Patriot Acts I and II and the edicts of the Department of Homeland Security? Debate the pros and cons of these types of policies with reference to the Constitution, the Bill of Rights, and international agreements such as the Genera Convection and the U.N. Charter on Human Rights, and so on.

Questions, Exercises, and Topics for Discussion and Debate (continued)

9) The struggle by former Japanese internees and groups such as the Japanese American Citizenship League for an apology and reparations to internees who were still alive in the late 1980s suggests that the government was willing to accept at least partial responsibility for a policy that the federal government and the U.S. military undertook.

a) What do you feel the government and/or the American people owe African Americans as a result of their suffering under slavery and decades of segregation, denial of voting rights, thousands of lynchings, and economic deprivation? Discuss the basis for your thoughts.

b) American Indians have faced massive genocide, loss of land, denial of religious freedom, and separation of children from their families due to boarding school education and removal of children into White Christian families. Should the government do anything to rectify historical past abuses or the horrible conditions that many Indians still face in the present on many reservations or urban areas? Explain.

10) What is the meaning of the term "model minority" as applied to Asian Americans, and what political implications does it have relative to Asians and other racial minorities?

11) Discuss the Vietnam War and the Indochina region in relation to the massive migration of Indochinese refugees to camps in various countries and ultimately to the United States, Australia, Canada, and other countries.

a) Distinguish between first- and second-wave Vietnamese and Indochinese refugees to America.

b) Who were the "boat people," and why was their exodus from Vietnam and Indochina so traumatic?

c) What is the meaning and significance of the term "the Killing Fields"?

12) Discuss the conflict between Blacks and Koreans on the East and West Coasts during the late 1980s and 1990s.

13) Discuss the murder of Vincent Chin in 1982. Was this a case of blatant racism as Asian activists contended, or an insignificant and isolated incident as the initial trivial findings against the culprits suggested?

14) Asian labor in the United States and in the labor markets around the world that serve the interests of transnational capital suggests that exploitation of Asian workers is an ongoing dynamic of corporate capitalism.
   a) What is meant by the term "Asians as a middle-man minority"?

   b) What conditions do many Asians and Latina women face in sweat shops or maquiladoras in the United States, Mexico, Latin America, and throughout Asia?

   c) Why was the migration of Asian Indians in the 1950s and 1960s referred to as the "South Asian brain drain"?

   d) What is meant by the term "outsourcing of labor," and how does this process help businesses and corporations to maximize their profits?

Bibliography

Acuña, Rodolfo. *Occupied America: A History of Chicanos.* Third Edition. New York, NY: Harper & Row Publishers, 1988.

Adams, David Wallace. *Education for Extinction: American Indians and the Boarding School Experience, 1875–1928.* Lawrence, KS: University Press of Kansas, 1995.

Adams, Howard. *Tortured People: The Politics of Colonization.* Revised Edition. Penticton, BC: Theytus Books Ltd., 1999.

Addai-Sebo, Akyaaba and Ansel Wong. Editors. *Our Story: A Handbook of African History and Contemporary Issues.* London, England: London Strategic Policy Unit, 1988.

Adovasio, J. M. With Jake Page. *The First Americans: In Pursuit of Archaeology's Greatest Mystery.* New York, NY: Modern Library, 2002.

Alland, Alexander, Jr. *Race in Mind: Race IQ, and Other Racisms.* New York, NY: Palgrave Macmillan, 2002.

Alkalimat Abdul and Associates. *Introduction to Afro-American Studies: A Peoples College Primer.* Chicago, IL: Twenty-first Century Books and Publications, 1986.

Allaton, Paul. *Key Terms in Latino/a Cultural and Literary Studies.* Malden, MA: Blackwell Publishing, 2007.

Allport, Gordon W. *The Nature of Prejudice.* Abridged. Garden City, NY: Doubleday Anchor Books, 1958.

Almaguer, Tomás. "Historical Notes on Chicano Oppression: The Dialectics of Racial and Class Domination in North America." *Aztlán* 5 (1 and 2) (Spring and Fall 1974): 27–56.

Anderson, Talmadge. *Introduction to African American Studies: Cultural Concepts and Theory.* Dubuque, IA: Kendall/Hunt Publishing Company, 1993.

Anderson, Terry H. *The Movement and the Sixties.* New York, NY: Oxford University Press, 1995.

Andrist, Ralph K. *The Long Death: The Last Days of the Plains Indian.* Norman, OK: University of Oklahoma Press, 2001.

Back, Les and John Solomos. Editors. *Theories of Race and Racism: A Reader.* New York, NY: Routledge, 2000.

Balderrama, Francisco E. and Raymond Rodríguez. *Decade of Betrayal: Mexican Repatriation in the 1930s.* Albuquerque, NM: University of New Mexico, 1996.

Bandon, Alexandra. *Asian Indian Americans.* Parsippany, NJ: New Discovery Books, 1995.

Banks, Dennis. With Richard Erdoes. *Ojibwa Warrior: Dennis Banks and the Rise of the American Indian Movement.* Norman, OK: University of Oklahoma Press, 2004.

Banks, James A. *Teaching Strategies for Ethnic Studies.* Fourth Edition. Boston, MA: Allyn and Bacon, Inc., 1987.

Banner, Stuart. *How the Indians Lost Their Land: Law and Power on the Frontier.* Cambridge, MA: Harvard University Press, 2007.

Barkan, Elazar. *The Retreat of Scientific Racism: Changing Concepts of Race in Britain and the United States between the World Wars.* Cambridge, NY: Cambridge University Press, 1992.

Barndt, Deborah. *Tangled Routes: Women, Work, and Globalization on the Tomato Trail.* Lanham, MD.: Rowman & Littlefield Publishers, Inc., 2002.

Bennett, Lerone Jr. *Before the Mayflower: A History of Black America.* Sixth Edition. New York, NY: Penguin Books, 1988.

Bernasconi, Robert and Tommy L. Lott. Editors. *The Idea of Race.* Indianapolis, IN: Hackett Publishing Company, Inc., 2000.

Berrios, Reynaldo. *Cholo Style: Homies, Homegirls & La Raza.* Los Angeles, CA: Feral House, 2006.

Berry, Mary Frances and John W. Blassingame. *Long Memory: The Black Experience in America.* New York, NY: Oxford University Press, 1982.

Better, Shirley. *Institutional Racism: A Primer on Theory and Strategies for Social Change.* Second Edition. Lanham, MD: Rowman & Littlefield Publishers, Inc, 2008.

Bhattacharyya, Gargi, John Gabriel, and Stephen Small. *Race and Power: Global Racism in the Twenty-First Century.* New York, NY: Routledge, 2002.

Biko, Steve. *I Write What I Like: Selected Writings.* Chicago, IL: The University of Chicago Press, 2002.

Black, Edwin. *War against the Weak: Eugenics and America's Campaign to Create a Master Race.* New York, NY: Thunder's Mouth Press, 2004.

Blassingame, John W. *The Slave Community: Plantation Life in the Antebellum South.* Revised and Enlarged Edition. New York, NY: Oxford University Press, 1979.

Blauner, Bob. *Black Lives, White Lives: Three Decades of Race Relations in America.* Berkeley, CA: University of California Press, 1990.

Blauner, Bob. *Still the Big News: Racial Oppression in America.* Philadelphia, PA: Temple University Press, 2001.

Bogle, Donald. *Prime Time Blues: African Americans on Network Television.* New York, NY: Farrar, Straus and Giroux, 2002.

Bogle, Donald. *Toms, Coons, Mulattoes, Mammies, and Bucks: An Interpretive History of Blacks in American Films.* New York, NY: Continuum, 2002.

Bonilla-Silva, Eduardo. *Racism without Racists. Color-Blind Racism and the Persistence of Racial Inequality in the United States.* Lanham, MD: Rowman & Littlefield Publishers, Inc., 2003.

Bonilla-Silva, Eduardo. *White Supremacy and Racism in the Post–Civil Rights Era.* Boulder, CO: Lynne Rienner Publishers, 2001.

Bowser, Benjamin P. Editor. *Racism and Anti-Racism in World Perspective.* Thousand Oaks, CA: Sage Publications, 1995.

Bowser, Benjamin P. and Raymond G. Hunt. Editors. *Impacts of Racism on White Americans.* Second Edition. Newbury Park, CA: Sage Publications, 1996.

Bradley, Michael. *The Columbus Conspiracy.* Brooklyn, NY: A & B Books Publishers, 1992.

Bradley, Michael. *Dawn Voyage: The Black African Discovery of America.* Brooklyn, NY: A&B Books Publishers, 1992.

Breitman, George. Editor. *Malcolm X Speaks: Selected Speeches and Statements.* New York, NY: Grove Press, Inc., 1965.

Browder, Anthony T. *Nile Valley Contributions to Civilization.* Washington, DC: The Institute of Karmic Guidance, 2004.

Brown, Dee. *Bury My Heart at Wounded Knee.* New York, NY: Washington Square Press, 1981.

Broyles-González, Yolanda. *El Teatro Campesino: Theater in the Chicano Movement.* Austin, TX: University of Texas Press, 1994.

Bulmer, Martin and John Solomos. Editors. *Racism.* New York, NY: Oxford University Press, 1999.

Bulosan, Carlos. *America Is in the Heart: A Personal History.* Seattle, WA: University of Washington Press, 1991.

Burbach, Roger and Jim Tarbell. *Imperial Overstretch: George W. Bush and the Hubris of Empire.* New York, NY: Palgrave Macmillan, 2004.

Burgett, Bruce and Glenn Handler. Editors. *Key Words for American Cultural Studies.* New York, NY: New York University, 2007.

Butler, Johnnella E. Editor. *Color-Line to Borderlands: The Matrix of American Ethnic Studies.* Seattle, WA: University of Washington Press, 2001.

Butler, Johnnella E. and John C. Walter. Editors. *Transforming the Curriculum: Ethnic Studies and Women's Studies.* Albany, NY: State University of New York Press, 1991.

Cagin, Seth and Philip Dray. *We Are Not Afraid: The Story of Goodman, Schwerner and Cheney and the Civil Rights Campaign for Mississippi.* New York, NY: Bantam Books, 1989.

Calleman, Carl Johan. *Solving the Greatest Mystery of Our Time: The Mayan Calendar.* Pine Grove-Coral Springs, FL: Garev Publishing International, 2001.

Cantú, Robert Tijerina. *MECHA Leadership Manual: History, Philosophy, & Organizational Strategy.* Riverside, CA: Coatzacoalco Publications, 2007.

Cao, Lan and Himilce Novas. *Everything You Need to Know about Asian American History.* New York, NY: A Plume Book, 1996.

Caplan, Nathan, John K. Whitmore and Marcella H. Choy. *The Boat People and Achievement in America.* Ann Arbor, MI: University of Michigan Press, 1989.

Carew, Jan. *Fulcrums of Change.* Trenton, NJ: African World Press, Inc., 1988.

Carew, Jan. *The Rape of Paradise: Columbus and the Birth of Racism in the Americas.* Brooklyn, NY: A & B Books Publishers, 1994.

Carmichael, Stockley and Charles V. Hamilton. *Black Power: The Politics of Liberation in America.* New York, NY: Vintage Books, 1967.

Carr, Leslie G. *"Color-Blind" Racism.* Thousand Oaks, CA: Sage Publications, 1997.

Cashmore, Ellis and James Jennings. Editors. *Racism: Essential Readings.* Thousand Oaks, CA: Sage Publications, 2001.

Cavalli-Sforza, Luigi Luca. *Genes, Peoples, and Languages.* Berkeley, CA: University of California Press, 2000.

Chacón, Justin Akers and Mike Davis. *No One Is Illegal: Fighting Racism and State Violence on the U.S.–Mexico Border.* Chicago, IL: Haymarket Press, 2006.

Chambers, Bradford. Editor. *Chronicles of Black Protest.* New York, NY: A Mentor Book, 1969.

Chan, Jeffrey Paul, Frank Chin, Lawson Fusao Inada, and Shawn Wong. Editors. *The Big AIIIEEEEE! An Anthology of Chinese American and Japanese American Literature.* New York, NY: A Meridian Book, 1991.

Chan, Sucheng. *Asian Americans: An Interpretive History.* Boston, MA: Twayne Publishers, 1991.

Chan, Sucheng. Editor. *Hmong Means Free: Life in Laos and America.* Philadelphia. PA: Temple University Press, 1994.

Chang, Iris. *The Chinese in America: A Narrative History.* New York, NY: Penguin Books, 2003.

Chavez, Ernesto. *"¡Mi Raza Primero!" (My People First!): Nationalism, Identity, and Insurgency in the Chicano Movement in Los Angeles, 1966–1978.* Berkeley, CA: University of California Press, 2002.

Chavez, John R. *The Lost Land: The Chicano Image of the Southwest.* Albuquerque, NM: University of New Mexico Press, 1991.

Chesler, Mark. "Contemporary Sociological Theories of Racism." In Phillis A. Katz. Editor. *Towards the Elimination of Racism* (pp. 21–77). New York, NY: Pergamon, 1976.

Choy, Philip. Editor. *The Coming Man: 19th Century American Perceptions of the Chinese.* Seattle, WA: University of Washington Press, 1995.

Churchill, Ward. *Fantasies of the Master Race: Literature, Cinema and the Colonization of American Indians.* Edited by M. Annette Jaimes. Monroe, ME: Common Courage Press, 1992.

Churchill, Ward. *A Little Matter of Genocide: Holocaust and Denial in the Americas 1492 to the Present.* San Francisco, CA: City Lights Books, 1997.

Churchill, Ward. *Perversions of Justice: Indigenous Peoples and Anglo American Law.* San Francisco, CA: City Lights Books, 2003.

Cleaver, Eldridge. *Soul on Ice.* New York, NY: A Delta Book, 1968.

Clow, Barbara Hand. *The Mayan Code: Time Acceleration and Awakening the World Mind.* Rochester, VT: Bear & Company, 2007.

Cocker, Mark. *Rivers of Blood, Rivers of Gold: Europe's Conquest of Indigenous Peoples.* New York, NY: Grove Press, 1998.

Cohn-Sherbok, Dan. *Understanding the Holocaust: An Introduction.* New York, NY: Cassell, 1999.

Cone, James H. *Martin & Malcolm & America: A Dream or a Nightmare?* Maryknoll, NY: Orbis Books, 1992.

Cook-Lynn, Elizabeth. *Anti-Indianism in Modern America: A Voice from Tatekeya's Earth.* Urbana, IL: University of Illinois Press, 2007.

Cornell, Stephen and Douglass Hartmann. *Ethnicity and Race: Making Identities in a Changing World.* Thousand Oaks, CA: Pine Forge Press, 1998.

Crawford, James. *Hold Your Tongue: Bilingualism and the Politics of "English Only."* Reading, MA: Addison-Wesley Publishing Company, 1992.

Cronon, Edmund David. *Black Moses: The Story of Marcus Garvey and the Universal Negro Improvement Association.* Madison, WI: The University of Wisconsin Press, 1969.

Daniels, Jessie. *White Lies: Race, Class, Gender, and Sexuality in White Supremacist Discourse.* New York, NY: Routledge, 1997.

Daniels, Roger. *Asian American: Chinese and Japanese in the United States since 1850.* Seattle, WA: University of Washington Press, 1988.

Daniels, Roger. *Coming to America: A History of Immigration and Ethnicity in American Life.* New York, NY: HarperCollins Publishers, 1990.

Daniels, Roger. *Prisoners without Trial: Japanese Americans in World War II.* New York, NY: Hill and Wang, 1993.

Davis, Angela Y. *Are Prisons Obsolete?* New York, NY: Seven Stories Press, 2003.

De León, Arnoldo. *They Called Them Greasers: Anglo Attitudes toward Mexicans in Texas, 1821–1900.* Austin, TX: University of Texas Press, 1991.

Debo, Angie. *A History of the Indians of the United States.* Norman, OK: University of Oklahoma Press, 1989.

Deloria, Vine, Jr. *Custer Died for Your Sins: An Indian Manifesto.* Norman, OK: University of Oklahoma Press, 1988.

Deloria, Vine, Jr. *Red Earth, White Lies: Native Americans and the Myth of Scientific Fact.* New York, NY: Scribner, 1995.

Diamond, Sara. *Roads to Dominion: Rightwing Movements and Political Power in the United States.* New York, NY: The Guilford Press, 1995.

Dobratz, Betty A. and Stephanie L. Shanks-Meile. *The White Separatist Movement in the United States: "White Power, White Pride!"* Baltimore, MD: The Johns Hopkins University Press, 2000.

Doob, Christopher Bates. *Racism: An American Cauldron.* New York, NY: HarperCollins Publishers, 1993.

Douglass, Frederick. *Narrative of the Life of Frederick Douglass: An American Slave.* New York, NY: A Signet Book, 1968.

Dray, Philip. *At the Hands of Persons Unknown: The Lynching of Black America.* New York, NY: Random House, 2002.

Drinnon, Richard. *Facing West: The Metaphysics of Indian-Hating and Empire-Building.* New York, NY: Schocken Books, 1990.

Duran, Livie Isauro and H. Russell Bernard. Editors. *Introduction to Chicano Studies.* Second Edition. New York, NY: Macmillan Publishing Co., Inc., 1982.

Duvall, Lynn. *Respecting Our Differences: A Guide to Getting Along in a Changing World.* Edited by Pamela Espeland. Minneapolis, MN: Free Spirit Publishing Inc., 1994.

Erdoes, Richard and Alfonso Ortiz. Editors. *American Indian Myths and Legends.* New York, NY: Pantheon Books, 1984.

Espiritu, Yen Le. *Asian American Panethnicity: Bridging Institutions and Identities.* Philadelphia, PA: Temple University Press, 1992.

Espiritu, Yen Le. *Filipino American Lives.* Philadelphia, PA: Temple University Press, 1995.

Esquibel, Antonio. Editor. *Message to Aztlán: Selected Writings of Rudolfo "Corky" Gonzales.* Houston, TX: Arte Público Press, 2001.

Essed, Philamena. *Everyday Racism: Reports from Women of Two Cultures.* Claremont, CA: Hunter House, 1990.

Essed, Philamera. *Understanding Everyday Racism: An Interdisciplinary Theory.* Newbury Park, CA: Sage Publications, 1991.

Estrada, Leobardo F. et al. "Chicanos in the United States: A History of Exploitation and Resistance." *Daedalus* 110(2) (Spring 1981): 103–131.

Fanon, Frantz. *The Wretched of the Earth.* New York, NY: Grove Press, Inc., 1968.

Feagin, Joe R. *Racial and Ethnic Relations.* Second Edition. Englewood Cliffs, NJ: Prentice-Hall, Inc., 1984.

Feagin, Joe R. *Racist America: Roots, Current Realities, and Future Reparations.* New York, NY: Routledge, 2001.

Feagin, Joe R. and Hernán Vera. *White Racism: The Basics.* New York, NY: Routledge, 1995.

Feagin, Joe R. and Melvin P. Sykes. *Living with Racism: The Black Middle-Class Experience.* Boston, MA: Beacon Press, 1994.

Fenton, Steve. *Ethnicity.* Malden, MA: Polity, 2003.

Ferber, Abby L. *White Man Falling: Race, Gender, and White Supremacy.* Lanham MD: Rowman & Littlefield Publishers, Inc., 1999.

Fernández-Armesto, Felipe. *The Americas: A Hemispheric History.* New York, NY: Palgrave, 2002.

Fischer, Steven Roger. *A History of the Pacific Islands.* New York, NY: Palgrave, 2002.

Foner, Philip S. Editor. *The Black Panthers Speak.* New York, NY: Da Capo Press, 1995.

Fong, Timothy P. *The Contemporary Asian American Experience: Beyond the Model Minority.* Upper Saddle River, NJ: Prentice Hall, 1998.

Fraser, Steven. Editor. *The Bell Curve Wars: Race, Intelligence, and the Future of America.* New York, NY: Basic Books, 1995.

Fraser, Steve and Gary Gerstle. Editors. *Ruling America: A History of Wealth and Power in a Democracy.* Cambridge, MA: Harvard University Press, 2005.

Fredrickson, George M. *Racism: A Short History.* Princeton, NJ: Princeton University Press, 2002.

Fredrickson, George M. *White Supremacy: A Comparative Study in American and South African History.* New York, NY: Oxford University Press, 1982.

Freeman, James M. Changing Identities: Vietnamese Americans, 1975–1995. Boston, MA: Allyn and Bacon, 1995.

Freire, Paulo. *Pedagogy of the Oppressed.* New York, NY: Continuum, 1990.

Fujino, Diane C. *Heartbeat of Struggle: The Revolutionary Life of Yuri Kochiyama.* Minneapolis, MN: University of Minnesota Press, 2005.

Gabaccia, Donna R. *Immigration and American Diversity: A Social and Cultural History.* Malden, MA: Blackwell Publishers, 2002.

García, Mario T. *Memories of Chicano History: The Life and Narrative of Bert Corona*. Berkeley, CA: University of California, 1994.

Gareau, Frederick H. *State Terrorism and the United States: From Counterinsurgency to the War on Terrorism*. Atlanta, GA: Clarity Press, Inc., 2004.

Gerstle, Gary. *American Crucible: Race and Nation in the Twentieth-Century*. Princeton, NJ: Princeton University Press, 2001.

Gibson, Arrell Morgan. *The American Indian: Prehistory to the Present*. Lexington, MA: D.C. Heath and Company, 1980.

Gibson, Nigel C. *Fanon: The Postcolonial Imagination*. Malden, MA: Policy, 2003.

Goldberg, David Theo. Editor. *Anatomy of Racism*. Minneapolis, MN: University of Minnesota Press, 1990.

Goldberg, David Theo. *Racist Culture: Philosophy and the Politics of Meaning*. Cambridge, MA: Blackwell, 1993.

Goldenberg, David M. *The Curse of Ham: Race and Slavery in Early Judaism Christianity, and Islam*. Princeton, NJ: Princeton University Press, 2003.

Gonzales, Manuel G. *Mexicanos: A History of Mexicans in the United States*. Bloomington, IN: Indiana University Press, 2000.

Gonzalez, Gilbert G. and Raul A. Fernandez. *A Century of Chicano History: Empire, Nations, and Migration*. New York, NY: Routledge, 2003.

Gonzalez, Juan. *Harvest of Empire: A History of Latinos in America*. New York. NY: Penguin Books, 2001.

Gordon, Milton M. *Assimilation in American Life: The Role of Race, Religion, and National Origins*. New York, NY: Oxford University Press, 1964.

Gossett, Thomas F. *Race: The History of an Idea in America*. New York, NY: Oxford University Press, 1997.

Gould, Stephen Jay. *The Mismeasure of Man*. New York, NY: W. W Norton & Company, 1981.

Grandin, Greg. *Empire's Workshop: Latin America, the United States, and the Rise of the New Imperialism*. New York, NY: Owl Books, 2007.

Gregory, Steven and Roger Sanjek. Editors. *Race*. New Brunswick, NJ: Rutgers University Press, 1994.

Griffin, Paul R. *Seeds of Racism in the Soul of America*. Naperville, IL: Sourcebooks, Inc., 2000.

Griswold del Castillo, Richard. *La Familia: Chicano Families in the Urban Southwest, 1848 to the Present*. Notre Dame, IN: University of Notre Dame Press, 1984.

Griswold del Castillo, Richard and Richard A. Garcia. *César Chávez: A Triumph of Spirit*. Norman, OK: University of Oklahoma Press, 1995.

Guerin-Gonzales, Camille. *Mexican Workers and American Dreams: Immigration, Repatriation, and California Farm Labor, 1900–1939*. New Brunswick, NJ: Rutgers University Press, 1994.

Guillaumin, Colette. *Racism, Sexism, Power and Ideology*. New York, NY: Routledge, 1995.

Gutiérrez, José Angel. *The Making of a Chicano Militant: Lessons from Cristal*. Madison, WI: The University of Wisconsin Press, 1998.

Hagedorn, Jessica Taraharta. Editor. *Charlie Chan Is Dead: An Anthology of Contemporary American Fiction*. New York, NY: Penguin, 1993.

Hall, Thomas D. *Social Change in the Southwest, 1350–1880*. Lawrence, KS: University Press of Kansas, 1989.

Haller, John, S., Jr. *Outcasts from Evolution: Scientific Attitudes of Racial Inferiority, 1859–1900*. Carbondale, IL: Southern Illinois University Press, 1995.

Hampton, Bruce. *Children of Grace: The Nez Perce War of 1877*. New York, NY: A John MacRae Book, 1994.

Handlin, Oscar. *The Uprooted*. Second Edition Enlarged. Boston, MA: An Atlantic Monthly Press Book, 1973.

Harman, Chris. *A People's History of the World*. New York, NY: Verso, 2008.

Harmer, Harry. *The Longman Companion to Slavery, Emancipation and Civil Rights*. Harlow, England: Longman, 2001.

Harris, Joseph E. *Africans and Their History*. Second Revised Edition. New York, NY: A Meridian Book, 1998.

Healey, Joseph F. and Eileen O'Brien. Editors. *Race, Ethnicity, and Gender: Selected Readings*. Second Edition. Los Angeles, CA: Pine Forge Press, 2007.

Honoré, Pierre. *In Search of Quetzalcoatl: The Mysterious Heritage of American Civilization*. Kempton, IL: Adventures Unlimited Press, 2007.

Hoogvelt, Ankie. *Globalization and the Postcolonial World: The New Political Economy of Development*. Baltimore, MD: The Johns Hopkins University Press, 1997.

Horsman, Reginald. *Race and Manifest Destiny: The Origins of American Racial Anglo-Saxonism*. Cambridge, MA: Harvard University Press, 1981.

Horton, James Oliver and Lois E. Horton. *Hard Road to Freedom: The Story of African America.* New Brunswick, NJ: Rutgers University Press, 2001.

Houston, Jeanne Wakatsuki and James D. Houston. *Farewell to Manzanar.* New York, NY: Bantam Book, 1985.

Howe, Stephen. *Afrocentrism: Mythical Pasts and Imagined Homes.* New York, NY: Verso, 1998.

Hraba, Joseph. *American Ethnicity.* Second Edition. Itasca, IL: F. E. Peacock Publishers, Inc., 1994.

Hurtado, Aída and Patricia Gurin. *Chicana/o Identity in a Changing U.S. Society: ¿Quién soy? ¿Quiénes somos?* Tucson, AZ: The University of Arizona Press, 2004.

Isaac, Benjamin. *The Invention of Racism in Classical Antiquity.* Princeton, NJ: Princeton University Press, 2004.

Jackson, John G. *Introduction to African Civilizations.* Secacus, NJ: The Citadel Press, 1970.

Jaimes, M. Annette. Editor. *The State of Native America: Genocide, Colonization and Resistance.* Boston, MA: South End Press, 1992.

Jaret, Charles. *Contemporary Racial and Ethnic Relations.* New York, NY: Harper Collins College Publishers, 1995.

Jennings, Francis. *The Founders of America: From the Earliest Migrations to the Present.* New York, NY: W. W. Norton & Company, 1994.

Jensen, Robert. *The Heart of Whiteness: Confronting Race, Racism, and White Privilege.* San Francisco, CA: City Lights, 2005.

Johansen, Bruce E. *The Native Peoples of North America: A History.* New Brunswick, NJ: Rutgers University Press, 2005.

Jones, James M. *Prejudice and Racism.* Second Edition. New York, NY: The McGraw-Hill Companies, Inc., 1997.

Jordane, Maurice "Mo." *The Struggle for the Health and Legal Protection of Farm Workers El Cortito.* Houston, TX: Arté Público Pres, 2004.

Joseph, Peniel E. *Waiting 'Til the Midnight Hour: A Narrative History of Black Power in America.* New York, NY: An Owl Book, 2007.

Karenga, Maulana. "Black Studies and the Problematic of Paradigm: The Philosophical Dimension." *Journal of Black Studies* 18 (1988): 395–414.

Karenga, Maulana. *Introduction to Black Studies.* Second Edition. Los Angeles, CA: The University of Sankore Press, 1993.

Katz, Phyllis A. Editor. *Towards the Elimination of Racism.* New York, NY: Pergamon, 1976.

Keen, Benjamin. Editor. *Latin American Civilization: History and Society, 1492 to the Present.* Fifth Edition. Revised and Updated. Boulder, CO: Westview Press, 1991.

Keller, Gary D., Rafael J. Magallán, and Alma M. García. Editors. *Curriculum Resources in Chicano Studies: Undergraduate and Graduate.* Tempe, AZ: Bilingual Review Press, 1989.

Kelley, Robert D. G. and Earl Lewis. Editors. *To Make Our World Anew Volume I. A History of African Americans since 1880.* New York, NY: Oxford University Press, 2000.

Kelley, Robert D. G. and Earl Lewis. Editors. *To Make Our World Anew Volume II. A History of African Americans since 1880.* New York, NY: Oxford University Press, 2000.

Kevles, Daniel J. *In the Name of Eugenics: Genetics and the Uses of Human Heredity.* Berkeley, CA: University of California Press, 1986.

Kibria, Nazli. *Family Tightrope: The Changing Lives of Vietnamese Americans.* Princeton, NJ: Princeton University Press, 1993.

King, Coretta Scott. Editor. *The Words of Martin Luther King, Jr.* New York, NY: Newmarket Press, 1987.

Kinzer, Stephen. *Overthrow: America's Century of Regime Change from Hawaii to Iraq.* New York, NY: Rutgers University Press, 2005.

Kivel, Paul. *Uprooting Racism: How White People Can Work for Racial Justice.* Gabriola Island, BC: New Society Publishers, 2002.

Kleg, Milton. *Hate Prejudice and Racism.* Albany, NY: State University of New York Press, 1993.

Kolchin, Peter. *American Slavery, 1619–1877.* New York, NY: Hill and Wang, 1993.

Koning, Hans. *The Conquest of America: How the Indian Nations Lost Their Continent.* New York, NY: Monthly Review Press, 1993.

Kwong, Peter. *The New Chinatown.* New York, NY: Noonday Press, 1987.

Kwong, Peter and Dušanka Miščević. *Chinese America: The Untold Story of America's Oldest New Community.* New York, NY: The New York Press, 2005.

Landau, Ronnie S. *The Nazi Holocaust.* Chicago, IL: Ivan R. Dee, 1994.

Laufer, Peter. *Wetback Nation: The Case for Opening the Mexican-American Border.* Chicago, IL: Ivan R. Dee, 2004.

Lazare, Bernard. *Antisemitism: Its History and Causes.* Lincoln, NB: University of Nebraska Press, 1995.

Lee, Joann Faung Jean. *Asian American Experiences in the United States: Oral Histories of First to Fourth Generation Americans from China, the Philippines, Japan, India, the Pacific Islands, Vietnam, and Cambodia.* New York, NY: New Press, 1992.

Lee, Robert G. *Orientals: Asian Americans in Popular Culture.* Philadelphia, PA: Temple University Press, 1999.

Lens, Sidney. *The Forging of the American Empire.* Chicago, IL: Haymarket Brooks, 2003.

Leonard, Karen Isaksen. *The South Asian Immigrants.* Westport, CT: Greenwood Press, 1997.

Levy, Jacques E. *Cesar Chavez: Autobiography of La Causa.* Minneapolis, MN: University of Minnesota Press, 2007.

Lewis, Bernard. *Semites and Anti-Semites: An Inquiry into Conflict and Prejudice.* New York, NY: W. W. Norton & Company, 1987.

Lewis, Jon E. *The Mammoth Book of Native Americans.* New York, NY: Carroll & Graf Publishers, 2004.

Lewis, Rupert Charles. *Walter Rodney's Intellectual and Political Thought.* Detroit, MI: Wayne State University Press, 1998.

Lewis, Rupert and Patrick Bryan. Editors. *Garvey: His Work and Impact.* Trenton, NJ: Africa World Press, Inc., 1991.

Lifschultz, Lawrence. *Bangladesh: The Unfinished Revolution.* London: Zed Press, 1979.

Lincoln C. Eric. *The Negro Pilgrimage in America.* New York, NY: Bantam Pathfinder Editions, 1967.

Litwack, Leon F. *Trouble in Mind: Black Southerners in the Age of Jim Crow.* New York, NY: Vintage Books, 1999.

Liu, John. "Towards an Understanding of the Internal Colonial Model." In Emma Gee. Editor. *Counterpoint: Perspectives on Asian America* (pp. 160–168). Los Angeles, CA: The Regents of the University of California, 1976.

López, Ann Aurelia. *The Farmworkers' Journey.* Berkeley, CA: University of California, Press, 2007.

Lopez, Ian F. Haney. *Racism on Trial: The Chicano Fight for Justice.* Cambridge, MA: The Belknap Press of Harvard University Press, 2003.

Louie, Miriam Ching Yoon. *Sweatshops Warriors: Immigrant Women Worker's Take on the Global Factory.* Cambridge, MA: South End Press, 2001.

Lowe, Lisa. *Immigrant Acts: On Asian American Cultural Politics.* Durham, NC: Duke University Press, 1996.

Lyman, Stanford M. *Chinese Americans.* New York, NY: Random House, 1974.

Macedo, Donald. *Literacies of Power: What Americans Are Not Allowed to Know.* Boulder, CO: Westview Press, 1994.

Malik, Kenan. *The Meaning of Race: Race, History and Culture in Western Society.* Washington Square, NY: New York University Press, 1996.

Marger, Martin N. *Race and Ethnic Relations: American and Global Perspectives.* Fifth Edition. Belmont, CA: Wadsworth/Thomas Learning, 2000.

Marine, Gene. *The Black Panthers.* New York, NY: A Signet Book, 1969.

Mariscal, George. *Brown-Eyed Children of the Sun: Lessons from the Chicano Movement, 1965–1975.* Albuquerque, NM: University of New Mexico Press, 2005.

Marrs, Jim. *The War on Freedom: The 9/11 Conspiracies.* Boyd, TX: Areas Publishing, 2003.

Martin, Tony. *Race First: The Ideological and Organizational Struggles of Marcus Garvey and the Universal Negro Improvement Association.* Dover, MA: The Majority Press, 1986.

Martínez, Elizabeth "Betita." *500 Years of Chicana Women's History/Años de historia de las Chicanas.* New Brunswick, NJ: Rutgers University Press, 2008.

Martínez, Elizabeth. *De Colores Means All of US: Latina Views for a Multicolored Century.* Cambridge, MA: South End Press, 1998.

Martinez, Glenn A. *Mexican Americans and Language: ¡Del dicho al hecho!.* Tucson, AZ: The University of Arizona Press, 2006.

Mazón, Mauricio. *The Zoot-Suit Riots: The Psychology of Symbolic Annihilation.* Austin, TX: University of Texas Press, 1989.

Mazrui, Ali A. *The Africans: A Triple Heritage.* Boston, MA: Little Brown and Company, 1986.

McCarthey, John T. *Black Power Ideologies: An Essay in African-American Political Thought.* Philadelphia, PA: Temple University Press, 1992.

McWilliams, C. Wayne and Harry Piotrowski. *The World Since 1945: A History of International Relations.* Sixth Edition. Boulder, CO: Lynne Rienner Publishers, 2005.

McWilliams, Carey. *North from Mexico: The Spanish-Speaking People of the United States.* New York, NY: Greenwood Press, Publishers, 1968.

Meier, Matt S. and Feliciano Ribera. *Mexican Americans, American Mexicans: From Conquistadors to Chicanos.* Revised Edition. New York, NY: Hill and Wang, 1993.

Melendy, H. Brett. *Asians in America: Filipinos, Koreans, and East Indians.* New York, NY: Hippocrene Books, 1981.

Melendy, H. Brett. *Chinese and Japanese Americans.* New York, NY: Hippocrene Books, Inc., 1984.

Meltzer, Milton. *Slavery: A World History.* Updated Edition. New York, NY: A Da Capo Paperback, 1993.

Memmi, Albert. *Racism.* Minneapolis, MN: University of Minnesota Press, 2000.

Miles, Robert. *Racism.* New York, NY: Routledge, 1989.

Miller, Mark Crispin. *Cruel and Unusual: Bush/Cheney's New World Order.* New York, NY: W. W. Norton & Company, 2004.

Mirandé, Alfredo. *The Chicano Experience: An Alternative Perspective.* Notre Dame, IN: University of Notre Dame Press, 2002.

Mirandé, Alfredo. *Gringo Justice.* Notre Dame, IN: University of Notre Dame Press, 1987.

Model, David. *Lying for Empire: How to Commit War Crimes with a Straight Face.* Monroe, ME: Common Courage Press, 2005.

Montagu, Ashley. *Man's Most Dangerous Myth: The Fallacy of Race.* Sixth Edition. Walnut Creek, CA: Altamira Press, 1997.

Moor, Marijo. Editor. *Eating Fire, Tasting Blood: Breaking the Great Silence of the American Indian Holocaust.* New York, NY: Thunder's Mouth Press, 2006.

Moquin, Wayne. Editor. With Charles Van Doren. *Great Documents in American Indian History.* New York, NY: Da Capo Press, 1995.

Moses, Wilson Jeremiah. Editor. *Classical Black Nationalism: From the American Revolution to Marcus Garvey.* New York, NY: New York University Press, 1996.

Mosse, George L. *Toward the Final Solution: A History of European Racism.* Madison, WI: The University of Wisconsin Press, 1985.

Muñoz, Carlos, Jr. *Youth, Identity, Power: The Chicano Movement.* New York, NY: Verso, 1990.

Murolo, Priscilla and A. B. Chitty. *From the Folks Who Brought You the Weekend: A Short, Illustrated History of Labor in the United States.* New York, NY: The New York Press, 2001.

Myrdal, Gunnar. *An American Dilemma: The Negro Problem and Modern Democracy.* New York, NY: Harper and Brothers, 1944.

Natambu, Kofi. *The Life and Works of Malcolm X.* Indianapolis, IN: Alpha, 2002.

Navarro, Armando. *The Cristal Experiment: A Chicano Struggle for Community Control.* Madison, WI: University of Wisconsin Press, 1998.

Navarro, Armando. *La Raza Unida Party: A Chicano Challenge to the U.S. Two-Party Dictatorship.* Philadelphia, PA: Temple University Press, 2000.

Navarro, Armando. *Mexican American Youth Organization: Avante-Garde of the Chicano Movement in Texas.* Austin, TX: University of Texas Press, 1995.

Neal, Jonathan. *A People's History of the Vietnam War.* New York, NY: The New Press, 2003.

Nee, Victor G. and Brett de Bary Nee. *Longtime Californ': A Documentary Study of an American Chinatown.* Stanford, CA: Stanford University Press, 1995.

Neihardt, John G. *Black Elk Speaks: Being the Life Story of a Holy Man of the Oglala Sioux.* New York, NY: Washington Square Press, 1972.

Neubeck, Kenneth J. and Noel A. Cazenave. *Welfare Racism: Playing the Race Card against America's Poor.* New York, NY: Routledge, 2001.

Newman, Richard and Marcia Sawyer. *Everybody Say Freedom: Everything You Need to Know about African-American History.* New York, NY: A Plume Book, 1996.

Nicholson, Philip Yale. *Who Do We Think We Are? Race and Nation in the Modern World.* Armonk, NY: M. E. Sharpe, 2001.

Nies, Judith. *Native American History: A Chronology of the Vast Achievements of a Culture and Their Links to World History.* New York, NY: Ballantine Books, 1996.

Niro, Brian. *Race.* New York, NY: Palgrave Macmillan, 2003.

Norton, Jack. *When Our Worlds Cried: Genocide in Northwestern California.* San Francisco, CA: The Indian Historical Press, 1997.

Novas, Himilce. *Everything You Need to Know about Latino History.* New York, NY: A Plume Book, 1994.

Novick, Michael. *White Lies/White Power: The Fight against White Supremacy and Reactionary Violence.* Monroe, ME: Common Courage Press, 1995.

Oates, Stephen B. *Let the Trumpet Sound: The Life of Martin Luther King, Jr.* New York, NY: A Plume Book, 1983.

O'Brien, Sean Michael. *In Bitterness and in Tears: Andrew Jackson's Destruction of the Creeks and Seminoles.* Guilford, CT: The Lyons Press, 2005.

Okihiro, Gary Y. *Margins and Mainstreams: Asians in American History and Culture.* Seattle, WA: University of Washington Press, 1999.

Olson, James Stuart. *The Ethnic Dimension in American History.* Second Edition. New York, NY: St. Martin's Press, 1994.

Olson, Steve. *Mapping Human History: Genes, Race, and Our Common Origins.* Boston, MA: A Mariner Book, 2003.

Omi, Michael and Howard Winant. *Racial Formation in the United States: From the 1960s to the 1980s.* New York, NY: Routledge, 1986.

Oppenheimer, Stephen. *The Real Eve: Modern Man's Journey Out of Africa.* New York, NY: Carroll & Graf Publishers, 2003.

O'Reilly, Kenneth. *"Racial Matters": The FBI's Secret File on Black America, 1960–1972.* New York, NY: The Free Press, 1991.

Packard, Jerrold M. *American Nightmare. The History of Jim Crow.* New York, NY: St. Martin's Press, 2003.

Pagán, Eduardo Obregón. *Murder at the Sleepy Lagoon: Zoot Suits, Race, and Riot in Wartime L.A.* Chapel Hill, NC: The University of North Carolina Press, 2003.

Page, Jake. *In the Hands of the Great Spirit: The 20,000 Year History of American Indians.* New York, NY: Free Press, 2003.

Pathfinder. *Malcolm X on Afro-American History.* New York, NY: Pathfinder, 1990.

Peet, Richard with Elaine Hartwick. *Theories of Development.* New York, NY: The Gilford Press, 1999.

Perea, Juan F. *Immigrants Out!: The New Nativism and the Anti-Immigrant Impulse in the United States.* New York, NY: New York University Press, 1997.

Pevar, Stephen L. *The Rights of Indians and Tribes: The Authoritative ACLU Guide to Indian and Tribal Rights.* Third Edition. Carbondale, IL: Southern Illinois University Press, 2002.

Pickering, Michael. *Stereotyping: The Politics of Representation.* New York, NY: Palgrave, 2001.

Pilger, John. *Freedom Next Time: Resisting the Empire.* New York, NY: Nation Books, 2007.

Pincus, Fred L. *Reverse Discrimination: Dismantling the Myth.* Boulder, CO: Lynne Rienner Publishers, 2003.

Pincus, Fred L. *Understanding Diversity: An Introduction to Class, Race, Gender, and Sexual Orientation.* Boulder, CO: Lynne Rienner Publishers, 2006.

Prashad, Vijay. *The Karma of Brown Folk.* Minneapolis, MN: University of Minnesota Press, 2000.

Prasso, Sheridan. *The Asian Mystique: Dragon Ladies, Geisha Girls, & Our Fantasies of the Exotic Orient.* New York, NY: Public Affairs, 2006.

Race & Class. "The Curse of Columbus." 33 (3) (January–March 1992): v–105.

Rawls, James J. *Chief Red Fox Is Dead: A History of Native Americans Since 1945.* Fort Worth, TX: Harcourt Brace College Publishers, 1996.

Reilly, Kevin, Stephen Kaufman, and Angela Bodino. Editors. *Racism: A Global Reader.* Armonk, ME: M. E. Sharpe, 2003.

Reimers, David M. *Still the Golden Door: The Third World Comes to America.* New York, NY: Columbia University Press, 1992.

Reinert, Erik S. *How Rich Countries Got Rich . . . and Why Poor Countries Stay Poor.* New York, NY: Caroll & Graf Publishers, 2007.

Reynolds, Edward. *Stand the Storm: A History of the Atlantic Slave Trade.* London: An Allison and Busby Book, 1989.

Rochín, Refugio I. and Dennis N. Valdés. Editors. *Voices of a New Chicana/o History.* Easy Lansing, MI: Michigan State University Press, 2000.

Rodney, Walter. *How Europe Underdeveloped Africa.* Washington, DC: Howard University Press, 1982.

Rodriguez, Luis J. *Always Running: La Vida Loca: Gang Days in L.A.* New York, NY: A Touchstone Book, 1994.

Rodríguez, Roberto. *Justice: A Question of Race.* Tempe, AZ: Bilingual Press/Editorial Bilingüe, 1997.

Rosales, F. Arturo. *Chicano: The History of the Mexican American Civil Rights Movement.* Houston, TX: Arte Público Press, 1997.

Rosales, F. Arturo. Editor. *Testimonio: A Documentary History of the Mexican American Struggle for Civil Rights.* Houston, TX: Arte Público Press, 2000.

Rothenberg, Daniel. *With These Hands: The Hidden World of Migrant Farmworkers Today.* Berkeley, CA: University of California Press, 2000.

Rothenberg, Paula. *Race, Class, and Gender in the United States: An Integrated Study.* Third Edition. New York, NY: St. Martin's Press, 1987.

Ruíz, Ramón Eduardo. *Triumphs and Tragedy: A History of the Mexican People.* New York, NY: W. W. Norton & Company, 1992.

Rutledge, Paul James. *The Vietnamese Experience in America.* Bloomington, IN: Indiana University Press, 1992.

Sale, Kirkpatrick. *The Conquest of Paradise: Christopher Columbus and the Columbian Legacy.* New York, NY: Alfred A. Knopf, 1990.

Samora, Julian and Patricia Vandel Simon. *A History of the Mexican-American People.* Notre Dame, IN: University of Notre, Dame Press, 1993.

San Juan, Epifanio, Jr. et al. *From Exile to Diaspora: Versions of the Filipino Experience in the United States.* Boulder, CO: Westview Press, 1998.

Sanders, Ronald. *Lost Tribes and Promised Lands: The Origins of American Racism.* New York, NY: Harper Perennial, 1992.

Saxton, Alexander. *The Indispensable Enemy: Labor and the Anti-Chinese Movement in California.* Berkeley, CA: University of California Press, 1971.

Schoch, Robert M. With Robert Aquinas McNally. *Voyages of the Pyramid Builders: The True Origins of the Pyramids from Lost Egypt to Ancient America.* New York, NY: Jeremy P. Tarcher/Penguin, 2004.

Scott, Daryl Michael. *Contempt and Pity: Social Policy and the Image of the Damaged Black Psyche, 1880–1996.* Chapel Hill, NC: The University of North Carolina Press, 1997.

Scott, Peter Dale and Jonathan Marshall. *Cocaine Politics: Drugs, Armies, and the CIA in Central America.* Updated Edition. Berkeley, CA: University of California Press, 1998.

Seale, Bobby. *Seize the Time: The Story of the Black Panther and Huey Newton.* Baltimore, MD: Black Classic Press, 1991.

Seed, Patricia. *American Pentimento: The Invention of Indians and the Pursuit of Riches.* Minneapolis, MN: University of Minnesota Press, 2001.

Segal, Ronald. *The Black Diaspora.* New York, NY: The Noonday Press, 1996.

Selden, Steven. *Inheriting Shame: The Story of Eugenics and Racism in America.* New York, NY: Teachers College Press, 1999.

Shorris, Earl. *Latinos: A Biography of the People.* New York, NY: Avon Books, 1994.

Sidel, Ruth. *Battling Bias: The Struggle for Identity and Community on College Campuses.* New York, NY: Penguin Books, 1994.

Sleeter, Christine E. *Multicultural Education as Social Activism.* Albany, NY: State University of New York Press, 1996.

Slotkin, Richard. *The Fatal Environment: The Myth of the Frontier in the Age of Industrialization, 1800–1890.* Middleton, CT: Wesleyan University Press, 1986.

Smedley, Audrey. *Race in North America Origin and Evolution of a Worldview.* Second Edition. Boulder, CO: Westview Press, 1999.

Smith, Anthony D. *Nationalism: Theory, Ideology, History.* Malden, MA: Polity, 2001.

Smith, Paul Chaat and Robert Allen Warrior. *Like a Hurricane: The Indian Movement from Alcatraz to Wounded Knee.* New York, NY: The New Press, 1996.

Smith, Robert C. *Racism in the Post–Civil Rights Era: Now You See It, Now You Don't.* Albany, NY: State University of New York Press, 1995.

Snowden, Frank M. Jr. *Before Color Prejudice: The Ancient View of Blacks.* Cambridge, MA: Harvard University Press, 1991.

Snowden, Frank M., Jr. *Blacks in Antiquity: Ethiopians in the Greco-Roman Experience.* Cambridge, MA: The Belknap Press of Harvard University Press, 1970.

Spickard, Paul. *Almost All Aliens: Immigration, Race, and Colonialism in American History and Identity.* New York, NY: Routledge, 2007.

Stannard, David E. *American Holocaust: Columbus and the Conquest of the New World.* New York, NY: Oxford University Press, 1992.

Steinberg, Stephen. *The Ethnic Myth: Race, Ethnicity, and Class in America.* Updated and Expanded Edition. Boston, MA: Beacon Press, 1995.

Steinberg, Stephen. *Race Relations: A Critique.* Stanford, CA: Stanford University Press, 2007.

Steinberg, Stephen. *Turning Back: The Retreat from Racial Justice in American Thought and Policy.* Boston, MA: Beacon Press, 1989.

Steiner, Stan. *Fusang: The Chinese Who Built America.* New York, NY: Harper Colophon Books, 1980.

Steiner, Stan. *La Raza: The Mexican Americans.* New York, NY: Harper Colophon Books, 1970.

Steiner, Stan. *The New Indians.* New York, NY: A Delta Book, 1968.

Stern, Kenneth S. *Loud Hawk: The United States versus the American Indian Movement.* Norman, OK: Red River Books, 2002.

Stocking, George W., Jr. *Victorian Anthropology.* New York, NY: The Free Press, 1991.

Takaki, Ronald. *From the Land of the Morning Calm: Koreans in America.* New York, NY: Chelsea House, 1994.

Takaki, Ronald. *Iron Cages: Race and Culture in 19th-Century America.* Revised Edition. New York, NY: Oxford University Press, 2000.

Takaki, Ronald. *Strangers from a Different Shore: A History of Asian Americans.* Boston, MA: Little, Brown and Company, 1989.

Tatum, Charles M. *Chicano Popular Culture: Que Hable el Pueblo.* Tucson, AZ: The University of Arizona Press, 2001.

The South End Press Collective. Editors. *What Lies Beneath: Katrina, Race, and the State of the Nation.* Cambridge, MA: South End Press, 2007.

Thompson, Richard Austin. *The Yellow Peril, 1890–1924.* New York, NY: Arno Press, 1978.

Thornton, Russell. *American Indian Holocaust and Survival: A Population History Since 1492.* Norman, OK: University of Oklahoma Press, 1990.

Tijerina, Reies López. *They Called Me "King Tiger."* Houston, TX: Arte Público Press, 2000.

Tong, Benson. *The Chinese Americans.* Revised Edition. Boulder, CO: University Press of Colorado, 2003.

Trask, Haunani-Kay. *From a Native Daughter: Colonialism and Sovereignty in Hawaii.* Revised Edition. Honolulu, HI: University of Hawai'i Press, 1999.

Treviño, Jesús Salvador. *Eyewitness: A Filmmaker's Memoir of the Chicano Movement.* Houston, TX: Arte Público Press, 2001.

Tuan, Mia. *Forever Foreigners, or Honorary Whites: The Asian Ethnic Experience Today.* Brunswick, NJ: Rutgers University Press, 1998.

Uchida, Yoshiko. *Desert Exile: The Uprooting of a Japanese American Family.* Seattle, WA: University of Washington Press, 1989.

Utley, Robert M. *The Indian Frontier of the American West, 1846–1890.* Albuquerque, NM: University of New Mexico Press, 1984.

Utter, Jack. *American Indians: Answers to Today's Questions.* Second Edition. Norman, OK: University of Oklahoma Press, 2001.

Valdez, Luis and Stan Steiner. Editors. *Aztlán: An Anthology of Mexican American Literature.* New York, NY: Vintage Books, 1972.

van Deburg, William L. Editor. *Modern Black Nationalism: From Marcus Garvey to Louis Farrakhan.* New York, NY: New York University Press, 1997.

van Deburg, William L. *New Day in Babylon: The Black Power Movement and American Culture, 1965–1975.* Chicago, IL: The University of Chicago Press, 1992.

Van Dijk, Teun A. *Communicating Racism: Ethnic Prejudice in Thought and Talk.* Newbury Park, CA: Sage Publications, 1987.

Van Dijk, Teun A. *Elite Discourse and Racism.* Newbury Park, CA: Sage Publications, 1993.

VanDevelder, Paul. *Coyote Warrior: One Man, Three Tribes, and the Trial That Forged a Nation.* Lincoln, NA: University of Nebraska Press, 2005.

Vázquez, Francisco H. and Rodolfo D. Torres. *Latino/a Thought: Culture, Politics, and Society.* Lanham, MD: Rowman & Littlefield Publishers, INC., 2003.

Vigil, Ernesto B. *The Crusade for Justice: Chicano Militancy and the Government's War on Dissent.* Madison, WI: The University of Wisconsin Press, 1999.

Vigil, James Diego. *Barrio Gangs: Street Life and Identity in Southern California.* Austin, TX: University of Texas Press, 1988.

Vigil, James Diego. *From Indians to Chicanos: The Dynamics of Mexican-American Culture.* Prospect Heights, IL: Waveland Press, Inc., 1998.

Villaseñor, Victor. *Rain of Gold.* New York, NY: Laurel, 1991.

Wade, Wyn Craig. *The Fiery Cross: The Ku Klux Klan in America.* New York, NY: A Touchstone Book, 1988.

Walch, Timothy. Editor. *Immigrant America: European Ethnicity in the United States.* New York, NY: Garland Publishing, Inc., 1994.

Weber, David J. Editor. *Foreigners in Their Native Land: Historical Roots of the Mexican Americans.* Albuquerque, NM: University of New Mexico Press, 1990.

Weber, Max. *The Protestant Ethic and the Spirit of Capitalism.* New York, NY: Charles Scribner's Sons, 1958.

Weglyn, Michi. *Years of Infamy: The Untold Story of America's Concentration Camps.* New York, NY: Morrow Quill Paperbacks, 1976.

Wei, William. *The Asian American Movement.* Philadelphia, PA: Temple University Press, 1993.

Weisbrot, Robert. *Freedom Bound: A History of America's Civil Rights Movement.* New York, NY: A Plume Book, 1991.

Wellman, David T. *Portraits of White Racism.* New York, NY: Cambridge University Press, 1977.

Weyler, Rex. *Blood of the Land: The Government and Corporate War against First Nations.* Philadelphia, PA: New Society Publishers, 1992.

Wieviorka, Michel. *The Arena of Racism.* Thousand Oaks, CA: Sage Publications, 1995.

Wilkinson, Charles. *Blood Struggle: The Rise of Modern Indian Nations.* New York, NY: W. W. Norton & Company, 2005.

Williams, Chancellor. *The Destruction of Black Civilization: Great Issues of a Race from 4500 B.C. to 2000 A.D.* Chicago, IL: Third World Press, 1997.

Williams, Juan. *Eyes on the Prize: America's Civil Rights Years, 1954–1965.* New York, NY: Penguin Books, 1988.

Williams, Robert A., Jr. *Like a Loaded Weapon: The Rehnquist Court, Indian Rights, and the Legal History of Racism in America.* Minneapolis, MN: University of Minnesota Press, 2005.

Wilson, Carter A. *Racism: From Slavery to Advanced Capitalism.* Thousand Oaks, CA: Sage Publications, 1996.

Wilson, James. *The Earth Shall Weep: A History of Native America.* New York, NY: Grove Press, 1998.

Wistrich, Robert S. *Antisemitism: The Longest Hatred.* New York, NY: Schocken Books, 1992.

Wolf, Eric R. *Sons of the Shaking Earth.* Chicago, IL: The University of Chicago Press, 1959.

Wolpert, Stanley. *A New History of India.* Third Edition. New York, NY: Oxford University Press, 1989.

Wolpoff, Milford and Rachel Caspari. *Race and Human Evolution.* New York, NY: Simon & Schuster, 1997.

Wormser, Richard. *The Rise and Fall of Jim Crow.* New York, NY: St. Martin's Griffin, 2004.

Wright, Ronald. *Stolen Continents: The Americas through Indian Eyes since 1492.* Boston, MA: A Peter Davidson Book, 1992.

Wu, Frank H. *Yellow: Race in America beyond Black and White.* New York, NY: Basic Books, 2002.

Wunder, John R. *"Retained by the People": A History of American Indians and the Bill of Rights.* New York, NY: Oxford University Press, 1994.

Yans-McLaughlin, Virginia. Editor. *Immigration Reconsidered: History, Sociology, and Politics.* New York, NY: Oxford University Press, 1994.

Young, Marilyn B. *The Vietnam Wars 1945–1990.* New York, NY: Oxford University Press, 1994.

Young, Vernetta D. and Rebecca Reviere. *Women behind Bars: Gender and Race in US Prisons.* Boulder, CO: Lynne Rienner Publishers, 2006.

Yung, Judy. *Unbound Feet: A Social History of Chinese Women in San Francisco.* Berkeley, CA: University of California Press, 1995.

Zhou, Min and James V. Gatewood. Editors. *Contemporary Asian America: A Multidisciplinary Reader.* New York, NY: New York University Press, 2000.

Zia, Helen. *Asian American Dreams: The Emergence of an American People.* New York, NY: Farrar, Stratus and Giroux, 2001.

Ethnic Studies Films

A Day without a Mexican	DVD
A Woman Called Moses	DVD
American Blackout	DVD
American Me	DVD
American Revolution 2	DVD
Amistad	DVD
Arlington West	DVD
BAADASSSS!	DVD
Battle for Diem Bien Phu	DVD
Black Robe	DVD
Blood in Blood Out	DVD
Born in East LA	DVD
Born into Brothels	DVD
Boulevard Nights	VHS
Bowling for Columbine	DVD
Broken Rainbow	DVD
Brother Minister: The Assassination of Malcolm X	DVD
Burn	DVD
Bury My Heart at Wounded Knee	DVD
Cheyenne Autumn	VHS
Chicano	DVD
Clara's Heart	VHS
Classified X	DVD
Claudine	DVD
Crash	DVD
Crucible of Empire: The Spanish–American War	DVD
Cry Freedom	DVD
Cry the Beloved Country	DVD
Dances with Wolves	DVD
Destination America	DVD
Dreamkeeper	DVD
El Che: Investigating a Legend	DVD
El Norte	DVD
Empire of the Sun	DVD
Eyes on the Prize: America's Civil Rights Movement	DVD
Fahrenheit 9/11	DVD
500 Nations	DVD
500 Years of Chicano History	DVD
Frida	DVD
Gandhi	DVD
Geronimo	DVD
Glory	DVD
Grey Owl	DVD
Higher Learning	DVD
Hotel Rwanda	DVD

I Am Joaquin	DVD
"I Will Fight No More Forever"	VHS
In the Time of the Butterflies	DVD
Incident at Oglala: The Leonard Peltier Story	DVD
Into the West	DVD
JFK: The Case for Conspiracy	DVD
King: Montgomery to Memphis	VHS
La Bamba	DVD
Lakota Woman	VHS
Life and Debt	DVD
Loose Change	DVD
Los Mineros	VHS
Lowriding in Aztlán	DVD
Luminarias	DVD
Lumumba	DVD
Malcolm X	DVD
Malcolm X: A Search for Identity	VHS
Malcolm X: His Own Story as It Really Happened	VHS
Malcolm X: Make It Plain (The American Experience)	VHS
Mandela: Son of Africa, Father of the Nation	DVD
Marcus Garvey: Look for Me in the Whirlwind	DVD
Maria Full of Grace	DVD
Martin Luther King Jr.: The Man and the Dream	VHS
Maxed Out	DVD
Men with Guns	DVD
Mighty Times: The Legacy of Rosa Parks	VHS
Mississippi Masala	DVD
My Family	DVD
911: In Plane Site: The Director's Cut	DVD
Outfoxed: Rupert Murdock's War on Journalism	DVD
Picture Bride	DVD
Pow Wow Highway	DVD
Rabbit in the Moon	DVD
Rabbit-Proof Fence	DVD
Real Women Have Curves	DVD
Revolution: Why It's Necessary, Why It's Possible	DVD
Roots	DVD
Salt of the Earth	DVD
Salvador	DVD
Sarafina	DVD
Schindler's List	VHS
Scottsboro: An American Tragedy	DVD
Selena	DVD
Skins	DVD
Skinwalkers	DVD
Slavery and the Making of America	DVD
Smoke Signals	DVD
Soldados: Chicanos in Viet Nam	DVD
Solving the Mayan Calendar Mystery	DVD
Stand and Deliver	VHS

Strange Fruit	VHS
The Ballad of Gregorio Cortez	VHS
The Battle of Algiers	DVD
The Burning Season	VHS
The Corporation	DVD
The Dark Wind	DVD
The Emerald Forest	DVD
The Fast Runner	DVD
The Fight in the Fields	DVD
The Fourth World War	DVD
The Gods Must Be Crazy	DVD
The Great Conspiracy: The 9/11 News Special You Never Saw	DVD
The Greatest Indian Wars, 1540–1890	DVD
The Hurricane	DVD
The Joy Luck Club	DVD
The Last Days of Malcolm X: Death of a Prophet	DVD
The Last Emperor	DVD
The Last of His Tribe	DVD
The Lemon Grove Incident	DVD
The Milagro Beanfield War	DVD
The Mission	DVD
The Power of Nightmares: The Rise of the Politics of Fear	DVD
The Revolution Will Not Be Televised	DVD
The Spook Who Sat by the Door	DVD
The Storm	DVD
The Ugly American	DVD
The Untold Story of Emmett Louis Till	DVD
The Wall	DVD
The War That Made America	DVD
Thunderheart	DVD
True Whispers	DVD
Truth and Politics: Unanswered Questions about 9/11	DVD
Tsotsi	DVD
Walkabout	DVD
Whale Rider	DVD
When the Levees Broke	DVD
When They Came for Ward Churchill	DVD
Work Harder	DVD
Yo Soy Chicano	DVD
Zoot Suit	DVD

CPSIA information can be obtained
at www.ICGtesting.com
Printed in the USA
LVHW012007050523
746182LV00002B/5